THE
SOUTH
WEST
COAST
PATH

For Stevie Owen, and the mini adventures
we all shared together xx

CONWAY
Bloomsbury Publishing Plc
50 Bedford Square, London, WC1B 3DP, UK
29 Earlsfort Terrace, Dublin 2, Ireland

BLOOMSBURY, CONWAY and the Conway logo are
trademarks of Bloomsbury Publishing Plc

First published in 2022

All internet addresses given in this book were correct
at the time of going to press. The author and publisher
regret any inconvenience caused if addresses have
changed or sites have ceased to exist, but can accept
no responsibility for any such changes

A catalogue record for this book is available from
the British Library

Library of Congress Cataloguing-in-Publication
data has been applied for

ISBN: PB: 978-1-8448-6617-5
       ePub: 978-1-8448-6616-8
       ePDF: 978-1-8448-6615-1

10 9 8 7 6 5 4 3 2

Typeset in Quicksand by Lee-May Lim
Based on design by Austin Taylor
Printed and bound in Dubai

FSC
www.fsc.org

MIX
Paper | Supporting
responsible forestry
FSC® C004800

To find out more about our authors and books visit
www.bloomsbury.com and sign up for our newsletters

THE
SOUTH WEST
COAST PATH

1,000 Mini Adventures Along Britain's Longest Waymarked Path

STEPHEN NEALE

CONWAY

LONDON · OXFORD · NEW YORK · NEW DELHI · SYDNEY

LYNTON MINEHEAD

ILFRACOMBE

SOMERSET

BUDE NORTH DEVON

DORSET

BOURNEMO

PADSTOW NORTH
CORNWALL SOUTH DEVON

LYME
REGIS

WEYMOU

Exmouth

NEWQUAY

PLYMOUTH TORQUAY

ST. IVES ST. AUSTELL

SOUTH CORNWALL

PENZANCE LIZARD

SOUTH WEST
COAST PATH

— — — — — NORTH DEVON
— — — — — NORTH CORNWALL
— — — — — SOUTH CORNWALL
— — — — — SOUTH DEVON
— — — — — DORSET

CONTENTS

Helford Passage

THE MAGIC PATH

THE MAGIC PATH

Something amazing is about to happen near Cornwall. Forget about work and chores for a minute. Do you want to go south? To experience a total eclipse?

A total solar eclipse is when the moon rolls in front of the sun. It's a multi-sensory experience – involving your eyes, nose, ears, tongue and skin. Your five senses all reacting to five aligned things: sun, moon, earth, cloudless sky and you. That perfect fix only happens because the moon sits exactly 400 times away from the sun, which is 400 times larger. Isn't that amazing? A coincidence (if you believe in them) that occurs in the same short moment in time that you, me and the rest of humanity happens to be on a planet (Earth) that is 4½ billion years old, next to a moon that is almost as old. What's more, total solar eclipses won't happen after you and I, and future generations, have exited Earth in the blink of a million years or so. Why? Because the moon will have moved out of that perfect orbit. Don't you love that?

People who have seen a total solar eclipse say it's literally unbelievable. Even scientists. The way they describe it, is like listening to someone in a lab on LSD or magic mushrooms. The air temperature suddenly cools, shadows grow longer, everything goes dark and then the stars come out. It happens in about two minutes but seems to pass in a few seconds. People say it can be life-changing, in a good way, and mildly addictive.

I wanted this book of 1,000 mini adventures to be like a solar eclipse. A 'dip in the toes' guide to altered states of consciousness via the five senses, immersed in nature. A total eclipse of the star that is 'you'. I've felt it, so I wanted to share it.

I met a retired doctor by chance one day. He'd spent his life working with children and adults suffering from mental illness.

'What's the single most important thing to fixing a mental illness?' I asked.

'Aim,' I mistakenly heard him say.

'I read that somewhere else,' I said. 'We all need an "aim" ... a purpose in our life!'

'No!' he said, 'Amines. Amino acids! The natural, "feel-good" chemicals our brains produce when we're outdoors in nature.'

Chance encounters such as this one are the life rafts that prop us up when we need them most. They are beyond coincidence. We don't always find the support we need, but it happens more than seems probable when we get out there ... on the coast path, for instance.

Once upon a time, the probability that a single eclipse would occur in your lifetime was beyond infinite. As you read this, however, there will be no fewer than 68 total solar eclipses in the 21st century. The next one on the South West Coast Path (SWCP) will happen on 4 June 2160, over Land's End.

But you don't need to wait that long. Just get on the path and go touch, taste, smell, hear and see nature in all her glory – from sitting under a waterfall by a deserted beach and hanging from a hammock in scented tamarisk to watching dolphins roll, and listening to waves in summer rain. A total eclipse ... of the star that is you.

Broadsands Beach

THE SOUTH WEST COAST PATH

This book has three objectives:

1 To serve as a guide to 1,000 places around England's South West Coast Path (SWCP).
2 To reset all your senses (sight, hearing, smell, touch, taste) so you can start to feel whole.
3 To share some path magic or knowledge.

WHAT?

You have in your hands a rough guide to sensing your way along a path. The SWCP is whatever you want it to be, but I hope it will be a slow journey through the senses that will change your life. If you go on to tell the tale, perhaps it may change other people's lives, too.

WHERE ARE THE 1,000 AMAZING PLACES AROUND THE SOUTH WEST COAST?

Skinny dipping in the surf under moonlight, watching dolphins breach in an azure bay, or finding a 50-million-year-old fossil on a Jurassic beach. Picking cherries on a tidal estuary, chewing bramble tips beside the shade of flowering mugwort. Feeling goosebumps on your skin while standing under the Milky Way by a hill fort crag; sheltering in a cold beach cave during a summer heatwave. Walking through damp mist that has seeped up from the sea on a dry June day. Sleeping in a cliff top lighthouse or wild camping on a mattress of samphire and sand; climbing down rope ladders or a scree path; scrambling between heather and gorse to secret beaches and mystic castle ruins.

A STATEMENT OF FACTS

The SWCP covers 630 miles and is a walking pipeline for visitors who spend more than £500 million a year, generating more than 10,000 jobs in coffee houses, cafes, B&Bs, hotels, farm shops, council-run car parks, ice-cream stalls, cottages for rent and campsites. The route takes in ancient rocks, stacks, caves and Arthurian myths. The walker who completes the entire path needs to climb Mt Everest ... four times. More than 17 rivers have to be ferried across, swum (not recommended) or bypassed. By the end, more than 300 bridges will have been crossed, 2,400 signposts followed, 900 stiles climbed, and 30,000 steps climbed or jumped.

The SWCP story

This is an English tale. Much like the England Coast Path that it is now part of, it involves thousands of people coming together to create something communal: a tribal legacy; a sacred and safer passage. The final section between Somerset and North Devon opened in 1978. Yet the path began life thousands of years ago as a track that was constantly trodden by our ancestors, who needed exactly the same things we do today: food, shelter, warmth, defence, stories, magic.

HOW?

This book was walked, researched, written, edited and put together by more than 100 people during, between and after 2020/21 Covid-19 lockdowns. The pandemic made it what it is.

There were three key themes that made it possible to finish in 2021: water, wild camping and ... nettles. Those three things were the foundation stones that replaced the B&Bs, hotels, seafood meals, ferries and coffee bars taken for granted in previous trips. Now things have reopened, the cafes and hotels are back, but with a caveat: adventures should never be reliant on the magic of a hotel, shop or ferry boat crossing.

All that's needed to survive a deficit of domesticity and order is a little planning, access to fresh water, nettles and the ability to catch a crab or two.

If you choose, or are lucky enough to have, the option of bathing in the milk of a five-star cottage or villa, rather than 'roughing it', then keep enjoying nature, too. It has a lot to offer: everything from blackberries, line-caught mackerel and hand-picked spider crabs, to snorkelling, and – not infrequently - al fresco wild sleep. If you've got a headache right now, all of that last sentence adds up to a dopamine fix so powerful it will cure you in an instant.

This is not a walking guide. It's a guide through your five senses, and it'll work for you whether or not the cafes, hotels and campsites stay open.

HOW MANY MILES?
Go at your own pace.

The path for this book was explored in 100 days. 6.3 miles a day. 630 miles. If you haven't got a spare 100 days, maybe something in your life needs changing?

Walking 6.3 miles a day allows you time to notice the size of the bee on the honeysuckle. To stop to talk to the person by the bench who looks lonely, or who thinks you look needy. Accept an invitation to their home.

Just 6.3 miles a day will fire you into the future like time travel. The slow day passes quicker than a few hours, but fills with a thousand more thoughts and encounters. Walking 15-30 miles a day can do the opposite. For some it's a slog. Like waiting for a pot to boil. You're not in the moment. For others, not. Either way, to walk through a place unchallenged is to own it.

Some parts of the path are good for a quick grind. Others for long, easy, tortoise steps. Keep moving, but keep pace with the rhythm of place and yourself.

Water – yin and yang

There's a theme running around the SWCP: the link between fresh water and salt water. Yin and yang. Life and death. Two worlds colliding that give birth to life under the canopy of an English rainforest.

The wonder of tidal pools is that they are flushed every 12 hours by the magnetic pull of the moon, while being infilled from the rear with freshwater streams, springs and rivers. They are warmed once a day by the heat of sunshine so that we can choose to (sun)bathe and/or swim.

That feeling of sun, breeze and water on skin is an intimate part of touching nature, only bettered by the serotonin-laden sleep it induces.

If you can, bathe in cold sea water every morning or night. Even if just for five seconds. It will keep you oiled.

Sacred places

English history – just like the history of anywhere else – is bound up in a pendulum that swings between the competing needs of survival: food, water, warmth and shelter. Long ago, those four things rarely came together in one place because the hunting of migratory animals was a big part of our survival. There was a need to keep moving in order to eat.

Aside from being convenient for hunting, the most important camps were created at places where fresh and salt water came together. The practicality and convenience of having fresh water to drink each day was irresistible to people who wanted to survive.

Water fulfilled other needs, too: fast travel by sea or river, water for washing and bathing and – perhaps more important as our numbers grew – defence. A camp made in the meander of a river is invariably easier to defend or escape from than one far from water.

These watery coastal locations became valued because of their ability to provide for survival. At some point – no one knows exactly when – they went from being purely practical to becoming something more important. They became sacred. And that status protected them for future generations – an idea that we have perhaps lost touch with.

Long before humans took up farming, they discovered something much more meaningful: the spirit world. And it was this non-material world – beyond food, water, shelter and warmth – that elevated these water-based camps and places into communal reserves of wealth. We pretend to celebrate these locations today, but we don't hold them as sacred. Because we still flush our antibiotic-laden sewage into them, with an odourless rinse of chemical pesticides to ensure our onions and tomatoes are as cheap as possible. We are all to blame. But things can, and will, get better.

Sleeping outdoors, going for wild swims and foraging for food are an important part of making and remaking that intimate connection with nature. They return our senses to an appreciation of the value we collectively hold for nature, but fail to act upon with any genuine patience or tenacity of purpose.

Woody Bay Waterfall

So much more needs to be done, but the creation, celebration and your access to the SWCP is a big part of the shift towards reconnection. It embodies places linked to the past, to the future and to the now. Locations that if we can begin to invest in and look after again, will continue to provide and cater for for local communities, individual travellers and 'pilgrims' long into the future.

Chew on this: foraging and eating wild foods - even if it's a bramble tip - is an important part of that connection with nature. Because it makes you think differently. And if you can say, 'Thank you!' to the plant, that's a fun and fabulous start.

Practicalities

FORAGING

Dip your toes and keep it simple. There are abundant blackberries, of course, in August and September. Venture out from summer and autumn into spring and winter with nettles. The tops can be picked and chewed all day as you walk.

The first edible fruits of winter include cleaver in February, lasting through until late July. The green straggly plant has those stems that stick to your trousers and socks. If you spot cleaver, snap it into several 4-inch segments and push them into a water bottle. After less than an hour, the flavour and scent is addictively fresh ... and cleans the liver. Cleaver can also be brewed in a tea.

The coast is covered in both edible plants and seafood. Pick samphire in late June with scissors. Purslane and sea beet are around all year. Limpets, too, are everywhere. They are grazers, not filter feeders, so are safer than mussels. Shore crabs - the type we found and fished as kids - are great for soups. Whelks can be collected and picked out of their shells with hawthorn or blackthorn twigs after being cooked on a fire.

DRINKING WATER

A water strategy can be based around topping up bottles at every opportunity, preferably by asking for reusable bottles to be filled at cafes and restaurants, rather than

Budleigh Salterton Beach

by buying plastic bottles as you go. Ideally, I drink 1–2 litres over 30 minutes before setting off on a walk from a town or village, whether I leave at 5am or 9pm. I then carry a further 3 litres. The combination of 2 litres drunk before setting off and 3 litres to be drunk for the journey to the next village or town will provide enough water on the hottest day and climbs. By the time I arrive, I'll be out of water, have a light bag, but will be well hydrated – even if I've used ½ litre for cooking or making coffee.

I also carry a filter for emergencies. Or for if/when shops and cafes are closed. There are plenty out there, so do some research to find the lightest and finest.

DANGER

The most important thing to remember about danger is it cannot be avoided, but it can be survived. It's always coming: around the next bend; at the entrance to the next cave; on the rim of the next cliff or heath.

Apart from anticipating trouble and avoiding taking too many risks, one of the best ways to increase your chances of surviving is through slow breathing and keeping calm. I learned how to slow breathe from a singing teacher when I wanted to overcome stage fright 30 years ago. Today, I use it when I walk.

Breathing 'properly' involves breathing less. It can be a bit burdensome at times, and even mildly painful if you're going uphill, but no more so than getting stung by nettles. And just like the sting from those nettles, breathing a little less is healthy.

It involves breathing slowly and rhythmically in through the nose for a slow count of five, and out through the mouth for a slow count of ten. There are many variations on this, but all serve to slow the heart rate, increase carbon monoxide in the body and decrease oxygen; ie controlled breathing stops the oxygen overdose we experience when we breathe rapidly through our mouth.

STAY SAFE

- Ask locals about dangers and risks.
- Carry a personal locator beacon.
- Check the weather before you set out.
- Carry emergency items such as a first aid kit, fire lighter and tinder, and a whistle.
- Carry a micro-light bivvy for rain shelter.
- Wear the right clothes and carry thermal and waterproof shells for emergencies.
- Don't eat anything you are not 100 per cent sure is safe.
- Don't drink water without boiling and filtering it first.
- Don't swim anywhere unless you know it to be safe – even if it's listed over the following pages as a potential swim spot.
- Stay away from cliff edges and tops.
- Pay attention to signage – even when it reads like it's written for someone else or doesn't apply to you.
- Remember, everything changes; safe places get dangerous; calm waters get rough; shallow waters get deep; firm ground can become flimsy. Stay alert and ready.

The effects of controlled breathing make me more alert and my limbs more supple, and decrease fatigue. I can walk further. Most importantly, controlled breathing prepares me.

DIRECTIONS AND PARKING

Many of the directions to the wild places are linked to public car parks. There's a cost to that – usually from £5 upwards. The best-

value parking in England is National Trust membership. This buys free parking and access to some of the best coast around the path (and the adjoining England Coast Path), as well as all of their properties.

Where parking fees have crept up to £7 or £8 per car, it's sometimes better value to make use of the many tearooms, and their car parks, along the SWCP, and invest in a cuppa or cream tea or three. The other upside of investing in a private business is that it makes their day, and keeps their business ticking over. Best of all, you often get access to sea views and beachfronts that would otherwise be inaccessible.

PUBLIC TRANSPORT

If you don't or can't drive, then you could use public transport. Bus and train journeys are invariably an adventure that is almost as much fun as travelling the paths themselves. This mode of transport is almost always efficient, but it's too fast to allow you to take in the scenery along the way. On buses along country lanes, I feel like a rag doll in a space shuttle re-entering Earth's atmosphere. The drivers are never ahead of the clock, so I must assume their timetables are fixed at obscene levels of haste, especially around villages. When you next cling on with white knuckles, consider how the drivers cope and whether they might need a night or two on the path, rather than beside it...

PUBS, B&BS, RESTAURANTS, CAFES, CAMPSITES AND HOTELS

Food and drink are the fuels that power outdoor adventures. Carrying water and a packed lunch is important; but combining a coast path trek with a treat at a pub, cafe or restaurant – or even an overnight stay at a special hotel or campsite – is a magical pleasure.

The accommodation and eateries featured in this book are not always the cheapest or best value along the SWCP, but many offer unique coastal access and views. What's more, as mentioned, even if you pay £5 for an overpriced coffee or £10 for a duff sandwich, it might come with free parking, wonderful views or even a place from which to launch a kayak or paddleboard that others have no access to.

Almost all the good restaurants and bars around the SWCP specialise in locally caught fresh fish and seafood. Most of the restaurants listed also cater for vegans, veggies and those with other diets and tastes. It's partly why they're in here. This is not an apology for the fishy focus of the food joints listed, it's justification for it.

LONG-STAY ACCOMMODATION

Some of the accommodation – usually holiday cottages – is only available for long stays. In other words, a minimum of a week. These were included because there's nothing that says you have to keep moving or that you can't stay in one place for more than a few days. Adventures have as much to do with setting up a temporary base camp as transient visits.

The locations chosen in this book are surrounded by many places and things to see. Take a bike, a boat, a kayak or just your imagination with you, and do something different every day.

CHURCHES

There are a good number of church entries here. There are two reasons for this:
1 Church wardens and parishioners are welcoming most of the time.
2 Old churches are usually built on the places our pagan and non-pagan ancestors considered most valuable and sacred – usually high ground where fresh water (springs, waterfalls and rivers) meet the tide.

Irrespective of your faith, atheism or religion, church grounds retain something of the life-sustaining beauty associated with precious locations around the SWCP that our ancestors considered vital to life.

DISABILITY

Some of the most remote locations inside do not have disabled access. Many do – and I hope that's a start for a new book where every listing has full access.

St Agnes

The senses

The SWCP is an opportunity for anyone – able, disabled or otherwise – to explore their senses. The ability after a swim to hear a tiny bee on a flower, while smelling the scent of the wet wood as warm water laps ankles, toes grip sand, and salt water kisses lips. Yin and yang. In that moment, the reconnection of self with the outside world is one of overwhelming calm.

Escaping the everyday through smell, sound, touch, sight and taste where tide meets terra is a fix better than anything you'll experience in any bar, coffee shop or bakery on earth.

Our senses are dulled by the pollution of urban living, domesticity and routine, and then overwhelmed by the fixes we rely on as a pick-me-up.

In most situations, we really only make proper use of one of our senses: sight. Two of our other senses – smell and touch – are underused, and the other two are drowned out altogether by pollution. Hearing is constantly overwhelmed by noise. We sometimes use masks to shield the noise – earphones and music are the most common. But these too can detach us from reality. The final polluted sense is taste, which is mostly overwhelmed by overeating and sugars and salt.

Nature is a respite from all of that. It's a balance. A resetting of the overused senses, and an ignition of the ones we may have neglected.

FOR THE UNDERUSED SENSES OF TOUCH AND SMELL, TRY:

1 SECRET SWIMS AND HIDDEN BEACHES
TOUCH: Feel the sea breeze of your face. Dip your feet in rock pools. Sit on a tidal riverbank and gently stoke the grass with your palm. Or, even better, strip off and float on water so

the tide runs over your body. If it's winter, buy a £350 wetsuit and float in ice. Feel hot sand under your feet. Or rest your toes on a shell bank. Sink your feet into warm estuary mud.

2 WATERSIDE WOODLAND
SMELL: Enter a coastal pine forest and inhale the fumes. Walk through the dense, broadleaf trees of an ancient English wood when it's raining. Smell the tree bark and the garlic around the roots. Walk from the wood out on to dunes and fill your nostrils and lungs with the scent of salty, fresh air.

FOR THE OVER-STIMULATED TASTE BUDS AND NOISE-WEARY EARS:

3 WILD CAMPS AND FORAGING
TASTE: We've touched on it already, but forage for leaves along the hedgerows. Chew on an oak twig. If you can find a safe water source, drink from the 'holy' wells and springs that feed into the tidal edges of the sands and rocks.

4 WONDERFUL WILDLIFE
HEAR: Listen out for the crows over castle ruins; the buzzards mewing around church fields; the trickle of water from the brook that runs along the old path. The wind in the canopy of the great elms; the fat bee around the mauve flowers; the rustling blackbird in the autumn leaves.

FOR OUR CONSTANTLY BOMBARDED SENSE OF SIGHT:

5 ANCIENT, SACRED AND NIGHT SKIES
SIGHT: Look down from the top of a hill fort over a sand bay. Sit on the estuary and watch the tide rise and fall around the creeks and rivers. Notice the changing landscapes, the beacons on the horizon. Catch a fleeting glimpse of the merlin swooping over the marshes or a seal as it pops its head up briefly. Watch dolphins and porpoises

offshore on the bay, from a cliff top. Gaze at the stars at night. See shooting stars from the corner of your eye. Marvel at your ability to witness night in the wildest, darkest places. See the foxes' eyes illuminated by the full moon, and bats dipping over water at dusk. Spot a fossil on a beach.

FOR ALL OF OUR SENSES:

6 SIXTH SENSE

CALM CONTENTMENT: This comes about as a combination of all the senses. It may be encountered while you are enjoying ice creams with your children at the beach with the sun on your face, or while eating fish, chips and tartare sauce at the estuary bar overlooking a harbour, admiring the gulls on mud flats.

However it happens, reflect on what you experienced and enjoyed and what you want to return to. There are more than 1,000 places in this book. They don't begin to scratch the surface of what's possible. There are countless more places, sights, sounds, smells, noises and sensations all just waiting for you. This is what is to escape into nature. And apart from the cost of an occasional afternoon tea, a parking or rail ticket, or night in a B&B ... it's still relatively free.

KEY TO SYMBOLS

These symbols appear alongside location titles as a guide to the habitat, geology or theme of a place:

 Woodland

 Mother nature

 Ancient and sacred

 Good for dark skies

 Beach or coast

 Accommodation

 Restaurant or cafe

KEY TO ABBREVIATIONS

This is a guide to the directional abbreviations used within the location texts:

N – north	R – right	SWCP – South West Coast Path
S – south	L – left	
E – east	FP – footpath	Rd – road
W – west	BW – bridleway	Ln – lane

18 WONDERS

OF THE
SOUTH WEST
COAST PATH

BEST FOR ...

1 HIDDEN BEACHES
2 SECRET SWIMS
3 WILD WOODS
4 CANOES AND WILD CAMPING
5 MAGIC AND MYSTERY
6 CAVES, SEA ARCHES AND TUNNELS
7 MOTHER NATURE
8 FORAGING AND FREE FOOD
9 RUINS AND HISTORIC PLACES
10 SACRED AND HOLY PLACES
11 STAR WATCHING
12 FOSSIL HUNTING
13 SUNSETS AND CLIFF TOP VIEWS
14 WATERFALLS, SPRINGS AND WELLS
15 SUMMER SOLSTICE
16 MABON – AUTUMN EQUINOX
17 WINTER SOLSTICE
18 OSTARA – SPRING EQUINOX

1 Best for…
HIDDEN BEACHES

The South West coast has the greatest variety of beaches in the world. Different states of the tide can reveal a raging boulder quarry or a tropical sunken paradise on the same beach in a few hours. Coves can change from golden sands to black rock, and back to sand, every few miles. Both space and time play a role.

Finding hidden and quiet places means different things in different areas at different times. Your timing, luck and preparation need to be impeccable. A hidden, isolated beach will sometimes be that way for a reason: it's hazardous – either to get to, to swim at, or to escape from. Sometimes, it will be fine. You might just need to take a 45-minute hike around a cliff edge. Other times, it will mean skipping down from one of the busiest beach car parks at Padstow, in Cornwall, to a rocky corner of sand that is all yours.

Speak to local people. But also learn about the tides and the moon. This is the key to finding 'hidden places'. Research spring tides and the lowest equinox tides. It doesn't take much effort. At the very least, search the internet for tide times and extreme lows. Even better, buy a tidal watch and set it to your location.

Remember that tide times are subject to change, just like buses. Not because of human error, but because of weather, wind and the pull of the moon. Try to arrange your coastal trips to coincide with the moons and the tides. That way, you'll get to see it all at both high and low tide.

Reaching a remote beach doesn't always require a canoe or kayak, and there's a huge sense of empowerment and freedom to be gained from being able to get somewhere that you'll have all to yourself for a few moments or hours – especially if it involves an old rope ladder or a scramble down a worn cliff path. A naked swim followed by a hot coffee over a campfire of driftwood is a moment beyond magical.

STAY SAFE

Make a note of when low tide occurs, and make sure you're back long before the water starts to come in. It will always return quicker than it goes out – both psychologically speaking and in real terms. There are so many deaths around this coast each year of people who either didn't time it properly or who took on an old cliff path that was too eroded, worn or fragile to support one eager swimmer. Don't let that be you. None of the beaches below is safe. But they struck me at the time – maybe just before sunrise, maybe just after sunset, or perhaps after a long walk – as being worthy of mention.

North Devon (and Somerset)
Sillery Sands – *Lynton*
Red Cleave – *Combe Martin*
Peppercombe Beach – *Bideford*
Shipload Bay – *Hartland*

North Cornwall
Cleave Strand and Waterfall – *St Gennys*
The Strangles Beach – *St Gennys*
Lill Cove – *Trebarwith*

South Cornwall
Durgan Beach – *Mawnan Smith*
Great Molunan Beach – *Roseland Peninsula*
Towan Beach – *Portscatho*
Trevean Cove Beach – *Perranuthnoe*

South Devon
Carswell Cove Beach – *Holbeton*
The Beacon Beach – *Kingston*
Mill Bay – *East Portlemouth*
Venerick's Cove Beach – *East Portlemouth*

Dorset
Middle Beach – *Studland*
East Ebb Cove Beach – *Chideock*
Ringstead Ledge – *Ringstead*

2 Best for...
SECRET SWIMS

The coastal waters around Dorset, Devon, Cornwall and Somerset are among the cleanest in Europe. They are also treacherous – even when taking a dip surrounded by literally hundreds of other swimmers.

So, why bother with swims?

Swimming overwhelms the five senses in a passive-aggressive encounter with nature. OK, the shock of cold water is a ... shock. But the after-effect, a few minutes later, is nirvana-like. That's why people do it. They are literally taking the plunge to experience something beyond normal. Floating on the surface or simply dipping your bare feet into surf maximises the sensations by multiples that are impossible to quantify. It is a form of magic beyond eating, music and good company, because it overwhelms the senses of touch, hearing, taste and smell in an environment of intimacy with nature that can only be bettered by sleeping under the stars. If wild camping outdoors, or in your back garden, is not your thing, then swim. It's as close to being intimate with nature as it's possible to get while awake. Much like forming a healthy, intimate relationship with a partner, it stimulates, lightens and fixes the baggage we all pick up day to day.

If you feel you need a wetsuit, invest in a good one – one that costs about £350 will keep you super warm, slightly buoyant and enable more time in the water. Make sure you get a proper fit.

Labrador Bay

North Devon (and Somerset)
Crook Point Sands – *Lynton*
Woody Bay Pool – *Parracombe*
Wild Pear Beach – *Combe Martin*
Zulu Bank – *Northam*

North Cornwall
Benoath Cove – *Tintagel*
Porthmeor Beach – *St Ives*
Porth Ledden Pools – *St Just*

South Cornwall
Porthoustock Beach – *St Keverne*
Chapel Pool – *Polperro*
The Grotto – *Freathy*
Freathy Beach – *Freathy*

South Devon
Bovisand Bay
Bugle Hole – *Mothecombe*
Leek Cove – *East Portlemouth*
Scabbacombe Sands – *Kingswear*

Dorset
Redend Point – *Studland*
West Cliff – *Eype*
Dancing Ledge Pool – *Langton Matravers*

STAY SAFE

If you're in any doubt about safety, enjoy the view and stay back from the water's edge.

- Never swim alone.
- Take local advice wherever possible.
- Even when wearing a wetsuit, be wary of cold water, which can cause limbs to seize up and you to panic-inhale water.
- Beware of waves and currents that can sweep you out from the shore.
- Look out for motor craft – wear a hat or a drag a brightly coloured float behind you.
- Look out for dangerous obstacles that can cause injury below the surface of the water.

3 Best for...
WILD WOODS

Coastal woodland is rare in England, but it's among our most precious habitats. Experience shade, smells, creaking limbs, rustling leaves, cool and warm air. Trees are the hairs on the dog that keep us cool in summer, and warm in winter. Trees are a powerful reminder of the past, but much like the water, they are also an important connector between us, the earth and the wild. If only we could reach out to them more – to taste, hug, smell and listen, obeying our primeval intuition, which we too often ignore in favour of solely focusing on trees' utility for fire, outdoor decking, or simply for providing shade in which we can park the car.

The last Ice Age entirely wiped out all England's trees. Then, when the changing climate thawed things about 10,000 years ago, pine and birch seeds blew in on the southerly winds. Those same trees dropped their leaves and composted the cold, barren ground, making it hospitable for almost 40 native trees that returned to these shores.

These native trees included alder, elder, ash, aspen, bay willow, crab apple, elm, hawthorn, hazel, holly, hornbeam, large-leaved lime, rowan, sessile oak, small-leaved lime, wild cherry, wild service tree and yew. Start to identify them around the path one by one. Maybe learn how to identify one tree species per year, starting with the most useful: oak – the root of the word 'druid'. Learn the names of trees, and then you can speak to them.

North Devon (and Somerset)
Culver Cliff – *Minehead*
Cuddycleave Wood – *Lynton*
The Gore – *Bucks Mills*
The Hobby (Drive) – *Higher Clovelly*

North Cornwall
Dizzard Point – *St Gennys*
Rocky Valley – *Tintagel*
Little Petherick Creek – *St Issey*

South Cornwall
St Loy's Cove – *St Buryan*
Great Wrea – *St Keverne*
Gillan Harbour – *Manaccan*
Ponsence Cove – *St Anthony-in-Meneage*

South Devon
Ferry Wood – *Newton Creek*
Wrinkle Wood – *Kingston*
Fir Wood – *Salcombe*
Tor Woods – *Salcombe*

Dorset
Whitecliff Wood – *Swanage*
Timber Hill – *Lyme Regis*
Gad Cliff – *Tyneham*
Black Head Spring – *Osmington*

Woody Bay

4 Best for...
CANOES AND WILD CAMPING

Kayaks, canoes, paddleboards and packrafts – all of them open up the possibilities to camp, explore and ditch the car for a few hours, days or even weeks. Hand-powered water craft give us access to areas that swimmers, walkers, power boats and even sails can't reach. Tidal navigation around the SWCP – apart from some exceptions that are unworthy of mention here – is a right enshrined in English law.

Some of the most precious coastal parts that the SWCP doesn't reach are almost always accessible from a sea kayak launched from somewhere along the SWCP. There's a thrill to combining two rights – Public Right of Way and the Right of Navigation. However, there is something that's more important than these rights: your responsibility to be safe, to get home. So, don't go on the water alone and don't go unprepared. Hook up with a local group or find at least one other person to go with. Stick to smaller, natural harbours, creeks and tidal rivers a little upstream of estuaries. Even the correct tide and wind can be hazardous when things inexplicably change or go wrong. And they will, at some point.

The coast is the best place in Dorset, Devon and Cornwall for wild camping. I'd say it's even better than Dartmoor. Sleeping on a heather heath above water or hammocking in tamarisk over sand provides a unique

Old Harry

connection between you and nature. And it gets even better. There are limitless opportunities for early morning swims, star watching and wild encounters with birds, insects, sea creatures and weather. It's not all idyllic, granted. There will be bee stings, late-night frights and wash-outs. But we still love a good partner, husband or wife in the morning after a bad row, don't we?

The two most important justifications for wild camping around England's coast are enshrined in English law: tidal fishing and tidal navigation.

Fishing and kayaking are not rights limited by daylight or, more importantly, time. That's an important distinction, because most of our domesticated world outside of the four walls of our home is controlled by time. Things close: libraries, shops, the gym, pubs, parking spaces, school, the work place.

Around the tidal coast, however, time is of no consequence. So if we choose to fish for cod or mackerel on a beach for three weeks that's a perfectly reasonable thing to do... And it's legal, 24 hours per day. As is the activity of sleep. There is no right to sleep, but it is a legitimate pursuit to sleep in a bivvie on the foreshore (below the high-tide mark) while waiting for the tide, and the fish, to return.

The same goes for kayaking or canoes. There is a right in law to be allowed to wait in the foreshore with your boat for the tide to return in six or seven hours' time before you navigate off to your next destination. The function of sleeping forms a legitimate part of that travel on the foreshore, below the high-tide mark.

RULES ON WILD CAMPING

- Keep it to small groups.
- Leave no trace.
- Take all rubbish home.
- Stay below the high-tide mark (foreshore).
- Pitch after dusk and pack down before dawn.
- Keep fires well below the high-tide mark.

North Devon (and Somerset)
Culver Cliff Sand – *Minehead*
Embelle Wood Beach – *Oare*
Velator Quay – *Braunton*
Appledore Pool – *Torridge Estuary*

North Cornwall
Porth Nanven – *Cot Valley*
Gwynver Beach – *St Just*
Trescore Islands – *St Eval*
Beacon Cove – *Mawgan-in-Pydar*

South Cornwall
Lamorna Cove Quay – *Lamorna*
Porthallow Cove – *Porthallow*
Helford Point – *St Anthony-in-Meneage*
The Bar – *Mawnan Smith*
Polkirt Beach – *Mevagissey*
Lower Porthpean – *Porthpean*

South Devon
Cellar Beach – *Wembury*
Saddle Cove – *South Hams*
Erme Mouth – *Holbeton*
Meadfoot Beach – *Torquay*

Dorset
Kimmeridge Bay – *Kimmeridge*
Clavell's Hard – *Kimmeridge*
Bowleaze Cove – *Weymouth*
The Fleet – *Wyke Regis*

5 Best for...
MAGIC AND MYSTERY

The South West abounds with stories of wizards, wise women and magic – everything from King Arthur, druids, shipwrecks and ghouls, to dungeons and dragons. Our mongrel past is bound up in a million stories involving ancient Britons, invaders, the conquered and conquerors. We have in common an inquisitive mind, the need for some magic, and a good mystery. Nowhere provides as much access to these as the South West coast.

Water is an important part of the secrets associated with magic: where to find the purest source, and how then to best make use of the plants, minerals and wildlife that thrive there.

It became obvious to most people during the Covid-19 lockdowns the extent to which we had been missing and had been deprived of the benefits of getting out in nature. Nature's power is as relevant today as it has ever been. Perhaps more so. Yet for all our science and technology, nature is more mysterious and further from us than ever. Our distance from it is how we often interpret what's 'good' about civil life, order and what it is to be safe. But it's a pendulum that has swung too far on the back of our own arrogance about the present and our dismissal of the wisdom from the past as being no more than folklore and old wives' tales. That's something we may need to redress.

North Devon (and Somerset)
Trentishoe Settlement and Tumuli – *Combe Martin*
Yelland Stone Rows – *East Yelland*
Seafield House ('Haunted House') – *Westward Ho!*

North Cornwall
Vicarage Cliff – *Morwenstow*
The Museum of Witchcraft and Magic – *Boscastle*
Merlin's Cave – *Tintagel*

South Cornwall
Giant's Rock – *Porthleven*
The Loe – *Porthleven*
Halzephron Cliff Cove – *Gunwalloe*

South Devon
Maer Rocks – *Exmouth*
The Geoneedle – *Exmouth*
Hooken Cliffs – *Beer*

Dorset
Durlston Bay
Burning Cliff – *Ringstead*
Church Ope Cove – *Portland*

Kimmeridge Bay

6 Best for...
CAVES, SEA ARCHES AND TUNNELS

The most dramatic coasts are areas of high-tide rock and headlands. Once the tide has gone out and the westerlies have dropped, the chance to explore newly exposed pools, arches and caves satisfies the most curious mind and soul. It's truly wonderful being the first down to a fresh bay after the tide has gone out.

Caves, stacks and arches are often tied up in myth, magic and tragedy. You don't always need to know the stories that surround them. You can feel them on the air like echoes from the past.

Many caves and stacks contain or are next to freshwater springs and wells that are also revealed at low tide. Our ancestors valued these places the way we celebrate cathedrals and their fonts today. Inevitably, our ancestors protected, stole and fought for these places. Don't be surprised to find waterfalls, springs and dry caves above the waterline close to or under the many castles and hill forts dotted around the South West coast. Fortification isn't about fighting. It's about defence from those you stole from or those who want to steal from you what is most precious: shelter, warmth and fresh water. They're the same things you will need to survive around the SWCP.

Lee Bay

North Devon (and Somerset)
Yenworthy Wood – *Lynton*
Giant's Rib Natural Arch – *Malmsmead*
Baggy Point Sea Caves – *Braunton*
Blackchurch Rock Arch Woods – *Clovelly*

North Cornwall
Ladies' Window – *Trevalga*
Port William Caves – *Trebarwith*
Port Quin – *St Minver Highlands*
Roundhole Point – *Trevone*

South Cornwall
Blackybale Point – *Lansallos*
Kynance Cove
Porthgwarra Cove – *St Levan*

South Devon
Berry Head Nature Reserve – *Brixham*
London Bridge – *Torquay*
The Pinnacles Cave – *Beer*

Dorset
Dancing Ledge Caves – *Langton Matravers*
Tilly Whim Caves – *Swanage*
Bat's Hole Natural Arch – *Chaldon Herring*
Durdle Door – *Wareham St Martin*

STAY SAFE

Caves and tunnels pose a risk – seek local advice before entering or exploring them.

- Visit caves and tunnels on calm days.
- Do not enter caves that contain moving tides.
- Always wear a helmet to protect your head from overhangs, falling rocks or other hazards.
- Do not explore deep caves or tunnels without carrying back-up torches.
- Beware caves that contain pipework, streams or flowing water that might be used by water companies as an emergency flush for large amounts of water.
- Beware of becoming trapped in a cave on either a high or low tide if it suddenly floods.
- Do not enter mine tunnels without professional assistance or advice.
- Use only bona fide groups that provide life jackets, wetsuits and helmets if you join a sea cave exploration group.

7 Best for...
MOTHER NATURE

Cornwall is one of the best places to see basking sharks. These huge plankton-eaters usually arrive in spring, and will stay until early autumn. Porpoises, dolphins and even killer whales, too, dance among kelp forests in the sea,
along with spider crabs, starfish and anemones. In the skies soar ospreys, sea eagles and choughs. This area is also home to some of the largest dune systems in England, alongside vast bogs, marshes and estuarine salt marshes. Deer are prolific, especially around north Devon.

For the best opportunity to see wildlife, sit still. For a long time. Better still, wild camp on a wooded beach or shelter in the porch of a prehistoric cave. Hidden from view.

North Devon (and Somerset)
Greenaleigh Sand – *Minehead*
Valley of Rocks – *Lynton*
Windy Cove – *Mortehoe*
Braunton Burrows Dunes – *Braunton*

North Cornwall
Steeple Point – *Morwenstow*
Duckpool – *Morwenstow*
Black Cliff – *Phillack*
Mutton Cove – *Gwithian*

South Cornwall
Hella Point – *St Levan*
St Michael's Mount – *Mount's Bay*
Devil's Frying Pan – *Cadgwith*
Porthleven Sands – *Porthleven*

South Devon
The Tomb – *Wembury*
Warren Point – *Wembury*
Gara Rock Beach – *East Portlemouth*
Cockle Sands – *Exmouth*
Otter Estuary – *Budleigh Salterton*

Dorset
South Beach – *Studland*
Black Ven – *Charmouth*
Mupe Rocks – *Wareham St Martin*
Sand Holes – *Portland*

Budleigh Salterton

8 Best for...
FORAGING AND FREE FOOD

The SWCP offers up more free food than anywhere else in England, and briny treats include giant bass, mackerel, spider crabs, razor shells, shrimps, clams and oysters. Almost all seaweed is also edible – from kelp to dulse, you will find bucket-loads of the stuff everywhere. This isn't a guide to foraging, so do a little research. Starting with seaweed is easier than mushrooms.

Samphire, sea beet and purslane are the most common plants to be found, after seaweed. They are tasty raw or cooked and are easy to identify. There's also sea kale, sea cabbage and so much more. Many of the edible plants have been over-picked in recent decades, so it's best not to pull plants up. Use scissors if you can – a knife is also OK, if a bit clumsy.

Shellfish is something to get excited about. Mussels, cockles, winkles, whelks and even oysters are easily found all around the coast. There are some areas where picking is protected by bylaws or archaic ownership rights, so look out for signs. But in most cases, collecting for personal use is OK.

Crabs make a great meal or snack, whatever their size. Shrimps netted out of a rock pool taste better than bought ones. Then there's the fish. Either use a telescopic rod with lures and feathers for mackerel, bass and wrasse, or else try small crayfish pots

Beer

that can be bought cheaply online and pack down really small.

Foraging is less about survival and more about interacting with the outdoors while either camping or exploring. But whether it's cooking a crab on a fire or eating nettle tips on the move, wild food is yet another powerful link between us and the natural world.

BASIC RULES
- Check with the beach owner before removing shellfish, plants or seaweed.
- Don't eat anything you haven't positively identified as safe.
- Check the status of waters to ensure that they're not polluted by recent outfalls of sewage.
- Ensure all foods – especially oysters and some seaweeds – are thoroughly soaked and washed before you cook them in line with expert advice.

North Devon (and Somerset)
Culver East Meadow – *Minehead*
Selworthy Sand – *Selworthy*
The Gore – *Bucks Mills*
Bothy Steps – *Bideford*
Marsland Water – *Hartland*

North Cornwall
Marsland Mouth – *Welcombe*
Curtis's Rock – *Northcott Mouth*
Pentire Point – *Pentire*
Porthminster Beach – *Porthminster*

South Cornwall
Kildown Cove – *Ruan Minor*
Batty's Point – *St Keverne*
Pendennis Point – *Falmouth*
Colona Beach – *Gorran Haven*

South Devon
Jennycliff Bay – *Hooe*
Rams Cliff – *Bovisand*
Wembury Bay
Black Head – *Torquay*

Dorset
Anvil Point View – *Swanage*
Furzy Cliff – *Weymouth*
Cogden Beach – *Burton Bradstock*

Cam Galver

9 Best for...
RUINS AND HISTORIC PLACES

The ruins of the South West come in different forms: from tin mines and Iron Age hill forts, to lost quays, pits and quarries.

Sit alone on a deserted tin mine with only yourself, the bats, the August breeze and a newly collapsed tunnel in the rock face for company. Or else saunter over a derelict stone quarry or quayside, which less than 100 years ago would have been a thriving hub of labour, trade, dreams, crimes and activity.

North Devon (and Somerset)
Selworthy Beacon – *Selworthy*
Beacon Point – *Ilfracombe*
Damage Barton Standing Stones – *Ilfracombe*

North Cornwall
Castle Point – *St Gennys*
Tintagel Castle – *Tintagel*
Stinking Cove Tumulus – *Dinas Head*
Trevelgue Head – *Porth*

South Cornwall
Kemyel Cliff – *Kemyel*
Pendennis Castle – *Falmouth*
St Mawes Castle – *St Mawes*
Rame Head – *Rame*

South Devon
Fort Bovisand – *Bovisand*
Burgh Island Fort – *Burgh Island*
Loam Castle – *Thurlestone*
Bolt Tail Hill Fort – *South Huish*

Dorset
Durlston Castle – *Durlston*
Rufus Castle – *Portland*
Portland Castle – *Castletown*
Sandsfoot Castle – *Weymouth*

10 Best for...
SACRED AND HOLY PLACES

The presence of henges, standing stones, churches and cairns tells us the importance the coast has always had for our species, in both life and death.

Although humans are still struggling with the meaning of life, they approach death by placing permanent reminders in the sites they value most. These places aren't exclusive to coastal regions – inland Stonehenge is testament to that – but the coast and tidal rivers do seem to multiply the significance we choose to give life.

Extant sacred places are generally much less visited in 21st-century England than historic ruins and fossil beaches. This is really quite nice, since it means that when you stumble upon empty churches by chance, they are wonderfully calm and peaceful.

North Devon (and Somerset)
Burgundy Chapel – *Minehead*
St Nicholas Chapel – *Ilfracombe*
Parish Church of St Nectan – *Stoke*

North Cornwall
Church of St Morwenna and St John the Baptist – *Morwenstow*
St Materiana's Church – *Tintagel*
St Enodoc Church – *Trebetherick*
St Helen's Chapel – *St Just*

South Cornwall
Church of St Mawnan and St Stephen – *Mawnan*
St Just In Roseland Church – *St Just*
St Saviour's Chapel Remains – *Polruan*

South Devon
St Clement's Church – *Powderham*
Giant's Rock – *Babbacombe Bay*

Dorset
Ballard Down Tumuli – *Swanage*
King Barrow – *Studland*
St Andrew's Church – *Portland*
St Catherine's Chapel – *Abbotsbury*

Barnoon Chapel, Porthmeor

11 Best for...
STAR WATCHING

The South West coast is one of the best placed in England for watching stars. Exmoor National Park became Europe's first International Dark Sky Reserve in 2011.

North Devon (and Somerset)
The Foreland – *Countisbury*
Gallantry Bower Tumulus – *Clovelly*
St Catherine's Tor – *Hartland*

North Cornwall
Efford Beacon View – *Bude-Stratton*
Willapark Settlement – *Forrabury and Minster*
Zennor Head – *Zennor*
Cape Cornwall – *St Just*
Tobban Horse – *Porthtowan*

South Cornwall
Minack Point – *St Levan*
Maenease Point – *St Goran*
Carrickowel Point – *Porthpean*
Downend Point – *Polperro*

South Devon
Muxham Point – *Kingston*
Sharp Tor View – *Salcombe*
Prawle Point – *East Prawle*
Shoalstone Point – *Berry Head*

Dorset
Peveril Point – *Swanage*
Ballard Point View – *Studland*
Golden Cap – *Stanton St Gabriel*

Artificial light pollution blocks terrestrial light from reaching the back of our retinas. It's an irony in some ways that a town awash with street lights has more dark corners and shadows because neither natural nor artificial light can reach them.

When we're in the wild, though, the night sky shines and bounces into the corners of both our eyes and the darkest places. The further we get from street lights, the closer we get to nature. The closer we get to nature, the better the skies. And the better the skies, the more we can see.

Wait for a clear night to visit an out-of-town location. It doesn't matter whether you're down on the beach waterside or high on a cliff top. Take a torch, but keep it off.

If you've got the time, arrive before sunset and allow your eyes to adjust to the changing phases. The skies, light and water can combine to create unique reflections of unimaginable beauty. Auras, green flashes, rainbows and unique cloud formations are common. Nature begins to do something strange and you'll start to see and hear things that are not entirely in keeping with the daylight norm. It can be unnerving, but it's good to walk into the darkness. Once the eyes have adjusted enough and the full moon lights up the way, looking skyward for the North Star is the anchor around which it's possible to start exploring the celestial map on a regular basis.

Consider combining star watching with night-time nature walks to see if you can spot bats or glow-worms, or hear nightjars.

Daddyhole, South Devon

12 Best for...
FOSSIL HUNTING

Time is an elastic concept that humanity has yet to come to terms with. All we know is that there remain a vast number of things about the past that we don't know. Fossils are a reminder of that lack of knowledge. Of our limits. Because to stand at Lyme Regis holding a 5-million-year-old ammonite and imagining what it was like back then is to imagine something beyond the scope of our current intellect.

The SWCP is a region dominated by geological changes. It is unravelling. Falling into the sea at such a rapid rate that it is visibly shocking and upsetting to those who have lived and seen it first-hand over little more than 70 years. The erosion of our cliffs exposes us to our own tiny, insignificant moment in time against the weight of history and the sum of its parts.

Collecting fossils is a way we can celebrate time without understanding it. The contrast is sometimes overwhelming and beautiful. Like staring at a mountain horizon of black clouds that is lit up by blue sky and sunshine that beams from behind us.

North Devon (and Somerset)
Porlock Weir
Broad Sands Beach – *River Taw*
Rugged Jack – *Wringcliff Bay*

North Cornwall
Northcott Mouth
Bude Cliffs – *Bude Bay*
Widemouth Bay
Rusey Beach – *St Gennys*
Portreath Submerged Forest – *Portreath*

South Cornwall
Portmellon Cove – *Portmellon*
Ropehaven Cliffs Reserve – *St Austell*

South Devon
Pinhay Bay – *Uplyme*
St Mary's Bay – *Brixham*
Hope's Nose – *Torquay*

Dorset
Devonshire Head – *Monmouth Beach*
Lyme Regis
The Spittles Beach – *Lyme Regis*

King Rock, Dorset

Trevalga

13 Best for...
SUNSETS AND CLIFF TOP VIEWS

The coastal hill forts are the best views we have of sea, sky and earth.

Where the peaks erode and fall into the sea you'll find the most dramatic and interesting landscapes in England, populated by birds and bats and maybe providing a glimpse now and then of the giant mammals that swim offshore.

Most of these highs are beacons – landmarks that have been used for thousands of years as markers, lookouts and safety points.

North Devon (and Somerset)
Highveer Point – *Martinhoe*
Great Hangman – *Combe Martin Bay*
Hele Bay View – *Ilfracombe*
Instow Dunes – *Instow*

North Cornwall
Hawker's Hut – *Morwenstow*
High Cliff – *St Juliot*
Willapark Lookout – *Forrabury and Minster*

South Cornwall
Treryn Dinas – *Treen*
Gerrans Point – *St Austell*
Gribbin Daymark – *Fowey*
Bass Point – *Lizard*

South Devon
Gara Point – *South Hams*
Bolt Head – *Malborough*
Salcombe Hill Cliff – *Salcombe*

Dorset
Old Harry Rocks – *Studland*
Pepler's Point – *Wareham St Martin*

14 Best for…
WATERFALLS, SPRINGS AND WELLS

The sound and sight of fresh water as it meets the sea is one of the most exciting things to discover on the SWCP. The fresh is yang to the tidal yin, where nature gives birth to life in a marriage of two worlds.

Waterfalls epitomise this tempestuous coming together of two worlds better than estuaries. The English coast isn't dotted with Niagara-style features, but look at an OS map and you'll be surprised by how many waterfalls there are around the SWCP.

Some will be inaccessible and others will run dry. Waterfalls are best, and most hazardous, after heavy rain.

Although tempting, it's best not to drink at freshwater streams and wells unless there is a very clear message that it's safe to do so. The chance of drinking contaminated water is perhaps slim – the longevity of our dogs is testament to that – but it's still a risk. At the very least, boil, filter and maybe sterilise the water first.

North Devon (and Somerset)
Sister's Well – *Lynton*
Hollow Brook Waterfall – *Martinhoe*
Greencliff – *Abbotsham*
Blackpool Mill Waterfall – *Hartland*
Mouthmill Beach Waterfall – *Hartland*

North Cornwall
Yeolmouth Cliff Waterfalls and Springs – *Morwenstow*
St Morwenna's Well – *Morwenstow*
Sandymouth Waterfalls – *Sandymouth*
Holywell Dunes and Beach – *Holywell*
Mot's Hole Cave and Waterfall – *St Gennys*

South Cornwall
Church Cove – *Gunwalloe*
Parson's Cove – *Lansallos*
Swanpool

South Devon
Shiphill Rock Waterfall – *Strete*

Dorset
Church Cliffs – *Lyme Regis*
St Gabriel's Mouth – *Stanton St Gabriel*
Burton Freshwater – *Burton Bradstock*

Church Cove

15 Best for…
SUMMER SOLSTICE

South West summers at the coast – much like the winters – are uniquely wonderful. No other English region enjoys such a temperate climate; ideal for surfing, walking, climbing and camping. English summers are famously wet, but the South West coast gets the most sunshine, with an average of almost five hours a day, 365 days a year, and an average maximum temperature of 10°C (51°F).

That said, if guaranteed sunbathing weather is your idea of a perfect holiday, the South West coast in summer is a coin toss. But if swimming, cycling, rock pooling, coasteering, horse riding, climbing or kayaking are your thing then there's nowhere better.

Summer is a time for late-night picnics and campfires under tarp or tree. Walks through meadows and cliff top rambles awash with butterflies and wild flowers; the screeching sound of swifts at dusk; and mewing buzzards over ripe cornfields in the weeks before the combine harvesters are sent out over another golden harvest.

If you measure value for money in daylight hours, the summer solstice usually occurs around 21 June, on the longest day of the year, with sunrise before 5am and sunset around 9.30pm.

North Devon (and Somerset)
Pebble Ridge, Sandymere – *Westward Ho!*
Bucks Mills Beach – *Bideford*
Clovelly Bay – *Clovelly*

North Cornwall
Devil's Hole – *Morwenstow*
Sandymouth Beach – *Sandymouth*
Porth Joke – *Cubert*
Cligga Head – *Perranzabuloe*

South Cornwall
Dolor Point – *St Keverne*
Porthbeor Beach – *Roseland Peninsula*

Dodman Point
Black Head – St Austell

South Devon
Sandy Bay – *Exmouth*
Dartmouth Castle – *Dartmouth*
Durl Head – *Brixham*

Dorset
Redcliff Point – *Osmington*
Abbotsbury Beach – *Abbotsbury*
St Aldhelm's Chapel – *Wool*
Doghouse Hill, Chideock

Durdle Door

MABON – AUTUMN EQUINOX

Marking the end of summer, the September equinox occurs between 21 and 24 September when the sun crosses the celestial equator, and rises directly in the east and sets directly in the west. Before this date, the sun rises and sets more to the north, and after the equinox it rises and sets more to the south.

The sun dips lower and lower in the sky, making this the best time to explore wooded shores, where beams of sunlight creep beneath the green leaf canopy on to the floor. Hedgerows still hang heavy with late berries and slow-moving dragonflies. As the autumn season moves on, look out for the dewy dawns and mist-filled mornings.

Late October and November are the best times to visit the wooded river valleys around south and north Devon. This is when they are bathed in sunshine and leaves are dappled red, yellow, brown and orange and seem to have the ability to hang forever ... until winter gales finally blow in on the first winter storms. October also sees the return of fieldfares, redwings, chestnuts and hazelnuts. Sloes are already black and getting fat. The larder is filling up for winter.

This is also probably the best season for foraging. Apart from shellfish, there are mushrooms, the last of the fattest and sweetest blackberries and elderberries, chestnuts, hazelnuts and the early sloes after an early frost.

North Devon (and Somerset)
Porlock Beach – *Porlock Weir*
Lynmouth Bay – *Lynmouth*
Chapman Rock – *Hartland*

North Cornwall
Prideaux Place – *Padstow*
Crantock Beach River – *Crantock*
Menachurch Point – *Northcott Mouth*
Broadagogue Cove – *St Minver Lowlands*

South Cornwall
Little Heaver – *Lamorna*
Praa Sands – *Sydney Cove*
Lansallos Cove – *Lansallos*
Captain Blake's Point – *Rame*

South Devon
The Landslip/Bindon Cliffs – *Axmouth*
Bolberry Down – *Malborough*
The Ness – *Shaldon*

Dorset
Seacombe Cliff View – *Seacombe*
Warren Wood – *Studland*
Chesil Beach – *Abbotsbury*
Mutton Cove – *Portland*

Westward Ho!

17 Best for…
WINTER SOLSTICE

The best-kept secret in England is winter. We miss its magic while tied up in the chaos of well-meaning Christmas chores and 'wishing away' the shorter days, pining for spring's rebirth.

Our ancient ancestors saw things a bit differently. Instead of mourning the changing seasons, they celebrated them. The 'deathly hallows' of modern winters were a celebration of nature for which holly, mistletoe and sloes were the iconic motifs.

During the colder months, dark footpaths and hedgerows lead out to the bright lights of coast and estuary, where wintering birds have arrived in Cornwall for thousands of years: dunlin from Scandinavia, knots from northern Canada, bar-tailed godwits from Russia. And then there are the starling murmurations, in Weymouth and West Bexington in Dorset; Paignton and Bigbury in Devon; Mullion and Marazion in Cornwall.

Solstice occurs a few days before Christmas, usually on 21 December, on the shortest day. It's a magical time in nature that mostly passes us by today.

'Solstice' comes from the Latin *sol* ('sun') and *sistere* ('to stand still'). It's literally a reference to the sun dying or appearing to stand still; its daily movement resting at its most northerly point before reversing its direction and moving south.

Whatever we think about the English climate, our winters – much like our summers – are uniquely temperate and mostly safe for expeditions and forays beyond the car parks and village greens towards the estuaries and coastal paths.

Meadfoot Beach

North Devon (and Somerset)
Yelland Marsh – *East Yelland*
Sloo Wood – *Torridge*
Sherrycombe Waterfall – *Combe Martin*

North Cornwall
Widemouth Sand – *Widemouth Bay*
Porthkidney Sands Caves – *St Ives*
Bedruthan Steps – *Bedruthan*
Carbis Bay

South Cornwall
Maenporth Beach – *Maenporth*
Charlestown Harbour – *Charlestown*
Polridmouth Cove – *Fowey*
Dollar Cove – *Gunwalloe*

South Devon
River Ledge – *Axmouth*
St Anchorite's Rock – *South Hams*
Kingswear Castle

Dorset
Osmington Mills – *Osmington*
St Gabriel's Chapel – *Stanton St Gabriel*
Bind Barrow – *Burton Bradstock*
Hambury Tout Barrows – *Oswald's Bay*

OSTARA – SPRING EQUINOX

The March equinox has a dramatic effect on low tides as the subsolar point leaves the southern hemisphere and crosses the celestial equator. The moon's pull will drag back waters to their absolute lowest in the days following the equinox, making this an incredible time to explore the rarely accessible coastal shallows for shellfish and fossils.

Sunken wrecks are perhaps one of the most interesting things to see around the South West coast at low tide. Nesting herons can be spotted around Helford.

The climate starts to warm quickly but not far past an average of 15°C (5°F). The bluebells that carpet ancient woodlands start to die back by April, as the air fills with the scent of wild garlic and hawthorn blossom.

It's a truly wonderful moment when this equinox combines with warm weather and low-pressure breezes. Nature literally sings its heart out as March moves into April.

This is the best time to wild camp with a view to whale watching along the Cornish coast, with the sun setting after 8.30pm and rising with the dawn chorus just before 5am.

Abbotsham Cliffs

North Devon (and Somerset)
Worthygate Wood – *Bideford*
Brownsham Cliff – *Hartland*
Rapparee Cove – *Ilfracombe*
Rockham Beach – *Mortehoe*

North Cornwall
Higher Sharpnose Point – *Morwenstow*
Treligga Cliff Tumuli – *Tintagel*
Stepper Point – *Padstow*
North Cliff Plantation – *Basset's Cove*

South Cornwall
St Anthony Head – *St Anthony-in-Roseland*
Caerhays Castle – *St Michael Caerhays*
Par Beach and Harbour – *Par*
Lizard Point – *Lizard*

South Devon
Southdown Cliffs – *Kingswear*
Branscombe

Dorset
Canary Ledges – *Lyme Regis*
Mouth Rocks – *Charmouth*
Burton Bradstock

Sillery Sands

PART 2

THE COAST PATH

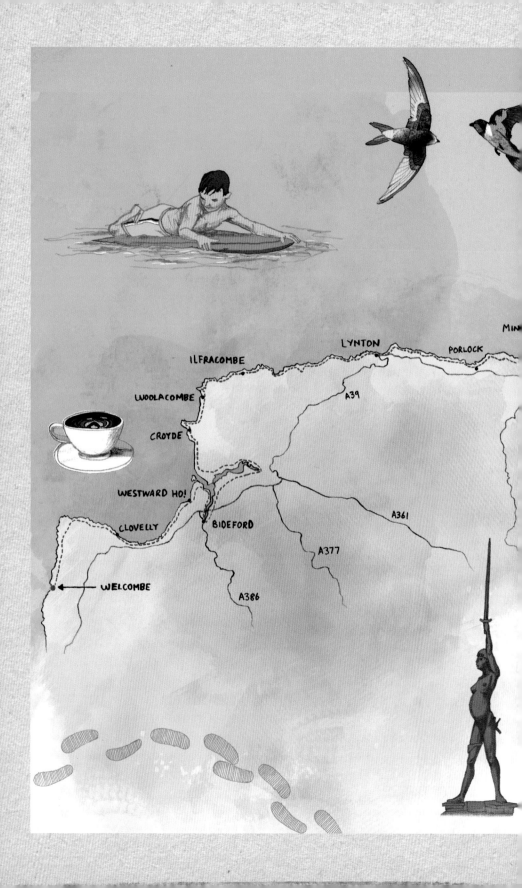

ILFRACOMBE

LYNTON

PORLOCK

MIN

WOOLACOMBE

A39

CROYDE

WESTWARD HO!

A361

CLOVELLY

BIDEFORD

A377

WELCOMBE

A386

NORTH DEVON (AND SOMERSET)

WATCH THE MOMENT – there was only sunlight at her back when she left you at Porlock. You wondered why she disappeared into Yearnor Wood. It puzzled you. Remember? Remembering her move. A magus' hand. A fawn crossing into the ether; where Exmoor unfolds into blue sea. Or was she ever there at all?

Minehead

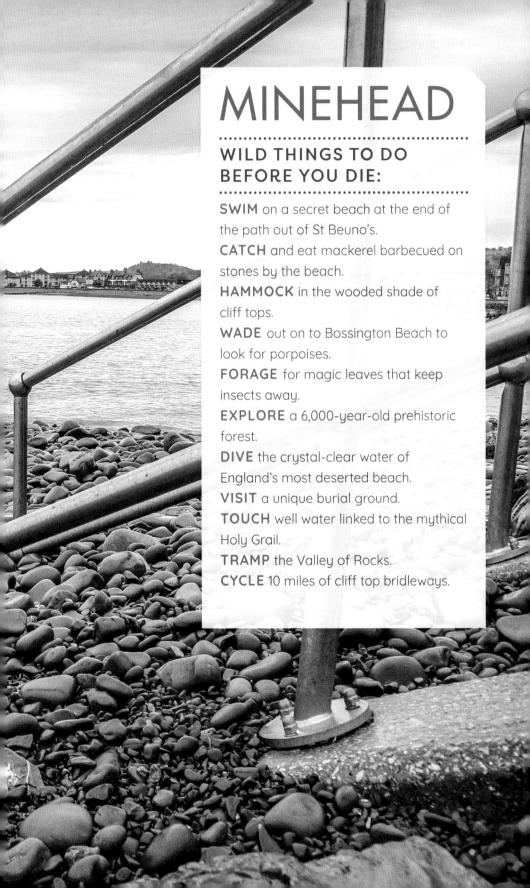

MINEHEAD

WILD THINGS TO DO BEFORE YOU DIE:

SWIM on a secret beach at the end of the path out of St Beuno's.

CATCH and eat mackerel barbecued on stones by the beach.

HAMMOCK in the wooded shade of cliff tops.

WADE out on to Bossington Beach to look for porpoises.

FORAGE for magic leaves that keep insects away.

EXPLORE a 6,000-year-old prehistoric forest.

DIVE the crystal-clear water of England's most deserted beach.

VISIT a unique burial ground.

TOUCH well water linked to the mythical Holy Grail.

TRAMP the Valley of Rocks.

CYCLE 10 miles of cliff top bridleways.

Minehead seafront, Minehead

Lay both palms on the SWCP bronze monument. Listen to herring gulls on the next beach. Inhale the smell of Minehead sea air. Taste the salt-spit of intrepid anticipation, and take a glug of water. Turn to the W side of the harbour beach, where anglers cast spells to catch dogfish on the flood tide. Move south with tempered excitement towards any of the next 1,000 mini adventures – all of which will be of your own making.

> **Find** Minehead station and walk 100 yards NW to the seafront at Jubilee Cafe for a cuppa on the terrace overlooking the sea. Facing the shore, turn L and walk 600 yards along the sea wall to the monument.

51.211056, -3.473928

Culver East Meadow, Minehead

Look for tiny grey rabbits in the meadow of Alexander flowers in June beneath the cliff face.

> **Find** RNLI Gift & Souvenir Shop (Quay St, Minehead, TA24 5UL) and the public car park next door overlooking the sea. Walk R, as you face the sea, past the small roundabout and on to the FP. The meadow is a few yards along the FP.

51.217302, -3.481787

Culver Cliff Wood, Minehead

Inhale the leafy scent along 1 mile of wooded cliff, ideally after rainfall. The FP runs above the rattle and hum of waves on stone.

> **Find** Culver East Meadow (see above). The cliff is 0.4 miles away, as the FP turns into the woodland. Park at North Hill Moor Wood Car Park (Hill Rd, Minehead, TA24 8SJ) and walk the bridleways of Minehead.

51.218282, -3.485900

Culver Cliff Sand, Minehead

Feel polished, red pebbles underfoot, beside the elder, oak and tamarisk shore. Walk from here to Greenaleigh Sand if you set off just after high tide. Beware incoming water and eddies. There are so many wooded overhangs and shaded places in which to rest that you'll wonder why you ever chose to leave this place. Look for red-and-white fly agaric mushrooms about birch roots in November.

> **Find** Culver Cliff Wood (see above), and scramble under the branches down the cliffside 50 yards. There are gaps in the trees and it's not too steep, but care is needed when it's muddy.

51.218282, -3.485900

THE QUAY INN, MINEHEAD

Seafront pub with views of the Bristol Channel. Food, rooms and ales close to the harbour and less than a five-min walk from the station. Perfect sleepover before a coast path stroll.

Quay St, Minehead, TA24 5UJ
www.thequayinn
minehead.co.uk

HARBOUR COTTAGE, MINEHEAD

Three-storey cottage on the harbour. On the SWCP, at the start of the foothills of Exmoor National Park.

55 Quay St, Minehead, TA24 5UL
http://harbourcottage
minehead.co.uk

Burgundy Chapel, Minehead

Listen to rutting barks of red deer around the chapel ruins in late autumn, between the wooded pine combes.

➤ **Find** North Hill Moor Wood Car Park (Hill Rd, Minehead, TA24 8SJ). Follow the SWCP S for a few yards and then take the FP fork (leaving the SWCP) down through the chapel combe.

51.222321, -3.507465

Greenaleigh Sand, Minehead

Look for porpoises between the roll of water over boulders at high tide in late July. Walk and paddle down in the bay, via the remains of Burgundy Chapel (see above). Hammock in the trees towards the back of the stone beach.

➤ **Find** North Hill Moor Wood Car Park as for Burgundy Chapel (see above), but keep walking down to the beach via Greenaleigh Farm FP and Greenaleigh Point. The wooded walk is just over 1 mile long.

51.220595, -3.516201

North Hill, Minehead

Listen for Dartford warblers in the bristle bent heath on North Hill.

➤ **Find** North Hill Moor Wood Car Park (Hill Rd, Minehead, TA24 8SJ). Walk W on the SWCP 700 yards.

51.220595, -3.516201

North Hill

Furzebury Brake, Minehead

A deserted prehistoric settlement, ripe with the odour of feral ponies and coconut-scented gorse flowers in late May.

> **Find** North Hill (see page 49) and walk on for another ¾ mile. There is no direct access to the settlement, but the FP passes within 300ft.

51.224136, -3.525511

Western Brockholes Spring, Minehead

Listen out for male stonechats calling and chasing females in spring, perched on top of gorse. They sound, as you'd expect, like two stones being knocked together on the beach below. Look out for the birds' red breasts and black heads. Exmoor has the highest coastline in England. Savour awhile the cliff view ... 800ft above sea level.

> **Find** Furzebury Brake (see above) and walk on another 1½ miles.

51.229254, -3.550032

Selworthy Beacon, Selworthy

Feel the cool breeze on Selworthy Beacon, 1,013ft above the Bristol Channel. You'll only make it here if you take the higher section of the SWCP rather than the lower route that takes you along by Western Brockholes Spring.

> **Find** at North Hill Moor Wood Car Park (Hill Rd, Minehead, TA24 8SJ). Walk ¾ mile E either along the road and BW, or a little N and then E on the SWCP.

51.221030, -3.549588

Selworthy Sand, Selworthy

Fish for the first run of mackerel in early June and cook them on a beach barbecue. The beach is best at low tide when lighter sands and rock pools are exposed.

> **Find** Bossington Beach (see opposite) and walk around Hurlstone Point after high tide. Avoid getting cut off by the incoming tide.

51.220736, -3.549308

Bossington Hill, Allerford

Listen for tawny owls around the trees at the bottom of the hill. The surrounding hills stay lit up in sunshine even on overcast days, and buttercups add to the cheer when they are in full yellow flower.

> **Find** Hurlstone Point (see opposite) and then take the SWCP NE, and then W, 1 mile up the hill.

51.224352, -3.570311

Hurlstone Point

EXMOOR COUNTRY HOUSE, PORLOCK WEIR

 Georgian-style house set in Exmoor National Park offering breakfasts, meals and rooms.

Porlock Rd, Porlock, TA24 8EY
exmoor-house.co.uk

PORLOCK VALE HOUSE, PORLOCK WEIR

 Edwardian house with 15 bedrooms and two self-contained two-bedroom apartments within the Exmoor National Park, 250 yards from the sea.

Porlock Weir, TA24 8PE
www.porlockvale.co.uk

Hurlstone Point, Bossington

Watch shags fish around the rocks below the lighthouse ruin on the breezy, 300ft cliff. On clear days, there are views over Wales, Porlock Bay and Bossington Beach.

➤ **Find** the NT Car Park for Bossington (Minehead, TA24 8HQ). Turn L out of the car park on to the road and then follow the SWCP L over North Bridge and follow the FP for 1 mile to the point.

51.231621, -3.578508

Bossington Beach, Bossington

Look out for porpoises, while counting how many stones you can stack in a single tower.

➤ **Find** the NT Car Park for Bossington (Minehead, TA24 8HQ). Walk out of the car park on to the road and turn R. Walk down the lane ½ mile to the beach.

51.231621, -3.578508

Porlock Beach, Porlock Weir

Paddle or swim at low tide. The beach is better in September after the crowds have gone, and when the water is at its warmest.

➤ **Find** the car park at Porlock Weir (Minehead, TA24 8PB). The beach is to the R.

51.217484, -3.619521

Porlock Weir coastline, Porlock Weir

Walk in a sunken woodland at low tide. Fossilised stumps mark the 6,000-year-old treeline that turned to stone. Also look for bones from Porlock aurochs, the large oxen that grazed here more than 3,000 years ago.

➤ **Find** the car park at Porlock Weir (Minehead, TA24 8PB).

51.218234, -3.624366

 ## Worthy Wood, Porlock

Listen for red deer roaring in the autumn rut, over the sound of feet crunching on fallen leaves.

➤ **Find** the car park at Porlock Weir (Minehead, TA24 8PB), then walk NW ½ mile on the SWCP to where it meets Worthy Toll Rd. A few yards on, take the BW L and leave the SWCP to follow the trail into the wood. Walk 1 mile to Yearnor Mill Bridge and come back to Porlock Weir in a circle via the Coleridge Way BW.

51.216503, -3.633554

The Gore, Porlock

Isolated rocky beach, good for collecting driftwood to either burn or make things with. Look for mugwort around the woodland edges for making tea or dried smudge sticks to ward off insects.

➤ **Find** the car park at Porlock Weir (Minehead, TA24 8PB), then walk ¾ mile NW through the dock to the isolated rocky beach and point via the BW that runs next to the SWCP.

51.224795, -3.635721

Porlock Weir

St Beuno's Church, Culbone

Smell the sweet scent of summer honeysuckle around the smallest parish church in England, then follow a woodland FP down to the shore.

> **Find** The Bottom Ship (see opposite) and the public car park that looks over the quay. Either walk past the quay and follow the beach round the bend to the base of the wood, or else follow the SWCP through the heart of the wood to the beach. Find signposts for the SWCP down by the quay beside a staircase. The FP includes a 110-yard section of Worthy Toll Rd before it forks off L under the house arch. It's a 1.4-mile walk to the church.

51.221383, -3.659397

Culbone Wood, Culbone

Inhale the musky air of an old oak wood. Look for rare endemic Sorbus trees or a glimpse of red deer in between the views over Exmoor and the Welsh coast. Colonies of lepers once burned charcoal here. The remains of their huts are still scattered about.

> **Find** St Beuno's Church (see above) and walk 1 mile W.

51.225642, -3.677380

Embelle Wood Beach, Oare

Deserted low-tide beach beneath trees. Chew hawthorn blossom towards the end of May.

> **Find** There are many tricky ways in, but perhaps the most enjoyable is the 3-mile walk along the beach from The Gore at Porlock (see opposite) while looking for fossils. Leave plenty of time to allow for the tide and to avoid getting cut off. Set off as soon as possible after high tide.

51.21393, -3.702035

PEOPLE OF THE PATH

**The Kiter,
Airy Point, North Devon**
Sometimes my feet leave the ground. I literally take off. Other people like to attach their kite to wheels, but I prefer to just ski the sand in my shoes.

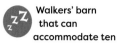

YENWORTHY BARN & YENWORTHY MILL, LYNTON

 Walkers' barn that can accommodate ten people in four bedrooms. This place is ideal for walkers since a FP leads from the farm to a secluded beach and the SWCP.

Lynton, EX35 6NY
www.thebestofexmoor.
co.uk/stay-in-
countisbury/yenworthy-
mill

Yenworthy Wood, Lynton

Walk from Porlock through the trees for a snap of solitude in the wild quiet. Look out for secret paths, ponds and tunnels. It's fun getting lost … but only before midday. Listen for barking nightjars.

➤ **Find** Culbone Wood (see page 53) and walk 1½ miles further W.

51.229552, -3.708155

Sister's Well, Countisbury

A well and spring with a mythical story: it was allegedly founded by Joseph of Arimathea, the 'secret disciple'. He has strong links to the Holy Grail and Arthurian legends, based on stories that gained in popularity in the 12th century.

➤ **Find** the County Gate Car Park on the A39 (Lynton, EX35 6NQ). Cross the A39 and follow the wooded, gated FP towards the sea, via Sister's Fountain, for ⅓ mile.

51.228831, -3.730352

Glenthorne Plantation, Countisbury

Rock arch surrounded by cliffs and trees. Explore the Roman fort and beautiful Wingate Combe stream. There is access to the beach (51.232681, -3.719968).

➤ **Follow** the same directions as for Sister's Well (see above). The plantation is ⅔ mile away from the car park, past the well.

51.233270, -3.731846

Giant's Rib Natural Arch, Countisbury

For low-tide exploits and explorers. Take a fishing rod.

➤ **Find** Sister's Well (see above) and then follow the FP N 1½ mile on to find a way down to the secluded beach.

51.235970, -3.731148

PEOPLE OF THE PATH

The Wild Swimmer, Braunton Burrows, North Devon

The sand dunes were twice as high when my children were young. I used to bring them here dune jumping. I cycle here now they're grown up, and like to swim at low tide.

THE LIGHTHOUSE KEEPER'S COTTAGE, LYNTON

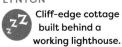 Cliff-edge cottage built behind a working lighthouse. The Lighthouse Keeper's Cottage has six bedrooms, so is suitable for large groups.

Foreland Point, Lynton, EX35 6NE
www.nationaltrust.org.uk/holidays/the-lighthouse-keepers-cottage-devon

Countisbury Cove, Countisbury

Wooded bay located at the very edge of total isolation.

> **Find** Giant's Rib Natural Arch (see opposite) and walk 1½ miles W on the SWCP.

51.236006, -3.769379

Gurney's Wood, Lynton

Smell the sweet flush of bluebells about the hills after leaving the wood. Fallow deer feed nervously around the steep grass banks here.

> **Find** the County Gate Car Park on the A39 (Lynton, EX35 6NQ). Walk W ½ mile to find the SWCP at Butter Hill, and turn R towards Foreland Point. Follow the FP for 1½ miles into the wood. To return, keep going and then loop back via Countisbury Cove (see above) for a 5-mile circular walk taking in many views and wild places.

51.237967, -3.775602

Goat Rock, Countisbury

Not visible from the FP but surely linked to feral acrobatics of the sure-footed beasts that navigate these treacherous climbs. Take a great deal of care, please.

> **Find** the County Gate Car Park on the A39 (Lynton, EX35 6NQ) and follow the same directions as for Gurney's Wood (see above), only leaving the SWCP after 1 mile at Coddow Combe to walk towards the Foreland Point and the rock.

51.245718, -3.784034

Foreland Lighthou

THE BLUE BALL INN, COUNTISBURY

A hikers' favourite, 1½ miles from Lynton and Lynmouth. Dog-friendly 13th-century coaching inn with low ceilings, blackened beams, stone fireplaces and a timeless atmosphere, 900ft above sea level, on the edge of Exmoor. Serves traditional North Devon meals and desserts.

Countisbury Hill, Countisbury, EX35 6NE
www.blueballinn.com

BERRY LAWN LINHAY BOTHY, COUNTISBURY

Camping barn for up to four walkers set on England's highest cliffs, with views over the Bristol Channel, Watersmeet valley and Exmoor. No heating or electricity. About 2 miles from Lynmouth.

Countisbury, Lynmouth, EX35 6ND
www.nationaltrust.org.uk/holidays/berry-lawn-linhay-bothy

FORELAND BOTHY, COUNTISBURY

'Minimal light pollution, maximum sky watching,' they say. The nights here get very dark. Sleeps four, dogs welcome.

Lighthouse Rd, Countisbury, EX53 6NE
www.nationaltrust.org.uk/holidays/foreland-bothy-devon

Foreland Point, Countisbury

Leave the SWCP to explore Foreland Point. The hill climb west of the lighthouse can be risky in high wind with falling scree and path slippage but it's worthy of the hike for the daring on a dry day, albeit not alone. Signs warn against progress for safety reason, but the FP is a public right of way.

➤ **Find** Goat Rock (see page 55), by leaving the SWCP at Coddow Combe. Foreland Point is ½ mile down the hill. The circular walk on the other side can be hazardous.

51.245866, -3.787038

Butter Hill, Countisbury

Explore the hill by the graveyard of St John the Evangelist Church while looking for flocks of goldfinches feeding over gorse.

➤ **See** directions for Gurney's Wood (page 55).

51.235562, -3.796373

Sillery Sands Beach, Lynmouth Bay

Fish and paddle from this black-sand beach with N cliff access. Landslides have closed several paths. Ospreys sometimes pass overhead in April on their northerly migration.

➤ **Find** Butter Hill (see above). The beach is 1 mile W along the SWCP. Alternatively, find the mouth of the East Lyn River and walk E at low tide.

51. 233991, -3.807324

THE VILLAGE INN, LYNMOUTH

Home-cooked pub food and en suite rooms.

19 Lynmouth St, Lynmouth, EX35 6EH
thevillageinnexmoor.co.uk

THE RISING SUN, LYNMOUTH

Situated right on the edge of Exmoor National Park, by the river estuary. Specialises in lobster, sea bass and local mussels. Rooms with sea views.

Harbourside, Lynmouth, EX35 6EG
www.risingsunlynmouth.co.uk

THE ANCIENT MARINER, LYNMOUTH

Nautical-themed bar and restaurant where Exmoor meets the sea. Full-size torpedo inside, as well as an octopus sculpture made by a local artist. Part of The Bath Hotel, there are quirky rooms, some of which are dog friendly, overlooking Lynmouth harbour. Ask for one with a sea view.

10–14 Lynmouth St, Lynmouth, EX35 6EL
www.ancientmariner lynmouth.co.uk

Lynmouth Eastern Beach, Lynmouth Bay

Wade the yin and yang of where fresh water meets sea; feel stones underfoot and a cool current around tired calves. Paddle between the rocks of Lynmouth Bay and the mouth of the East Lyn River stream.

➤ **Find** the Valley of Rocks Upper Car Park (Lee Rd, Lynton, EX35 6JH), then walk across the road and N 400 yards to the SWCP. Turn R at the sea and walk 1 mile along the FP.

51.233005, -3.830017

Lynmouth Western Beach, Lynmouth Bay

Best visited in autumn when the beach backdrop is draped in golden leaf. Climb boulders, explore the many rock pools and take in the views of Wales on a clear morning as the days get cooler.

➤ **Find** the Valley of Rocks Upper Car Park (Lee Rd, Lynton, EX35 6JH), then walk W along the SWCP ¾ mile.

51.232883, -3.809316

Wester Wood, East Lyn River

River valley trail to the beach. This is a hike, but a joy. The water trail leads back inland 5 miles to Brendon. Enjoy a pub meal and hike back to the beach for a swim.

➤ **Find** the public car park at Watersmeet Rd (Lynmouth, EX35 6EP), beside the river. Facing the river, turn R and walk down to the steel-mesh bridge and cross into Tors Rd. Turn R. Follow the road all the way up to the parking bays and keep on going up along the wooded FP. Find the heart of Wester Wood ⅔ mile from the bridge crossed earlier. The wooded river FP goes all the way to Brendon 3½ miles away. The Staghunters Inn (1 Lea Villas, Brendon, EX35 6PS) is there. It's a long but beautiful walk back. Worth the hike!

51.224871, -3.816768

Hollerday Hill, Lynton

View to the west above Wringcliff Bay as the SWCP starts through the Valley of Rocks. Castle Rock towers over the landscape.

➤ **Find** the Valley of Rocks Upper Car Park (Lee Rd, Lynton, EX35 6JH), then walk 300 yards across the road and N then E up the hill.

51.232910, -3.843476

Highveer Point

WOODY BAY

WILD THINGS TO DO BEFORE YOU DIE:

TRAMP around prehistoric hut circles famous for UFO sightings.

PADDLE one of the highest waterfalls in Britain.

SWIM a sunken Victorian pool.

CLIMB a rope to a secluded beach.

SNORKEL the crystal waters of Golden Cove.

FORAGE for limpets.

LISTEN to falcons hunting over Exmoor.

EXPLORE caves at low tide.

TOUCH a hidden waterfall that German U-boats visited in WWII to restock with fresh water.

CATCH shore crabs at a naturist beach.

Valley of Rocks, Wringcliff Bay

Listen for peregrines that hunt where Exmoor meets the sea. Climb down to the beach along the steep, snaking FPs patrolled by nervous mountain goats and their kids.

➤ **Find** Mother Meldrums Tea Gardens & Restaurant (see left). Facing the sea, the rocks are 330 yards to the L. Loos and parking. Easy access from Lynton.

51.231553, -3.857470

Rugged Jack, Wringcliff Bay

Find the jagged tor known as Rugged Jack – supposedly ancient peoples who danced here on a Sunday were turned to stone. Keep your eyes peeled for fossils.

➤ **Find** Mother Meldrums Tea Gardens & Restaurant (see left) and walk W a few hundred yards.

51.233384, -3.854379

Cuddycleave Wood, Lynton

Listen for freshwater dripping about the cliff edge, which resembles a velvet-green wall, reminiscent of a fantasy Aztec sector from the 1990s show *The Crystal Maze*. Some surfers shower here, but watch for falling rocks and scree.

➤ **Find** the car park ¼ mile W of Lee Abbey, Lynton, EX35 6JJ. The beach and wood are next door.

51.228503, -3.874096

Lee Bay, Lynton

Swim and forage for limpets. Boulders are washed in freshwater from The Grove, and salt waves. Great place for rock art. Explore hidden caves at low tide.

➤ **Find** the car park for Cuddycleave Wood. The beach is right next to the wood.

51.228503, -3.874096

Crook Point Sands, Lynton

Swim at a secluded beach. Getting there is fun, involving a hedge tunnel via ropes that are occasionally available. On the way down, pick nettle tops to eat raw or to use to brew tea.

➤ **Find** and park in the lane at Lynton, EX35 6JJ, above Lee Bay. Walk down to the beach. Climb back up to the car park and exit on foot on to the lane and turn R. Walk 330 yards and the SWCP should be signposted forking off to the R. Follow the cliff edge another ⅓ mile to reach Crook Point.

51.226163, -3.883874

The Pines, Parracombe

Smell the perfume of elderflowers on the wild woodland walk to Woody Bay. It's harder and much longer coming up. You've been warned.

➤ **Find** the car park off Berry's Ground Ln (51.221148, -3.897382) and walk 1½ miles down the cobbled track signed Martinhoe Manor to the beach, passing an ancient limekiln as you go.

51.223962, -3.886072

Lee Bay

Hollow Brook Waterfall

Woody Bay, Parracombe

Swim at slack water on a high, rocky tide, but beware the currents.
> **Find** by following directions for the Pines (see page 61).

51.228503, -3.874096

 ## Woody Bay Pool, Parracombe

Hidden at the far E end of the beach is a man-made Victorian bathing pool carved into the rock – perfect for low-tide fun swims. Look for the remains of the old Victorian pier.
> **Find** by following directions for the Pines (see page 61). The pool is at the far E end of the beach.

51.228503, -3.874096

 ## Woody Bay Waterfall, Parracombe

Feel the spray of freshwater under the waterfall on the boulder-strewn beach.
> **Find** by following directions for the Pines (see page 61).

51.223881, -3.896672

 ## West Woody Bay Wood, Parracombe

Feel the warm westerly breeze in August under tree shade. Look 1 mile offshore to see if you can spot dolphins.
> **Find** by following directions for the Pines (see page 61) or walk 2 miles here from Heddon's Mouth Beach (see page 64).

51.226595, -3.903925

 ## Hollow Brook Waterfall, Martinhoe

Paddle through one of the highest waterfalls in Britain. It flows down nearly 1,300ft in a series of long cascades, the last one into the sea.
> **Find** Woody Bay, following directions for The Pines (see page 61), and walk E along the SWCP ¾ mile.

51.227789, -3.910810

PEOPLE OF THE PATH

**The Artist,
Broad Sands, Crow Point,
North Devon**

People say the coast path is better when the sun is shining. But sunshine is all in the mind.

MARTINHOE MANOR, PARRACOMBE

 Self-catering holiday apartments surrounded by woodland. Ask for one overlooking the bay and the Bristol Channel. It's a lovely walk down through the trees to the top of the beach.

Parracombe, Barnstaple, EX31 4QX www.marsdens.co.uk

THE HUNTERS INN, MARTINHOE

 B&B and home-cooked dining in 4 acres of gardens surrounded by Exmoor. Set in Europe's first Dark Skies reserve, the Hunters Inn provides a unique location for a spot of star gazing.

Heddon Valley, Jose's Ln, Martinhoe, EX31 4PY www.thehuntersinn exmoor.co.uk

HEDDON'S GATE HOTEL, MARTINHOE

 Hotel set in 2½ acres of garden and wood, midway between Lynton and Combe Martin. Situated 1 mile from the sea, tucked away at the end of a private drive. Dog friendly, with river walks on the W edge of Exmoor National Park.

Martinhoe, EX31 4PZ www.heddonsgate hotel.co.uk

Great Burland Rocks, Martinhoe

Listen for feral goats while walking E of the waterfall at Hollow Brook. There's a beacon and Roman fort nearby worth exploring (51.227651, -3.916160), but it's on a FP that runs parallel to the SWCP and access to that FP is best found back at Woody Bay Wood, just W of the car park.

➤ **Find** Woody Bay, following directions for The Pines (see page 61), and walk E along the SWCP 1 mile.

51.229401, -3.914587

Highveer Point, Martinhoe

The coolest place in Devon on a hot day. Locals call the ridge's west side 'the fridge'. Sit among campions and nibble primrose leaves and flowers while watching walkers below on Heddon's Mouth (see below).

➤ **Find** Great Burland Rocks (see above) and walk ¾ mile W, or find Heddon's Mouth Beach (see below) and walk uphill 1 mile NE.

51.232047, -3.926031

Heddon's Mouth Beach, Martinhoe

Small beach cove where the River Heddon gorge meets the sea, and seals come in to fish. Walk back up the river to meet heather and The Hunters Inn pub (see left).

➤ **Find** National Trust Heddon Valley car park (Jose's Ln, EX31 4PY) and walk back up the river BW (not FP) to the coast, past The Hunters Inn pub (see left).

51.230264, -3.928237

Ash Cove, Trentishoe

Series of secluded coves, with steep or no access (depending on rockfalls). Care needed.

➤ **Find** the car park off S Dean Ln, (Barnstaple, EX31 4QD; 51.213722, -3.946580). Facing the road, turn L and then R down S Dean Ln and walk ½ mile to Trentishoe Ln. Turn L and find the FP opposite down to the coast cliffs and coves.

51.221402, -3.952542

Heddon's Mouth Beach

Holdstone Hill Stones

THE OLD RECTORY HOTEL, MARTINHOE

Hotel in Exmoor National Park, 500 yards from the coastal FP with views of the highest hog-backed cliffs across the Bristol Channel towards Wales.

Berry's Ground Ln, Martinhoe, EX31 4QT
www.oldrectoryhotel.co.uk

Trentishoe Settlement and Tumuli, Combe Martin

Famous for UFO sightings and ancient hut circles, the old settlement is on the FP at the bottom of a hill. From the top, see the Brecon Beacons to the N and Exmoor to the rear (S). This is magic country.

➤ **Find** the drive to Coastal Path Cottage (Holdstone Down, Combe Martin, EX34 0PF). Keeping the cottage on your L, continue on 330 yards, where there is a small car park on the L. Walk towards the shore and the SWCP. The settlement's old location is between the car park and FP. Explore this important headland on all sides. And look out for UFOs! Circles are barely visible on the W side of the rock wall, but a telltale FP leads up the wall's E side and into the circles. Tread slowly to catch a glimpse of adders or lizards.

51.215638, -3.967077

Holdstone Hill Stones, Combe Martin Bay

Listen for mewing buzzards. The stones are overrun with bracken, gorse and heather, and there's magic in the air.

➤ **Find** the Trentishoe Settlement and Tumuli (see above) and walk ½ mile W.

51.211611, -3.973485

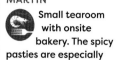

COMBE MARTIN BAKERY AND TEAROOM, COMBE MARTIN

 Small tearoom with onsite bakery. The spicy pasties are especially good.

King St, Combe Martin, EX34 0AL
01271 882865

 ## Red Cleave, Combe Martin Bay

Secluded bay: you'll be alone. There's crabbing to be had at low tide.

> **Find** Holdstone Hill Stones (see page 65) and walk N ⅓ mile to the SWCP, then look for occasional winding FPs down to the cove. The FP is long and hazardous at times and sometimes impassable. Care is needed.

51.217565, -3.994213

Sherrycombe Waterfall, Combe Martin Bay

Listen to the waterfall after heavy rain... There's a small stone beach at the bottom. German U-boats visited here in WWII to restock with fresh water.

> **Find** Red Cleave (see above) and walk ⅔ mile W after high tide if the water falls low enough. Take great care not to get cut off by the incoming tide.

51.217565, -3.994213

Combe Martin Bay

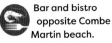

Great Hangman, Combe Martin Bay

Star watch from this spot, which, at 1,043ft, is the highest point of the SWCP.

> **Find** Holdstone Hill Stones (see page 65) and walk 1 mile W.

51.214521, -3.004343

Little Hangman Hill, Combe Martin Bay

Watch gannets diving offshore when they come in to feed on shoals of fish. Cormorants hang about the rocks close to the hill. Less than an hour's walk from Combe Martin.

> **Find** Kiln Car Park in Combe Martin beside the beach (1 Hangman Path, Combe Martin, EX34 0DN). Follow the SWCP to Wild Pear Beach (see below) and walk on another ¼ mile.

51.213610, -4.027386

Wild Pear Beach, Combe Martin Bay

Catch and cook shore crab soup after a swim. Add nettles. Both are around most of the year. As are the naturists ... naturally. Shingle beaches accessed by eroded steps, crumbling cliff and sometimes rope. On a low tide, access is possible from Combe Martin beaches to the W, but at the risk of getting cut off.

> **Find** Kiln Car Park (1 Hangman Path, Combe Martin, EX34 0DN). Pick up the SWCP and walk ¾ mile to the beach.

51.210964, -4.031533

Lester Point, Combe Martin Bay

Good for bass fishing. Entrance to one of Combe Martin's best beaches.

> **Find** Kiln Car Park (1 Hangman Path, Combe Martin, EX34 0DN). It's a short walk from there down to the beach.

51.207537, -4.039228

Newberry Beach

Tiny cove for snorkelling and swims. Best at low tide for rock pools and exploring.

> **Find** the beach W a few yards off Lester Point (see above).

51.207335, -4.041459

Golden Cove, Combe Martin Bay

Small, clear-water cove for snorkelling and relaxing.

> **Find** Newberry Beach (see above) and kayak W. Alternatively, use the directions for Broadsands Beach (see page 68).

51.210240, -4.054070

Watermouth Co

Broadsands Beach, Berrynarbor

Several hundred steps lead down to the beach, where there is a series of coves with caves, and sheltered swims. Paradise.

➤ **Parking** and provisions can be tricky around Combe Martin, but there is a store and post office for supplies and parking 1⅓ mile from the SWCP. Find the village shop in Castle Hill (Berrynarbor, EX34 9SE). Exit the car park on foot and turn L into Castle Hill and R into Barton Ln, with St Peter's Church on your L. Follow Barton Ln ⅔ mile, across the A399 until the T-junction at Barton Hill. Walk straight ahead into the lane marked Old Coast Rd. The beach is just under ½ mile down this lane, which is part of the SWCP.

51.212244, -4.058637

Briery Cave, Berrynarbor

Something to explore after relaxing for too many hours at Broadsands Beach.

➤ **Find** Newberry Beach (see page 67) and kayak W. Alternatively, use the directions for Broadsands Beach (see above).

51.214313, -4.063313

WATERMOUTH VALLEY CAMPING PARK, WATERMOUTH

 Camping on the edge of Exmoor National Park, near sandy beaches and the SWCP. Great views over the bay. Showers and all facilities right next to the coast FP. Explore Watermouth Cove. Boat launching facilities at Watermouth Harbour into the Bristol Channel. Kayaks can be launched for a small fee at the nearby cove, or for free at Hele Beach.

Watermouth,
Ilfracombe, EX34 9SJ
www.watermouthpark.co.uk

LITTLE MEADOW CAMPSITE, WATERMOUTH

 Tents, caravans, huts and luxury cottages. Showers and toilets on the campsite. Just across the A399, about 150 yards from the SWCP.

Watermouth,
Ilfracombe, EX34 9SJ
www.littlemeadow.co.uk

WIDMOUTH FARM COTTAGES, WATERMOUTH

 Ten self-catering, dog- and family-friend cottages with sea views and a private beach. At low tide, walk to Watermouth Harbour and return via the SWCP. There are also animals on site, along with daily handling and feeding sessions.

Watermouth,
Ilfracombe, EX34 9RX
widmouthfarmcottages.
co.uk

Small Mouth Cove

Stunning entrance to the bay and holiday park, either accessed by kayak or by asking permission of Watermouth Cove Holiday Park, just east of Watermouth. The Park's reception sometimes allow launch from there in return for a fee.

➤ **Find** Newberry Beach (see page 67) and kayak W. Alternatively, use the directions for Broadsands Beach (see opposite).

51.210240, -4.054070

Watermouth Harbour

Natural harbour and site of a perfect boat cafe. Best at high tide when the harbour functions.

➤ **Find** parking at either Berrynarbor or E Ilfracombe, then locate the SWCP and walk N from Berrynarbor or E from Ilfracombe. It's 1½ miles in both directions, but is well worth the effort.

51.215731, -4.073377

Watermouth Castle

This castle and theme park offers family fun but is also worth it for the views and historic curiosities. A great option on a bad-weather day.

➤ **Find** Watermouth, Ilfracombe, EX34 9SL

51.213221, -4.068967

PEOPLE OF THE PATH

The Angler, Horsey Island, North Devon

I fished here for mullet when I was a schoolboy. It was all farmers' field and just a small tidal pool. The weir was flooded by the tide in the last few years, and the fields were washed away. I still fish for mullet and bass in the creek.

Braunton Burrows

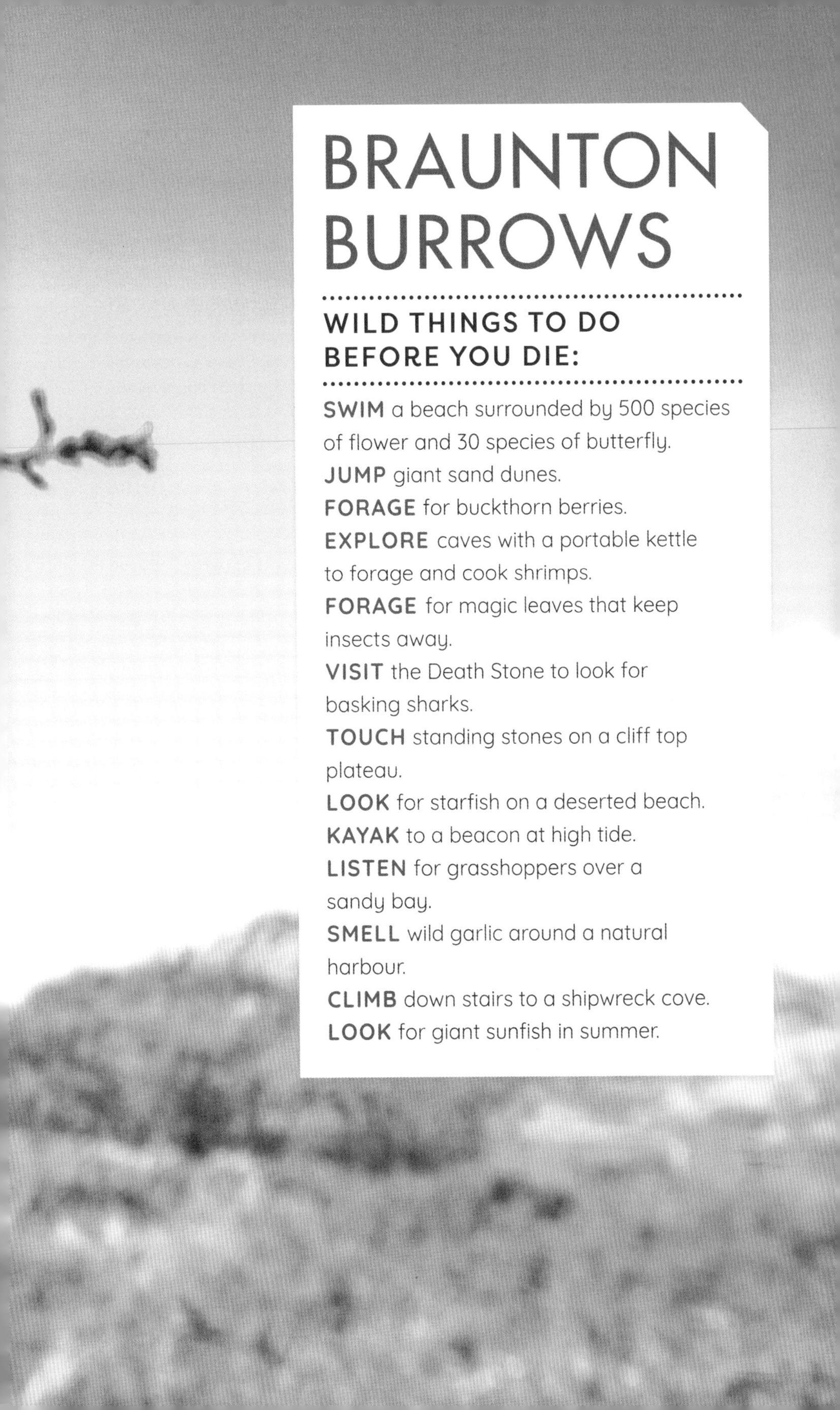

BRAUNTON BURROWS

WILD THINGS TO DO BEFORE YOU DIE:

SWIM a beach surrounded by 500 species of flower and 30 species of butterfly.
JUMP giant sand dunes.
FORAGE for buckthorn berries.
EXPLORE caves with a portable kettle to forage and cook shrimps.
FORAGE for magic leaves that keep insects away.
VISIT the Death Stone to look for basking sharks.
TOUCH standing stones on a cliff top plateau.
LOOK for starfish on a deserted beach.
KAYAK to a beacon at high tide.
LISTEN for grasshoppers over a sandy bay.
SMELL wild garlic around a natural harbour.
CLIMB down stairs to a shipwreck cove.
LOOK for giant sunfish in summer.

BEACH COVE COASTAL RETREAT, HELE BAY

Luxury beach hut-inspired accommodation with hot tubs, sea views, and situated just a few steps from the beach. The one-bed open-plan huts have a shower room, kitchen and outside decking, and floor-to-ceiling windows.

Hele Bay, Ilfracombe, EX34 9QZ
www.darwinescapes.co.uk

THE HELE BAY PUB, HELE BAY

Fish on Friday, steak on Saturday. Sunday is roast day. Lunchtime specials for fish fans and veggies.

39 Beach Rd, Hele Bay, Ilfracombe, EX34 9QZ
helebaypub.co.uk

SNACKING KRAKEN, HELE BAY

Food and drink with a spectacular sea view, next to Hele Beach and on the SWCP.

31 Beach Rd, Hele Bay, Ilfracombe, EX34 9QZ
snackingkraken.com

Hele Bay View, Ilfracombe

Star watch by night, dolphin watch by day. Fulmars hang about the headlands on either side.

> **Find** the car park at 33 Watermouth Rd (Ilfracombe, EX34 9QY). Take the SWCP R facing the harbour and walk ½ mile towards the rocks and cave E of Hele Bay, W of Samson's Bay.

51.214682, -4.091274

Hele Bay West, Ilfracombe

This is a popular swim spot. Explore the rock arch and hidden caves at low tide in neighbouring bays with a portable kettle so that you can cook foraged edible crabs and shrimps.

> **Find** Hele Bay View (see above), and then walk 600 yards SW along the FP.

51.211836, -4.097408

Beacon Point, Ilfracombe

Explore the point on foot on a spring low tide from Hele Beach, but heed the incoming tide. There is a small beach on the W side of the point that is popular with experienced kayakers.

> **Find** the car park at 33 Watermouth Rd (Ilfracombe, EX34 9QY), and walk NW on the SWCP ⅓ mile to the point.

51.213083, -4.102839

Hillsborough, Hele Bay

Smell and look for ramsons (wild garlic) in May. This place is known as the sleeping elephant, because that's what it looks like from Ilfracombe Harbour, with the trunk flat and out to sea. The old hill fort looks over Ilfracombe Harbour.

> **Find** Hele Bay Pub (39 Beach Rd, Ilfracombe, EX34 9QZ), and the large public car park. Follow the beach road down to the cove and walk along its L edge up and on to the SWCP. From here, follow the FP as it zigzags around the summit and leads up on to the plateau, some 330 yards back from the cliff face.

51.209587, -4.102976

Rapparee Cove

Climb the stairs to see a shipwreck at low tide or to swim the shallows.

> **Find** Larkstone/Marine Drive car park (Ilfracombe, EX34 9NU), then locate the SWCP and, facing the water, turn R and walk 200 yards.

51.209937, -4.108345

Beacon Point

THE SMUGGLERS, ILFRACOMBE

Located on the harbourfront, this pub is not much to look at from the outside. But inside ... great service, clean premises and good-value food.

The Quay, Ilfracombe, EX34 9EQ
01271 863620

ADELE'S CAFE, ILFRACOMBE

Harbourside cafe. Try the ginger cream tea.

8 Broad St, Ilfracombe, EX34 9EE
01271 867238

'Verity', Ilfracombe

Feel the power of a female deity bridging the space between sea and shore. This large steel and bronze statue of a pregnant Amazonian figure is on loan to North Devon Council from artist Damien Hirst. Visit at 5.30am in midsummer, when the parking is free, to make sense of it on your own terms - or at least before Hirst calls in his loan. Heavy, brash herring gulls that hang about the place add to the magnificence of it all.

➤ **Find** Larkstone/Marine Drive car park (Ilfracombe, EX34 9NU), then locate the SWCP and, facing the water, turn L and walk anticlockwise around the harbour ½ mile to the statue.

51.211317, -4.113104

St Nicholas Chapel, Ilfracombe

Harbour views and a steep climb to the 14th-century chapel and lighthouse. Look out for porpoises offshore on the bay. Best at 5.30am sunrise when the harbour is dead calm in June.

➤ **Find** 'Verity' (see above). The chapel overlooks the harbour.

51.211317, -4.113104

Tunnels Beaches, Ilfracombe

This Victorian sea-bathing complex is Ilfracombe's most popular beach attraction. It consists of four hand-carved tunnels next to a shingle beach with rock pools, and a tidal bathing pool that fills for three hours before and after low tide. Fees apply.

➤ **Find** Brookdale Car Park in the town centre (Brookdale Av, Ilfracombe, EX34 8DB). The tunnels are only 220 yards away, as you walk down into town towards the Tourist Information.

51.208523, -4.126966

 ## Brandy Cove Point, Ilfracombe

In summer, look for the seals that come to feed and bathe around the point and neighbouring Breakneck and Freshwater bays.

➤ **Find** St Nicholas Chapel (see page 73) and walk 2 miles W on the SWCP to the point.

51.207208, -4.142862

 ## Freshwater Bay, Ilfracombe

Touch the freshwater springs that feed into the bay at low tide, giving it its name. Access is limited and tricky due to constant erosion. Forage Alexander seeds in autumn.

➤ **Find** the bay 1 mile W of Brandy Cove Point (see above).

51.204726, -4.160796

 ## Shag Point, Ilfracombe

Deserted beach next to Freshwater Bay. Look for starfish at low tide around the rock pools and shallows.

➤ **Find** the bay 500 yards W of Freshwater Bay (see above).

51.202677, -4.167753

PEOPLE OF THE PATH

The Busker, Westward Ho!, North Devon

Perranporth to St Agnes is my favourite walk because of the tin mines, waterfalls and secret caves. I look for the cracks in the cliff to peer onto the tin mines. There are also some good waterfalls around Hartland.

THE MILL HOUSE, ILFRACOMBE

 Cottage on the water's edge, with sea views from every window. Built in 1572, it has been used previously as a smuggler's hideout, flour mill, bakery, sweet shop and tea room. Garden and terrace overlooking the bay. Sleeps eight.

Lee, Ilfracombe, EX34 8LR
www.themillhouse
devon.co.uk

THE OLD VICARAGE, MORTEHOE

 Georgian house surrounded by walled garden in Mortehoe village. The Old Vicarage sleeps up to ten and each cottage four. They can be rented separately or together. Play croquet, badminton and French cricket in the garden.

N Morte Rd, Woolacombe, EX34 7EE
www.oldvicarage
mortehoe.co.uk

NORTH MORTE FARM CARAVAN & CAMPING PARK, MORTEHOE

 Family-run campsite 500 yards from Rockham Beach (see right). Direct access to the SWCP and a five-min walk from Mortehoe village.

N Morte Rd, Mortehoe, Woolacombe, EX34 7EG
www.northmortefarm.co.uk

Lee Bay, Ilfracombe

Feel the magic of sandy Lee Bay at midsummer sunset as the sun falls behind Outer Appledore Rocks.
➤ **Find** Lee Car Park (Ilfracombe, EX34 8LW).

51.199588, -4.177068

Sandy Cove, Ilfracombe

Watch hobbies hunt from the main lookout along what was once known as the smugglers' coast. Great for exploring rocks and rock pools.
➤ **Find** Lee Bay (see above) and walk ⅓ mile W along the SWCP.

51.199483, -4.182018

Damage Barton Standing Stones, Ilfracombe

Three standing stones on the cliff top plateau NW of Lee Bay. A 1-mile detour from the SWCP but worthy of the sweat.
➤ **Find** Lee Car Park (Ilfracombe, EX34 8LW). Walk 300 yards W on the road and SWCP, but stay on the road where the FP leaves it. Keep walking another 400 yards S to Hillymouth until the BW on the right. Follow the BW for 400 yards until the T-junction and then take the BW right. Walk another 200 yards to see the standing stone on the right. There is also an informal note/map showing how to find the other stones.

51.194126, -4.190089

Bull Point Lighthouse, Mortehoe

Look for giant sunfish in summer. This 19th-century lighthouse is best seen at night when its light is visible for 20 miles.
➤ **Find** Damage Barton Standing Stones (see above) and walk W ⅔ mile along the SWCP to the lighthouse.

51.200373, -4.201155

Rockham Beach, Mortehoe

Find the shipwreck if you can manage to make your way down the hazardous cliff. High tides continue to erode the cliff and frequently wash away the steep wooden staircase down to the beach. Rock pools and cliffs are fab for fallow deer, foraging and seal spotting.
➤ **Find** Bull Point Lighthouse (see above) and walk ⅔ mile SW to the beach. Alternatively, find parking in Mortehoe and walk ½ mile on the FP 100 yards E of North Morte Farm Caravan & Camping Park (N Morte Rd, Mortehoe, Woolacombe, EX34 7EG).

51. 193247, -4.209309

THE SHIP AGROUND, MORTEHOE

Pub with a sun terrace overlooking the village square. Steeped in stories of historic shipwrecks. The pub features an anchor from the collier that was wrecked in 1914 outside the pub.

Mortehoe, Woolacombe, EX34 7DT
www.shipaground.co.uk

SEACROFT, MORTEHOE

Luxury five-bedroom self-catering holiday cottage with sea views. Situated a ten-min walk down the hill from Mortehoe village and its 13th-century church. Check out the village museum, pubs and cafe. There's also a haunted manor that dates back to the 11th century.

Chapel Hill, Mortehoe, Woolacombe, EX34 7DZ
www.seacroftdevon.co.uk

Morte Stone, Mortehoe

Gannets plunge to feed; sailors have plunged to their death. Known as the 'Death Stone', for obvious reasons.

> **Find** Mortehoe Car Park (Mortehoe Station Rd, EX34 7DR) and walk 400 yards SW along the main road to the front of the Parish Church of St Mary (1945 The Espl, EX34 7DT). Take the FP beside the church and walk 1 mile NW to Morte Point for a view of the stone 500 yards off the W shore.

51.187773, -4.229748

Morte Point, Mortehoe

Watch out for basking sharks, and seals basking on jagged rocks in the sunshine. Woolacombe Sand is 2 miles S.

> **Find** Morte Stone (see above).

51.187773, -4.229748

Windy Cove, Mortehoe

Feel wild flowers and grasses such as bird's-foot trefoil, wild thyme, common bent, sweet vernal and orchids. Look out for the dark green fritillary butterfly. Relax in wind-dried heathland and grass.

> **Find** the cove just S of Morte Point (see above).

51.186280, -4.227634

Grunta Beach, Mortehoe

Views, large pebbles and driftwood – perfect for exploring, as is Grunta Pool, which is located next door at low tide.

> **Find** Mortehoe Car Park (Mortehoe Station Rd, EX34 7DR) and walk 400 yards SW along the main road to the front of the Parish Church of St Mary (1945 The Espl, EX34 7DT). After 400 yards, take the FP R and follow it for 300 yards to where it joins the SWCP, beside where a spring flows into the beach. Follow the spring down to the beach.

51.180076, -4.215948

Potter's Hill, Woolacombe

Listen for bees on flowers that bloom here in spring and summer – eyebright, orchids, thyme and broomrape.

> **Find** parking at Sandy Burrows Car Park (Challacombe Hill Rd, Woolacombe, EX34 7BN).

51.165906, -4.205520

LUNDY HOUSE HOTEL, MORTEHOE

 B&B or self-catering accommodation on the cliffs between Mortehoe and Woolacombe, with views of Lundy Island.

Chapel Hill, Mortehoe, Woolacombe, EX34 7DZ
www.lundyhousehotel.co.uk

THE WATERSMEET HOTEL, WOOLACOMBE

 Hotel and restaurant with sea views over Woolacombe Bay and Combesgate Beach. Private steps down to the sandy beach.

The Espl, Woolacombe, EX34 7EB
www.watersmeethotel.co.uk

THE RED BARN, WOOLACOMBE

 Beer, food and surf. Feast on the special of mussels in cider, bream fillet and samphire.

Barton Rd, Woolacombe EX34 7DF
www.redbarnwoolacombe.co.uk

BEACHCOMBER CAFE, WOOLACOMBE

 Cafe overlooking the sandy beach. Lots of variety, including cream teas, falafel and vegan lunches.

The Espl, Woolacombe, EX34 7DJ
Facebook: @WoolacombeBeach Cafe

Woolacombe Sands, Woolacombe

Dune jumping. Feel the rush of surf. The water is cold, even in July and August, but warm yourself up by laying your bare skin against the hot sand dunes.

➤ **Find** Potter's Hill (see opposite) and walk down to sea and 2 miles of beach.

51.159850, -4.214457

Woolacombe Sands

THE PORTHOLE, WOOLACOMBE

Beachside cafe. Stuffed savoury croissants, vegan feast boxes, cakes, coffees, ice creams and more.

Marine Dr, Woolacombe, EX34 7ZZ
Facebook: @theportholewoolacombe

PUTSBOROUGH BEACH CAFE, CROYDE

Cafe and shop with a terrace on which to enjoy snacks and lunches overlooking the beach.

Croyde, EX33 1LB
www.putsborough.com

Putsborough Sands, Croyde

Summer surf beach with great swimming and golden sand. Rocks and pools to explore and forage at low tide. Fry shrimps on a portable cooker. Beware: access and parking is poor in high season.

➤ **Find** Putsborough Beach car park (Vention Ln, Croyde, EX33 1LB), then walk on to the beach.

51.147340, -4.221568

Napps Cliff, Croyde

Listen to grasshoppers over Morte Bay at dusk. There are 2 miles of sand below.

➤ **Find** the N end of Putsborough Sands (see above).

51.144399, -4.227340

Whiting Hole, Georgeham

Watch shags and cormorants swim and hunt on a calm day. Rock climbers enjoy this place, too.

➤ **Find** the point 1½ miles W of Napps Cliff (see above).

51.146667, -4.256923

Baggy Point sea caves, Braunton

Touch the caves and tunnels around the bays (Croyde Bay and Morte Bay) on either side of Baggy Point. Ponder history and reflect on the evidence of Mesolithic human occupation, or the more recent activities of US forces, who used Baggy Point as a training ground for the Normandy Landings.

➤ **Find** the NT car park (Moor Lane, Croyde, EX33 1PA). Walk NW 1.2 miles out of town to Baggy Point along the coast FP.

51.143897, -4.258975

PEOPLE OF THE PATH

The Beach Hut Owner, Westward Ho! North Devon

Kids love to have their picture taken with the mermaid. She's very popular. I get to meet some interesting people here who are walking the path. If you walk the sewage pipe out across the rocks, you'll get a good view of the old house. People call it The Haunted House, but I knew the lady who owned it. She was lovely.

PUTSBOROUGH MANOR COTTAGES, CROYDE

 Cottages 400 yards from Putsborough Sands, with access to a private tennis court. Dog friendly.

Croyde, EX33 1LB
putsboroughmanor
cottages.co.uk

BLUE GROOVE, CROYDE

 Laidback cafe/ bar/restaurant with a riverside beer garden. Locally landed fish specials, home-made curries and sharing platters.

2 Hobb's Hill, Croyde, EX33 1LZ
www.blue-groove.co.uk

THE THATCH, CROYDE

 A 16th-century inn and rooms. Try their famous nachos.

14 Hobb's Hill, Croyde, EX33 1LZ
www.thethatch
croyde.co.uk

SURFER'S PARADISE, CROYDE BAY CAMPSITE, CROYDE

 Wake up a few yards from sandy beaches, with the chance to dip your toes in the waves of England's best surf beaches. Surf shop and lesssons available.

Croyde, EX33 1NP
www.surfparadise.co.uk

Croyde Beach

Pencil Rocks, Croyde

Gannet watching. See them fall like spears one after the other on shoals of mackerel. Remember to take binoculars to spy on the rock stacks, birds or surfers at Croyde Bay.
➤ **Find** the rocks 500 yards SW of Baggy Point (see opposite).

51.139772, -4.255839

Middleborough Hill, Croyde

Find blue butterflies on an early morning climb to watch sunrise over Baggy Point.
➤ **Find** the NT car park (Moor Lane, Croyde, EX33 1PA). The FP leads out of the car park and up the hill.

51.129882, -4.235816

Croyde Burrows Dunes, Croyde

When you've had enough of dune jumping and surf rides, forage for buckthorn berries.
➤ Beach and dunes are 500 yards S of Middleborough Hill (see above).

51.129882, -4.235816

SAUNTON SANDS FARM HOLIDAY COTTAGES, BRAUNTON

Cottages in a nature reserve 1 mile from Saunton Sands (see right). The holiday park sits in 12 acres on the Tarka Trail and SWCP.

Gallowell Lane Burrows, Braunton, EX33 2NX
01271 814346

Saunton Sands, Braunton

Surfers' paradise, North Devon style. Big skies, vast low-tide sands.
➤ **Find** Sandy Lane Car Park (Braunton, EX33 2NX), then walk 1 mile to the shore ... 1½ miles at low tide. It's a fun walk over the dunes.

51.099318, -4.206271

Saunton Down Dunes, Braunton

Look out for rare pink-mauve flowers of the pyramidal orchid in June and July around the beach's quieter S dunes and marram grass. The spot is also good for rare sea holly flowers, which bloom in July. These were once used in folklore as an aphrodisiac. Holly root was eaten as a sweet late into the 20th century.
➤ **Find** Sandy Lane Car Park (Braunton, EX33 2NX), then walk N over the dunes towards Saunton.

51.099318, -4.206271

Saunton Sands

Braunton Burrows Dunes, Braunton

More than 30 species of butterflies feed on almost 500 species of flowering plant on the second largest dune system in the UK.
➤ **Find** Sandy Lane Car Park (Braunton, EX33 2NX), then walk S over the dunes towards Crow Point, which is almost 3 miles away.

51.102179, -4.214632

Bideford Bar North Tail, Braunton

Fish for dogfish and bass around the fast current and eddies on the ebb and flood. Beware the incoming tide.
➤ **Find** Sandy Lane Car Park (Braunton, EX33 2NX), then walk 2 miles W across the dunes and flat wet sand to the tail at low tide.

51.085023, -4.235298

Crow Point

CROW POINT

WILD THINGS TO DO BEFORE YOU DIE:

CATCH mullet in a flooded creek.

LISTEN to wailing curlews at dawn over Fremington Quay.

BELLY SURF at Westward Ho!.

FORAGE wild garlic to cook with hand-caught rock eel.

BECOME AN EXPLORER by rediscovering the avenue of lost stones at Isley Marsh.

PACKRAFT from the stone steps of Appledore Quay.

LOOK for porpoises on a wooded climb down to a waterfall.

TRAMP the historic bridge at Torridge.

LOOK for puffins.

KAYAK a sunken, lost island.

LISTEN to ravens around a 'Haunted House'.

FLOAT on the water of a Victorian rock pool.

TASTE bass cooked on kindling from King Alfred's cake.

South Burrow Cott, River Taw

Smell the smoke from nature's charcoal briquette. Forage, feel and beachcomb the high-tide mark for, of all things, King Alfred's cake. This incredible fungus, also known as coal fungus, allowed our prehistoric ancestors to carry fire into cold and inhospitable places. *Daldinia concentrica* grows exclusively on dead ash and beech branches, which are quite common among the driftwood around Airy Point. On warm, breezy days between May and September, the fungus is as dry as tinder and catches a steel spark in seconds.

➤ **Find** Bideford Bar North Tail (see page 81) and walk 1 mile SE at low tide or find Crow Point (51.0667063, -4.1904747), then walk 1.3 miles NW.

51.080086, -4.203513

Crow Point, River Taw

Like a wild scene from a real-life *Pirates of the Caribbean* saga. Pay a toll fee to drive up the FP to get to the beach. Or else walk in. Smell pineapple weed on the FP down.

➤ **Find** Crow Point Car Park off American Rd (Unnamed Rd, Braunton, EX33 2NX). Facing the River Taw, walk R along the SWCP ½ mile to Crow Point. Best at low tide. Watch out for mud.

51.0667063, -4.1904747

South Burrow Cott

WATERSIDE COFFEE HOUSE, BRAUNTON

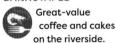 This place offers raised outdoor benches looking out across the Taw-Torridge estuary. Organic, Fairtrade coffee and gluten-free and vegan cakes on the waterside.

Chivenor Business Park, Braunton, EX31 4AY
waterside-coffee-house. co.uk

TEA BY THE TAW, BARNSTAPLE

Great-value coffee and cakes on the riverside.

The Strand, Barnstaple, EX31 1EU
Facebook: @teabythetaw

Broad Sands Beach, River Taw

Look and feel the starry, sunshine-shaped lines in the rocks between Crow Point and Crow Rock. The radiant shapes are the remnants of urchin fossils washed out by the tide.

> **Find** Crow Point Car Park off American Rd (Unnamed Rd, Braunton, EX33 2NX) and walk on to the beach.

51.072642, -4.189068

Horsey Island, River Caen

Fish for mullet and bass over marsh and creek. The island's land access is mostly lost because of erosion so consider a kayak or packraft from Velator Quay (see below) or walk in from Broad Sands Beach (see above). The SWCP once navigated the island's edge. The FP entrance points are still visible at the SW and NE ends of the island, but have been closed.

> **Find** Velator Quay car park (Braunton, EX33 2DX). With your back to the road, walk towards the River Caen and SWCP, then walk 1 mile S to Horsey Island entrance.

51.079834, -4.173387

Velator Quay, River Caen

Launch kayak or packraft after high tide to explore Horsey Island (above) and Crow Point. The tiny quay is lovely place to sit.

> **Find** Velator Quay car park (Braunton, EX33 2DX).

51.097814, -4.165689

Velator Quay

**FREMINGTON QUAY
CAFE, FREMINGTON**

Locally sourced seafood, bread, meats, fruit and veg. Delightful views over the river.

Fremington Quay, Barnstaple, EX31 2NH
Facebook: @fremington.quay

**TARKA TRAIL
CAMPING, YELLAND**

Family-owned campsite beside the beautiful Tarka Trail on the River Taw Estuary, between the surfing beaches of Croyde, Woolacombe and Westward Ho!.

Lower Yelland Farm, Yelland, EX31 3EN
https://tarkatrailcamping.co.uk

**SANDBANKS CAFE,
WEST YELLAND**

Coffees, cakes and breakfasts.

Unit 1 Sandbanks Business Park, West Yelland, EX31 3UH
01271 320650

Foxhole, River Taw

Listen to waders at dawn on low-tide sand banks opposite Penhill Point, on the S bank of the River Taw.

➤ **Find** Velator Quay car park (Braunton, EX33 2DX), then walk 2 miles E on the SWCP.

51.093923, -4.119743

Fremington Quay, Fremington

Hire bikes to explore Fremington Quay and Sticklepath. The Holy Well or Sacred Spring (51.075154, -4.076888) in Anchor Wood makes this a special place. Fremington Pill (Creek) and Rock are on the dead straight path, which means that if you're on foot, you have to run the gauntlet of cyclists in summer.

➤ **Find** the car park at Fremington Quay (Fremington, Barnstaple, EX31 2NH).

51.080525, -4.120208

Fremington Rock, River Taw

Listen to curlews, oystercatchers and egrets at dawn.

➤ **Find** the car park at Fremington Quay (Fremington, Barnstaple, EX31 2NH), then walk W 300 yards across the bridge on the SWCP over Fremington Pill.

51.079420, -4.124199

Saltpill Duck Pond, Fremington

Look for marsh harriers hunting over the water.

➤ **Find** the pond ½ mile W from Fremington Rock (see above).

51.077074, -4.135607

Yelland Stone Rows, East Yelland

An avenue of nine stones along the Isley Marsh harbour. The last time someone looked in 2018, the two rows were covered in silt and weren't visible. But don't let that stop you looking; it only takes one storm or high tide to wash the silt away.

➤ **Find** Sandhills car park (8 Sandhills, Instow, EX39 4LF), then walk 1.2 miles NE to East Yelland Marsh, 1⅓ miles E of Saltpill Duck Pond (see above).

51.075438, -4.155061

East Yelland Marsh, East Yelland

Listen to flocks of ducks in winter on these salt marsh and intertidal mudflats.

➤ **Find** Sandhills car park (8 Sandhills, Instow, EX39 4LF), then walk 1.2 miles NE to East Yelland Marsh.

51.071533, -4.161464

Instow Dunes, Instow

A combination of stunning dunes and 360-degree views of both the Taw and Torridge estuaries. Keep walking to find the lonely places and one of the best sunset views, over Appledore and Westward Ho!, in North Devon.

➤ **Find** Sandhills car park (8 Sandhills, Instow, EX39 4LF), and walk S 100 yards into the dunes and 100 yards E to the beach on the River Taw.

51.058453, -4.179595

Torridge Bridge, Bideford

Feel the history of countless feet and wheels that have crossed the historic Long Bridge over the River Torridge. It has 24 spans – each one unique.

➤ **Find** Riverbank Long Stay Car Park (Bideford, EX39 2LG), and walk ½ mile S along the river to the bridge.

51.029665, -4.201188

Torridge Bridge

THE COMMODORE HOTEL, INSTOW

 Hotel overlooking the waterfront between the mouths of the sandy Taw and Torridge estuaries. Cycle or walk the Tarka Trail.

Marine Pde,
Instow, EX39 4JN
www.commodore
-instow.co.uk

THE WESTLEIGH INN, BIDEFORD

 Food and drink in a large outside space with estuary views.

Westleigh, EX39 4NL
www.thewestleighinn.co.uk

OLD KEEPERS COTTAGE B&B, BIDEFORD

 How to turn poacher: B&B in a gamekeeper's cottage. Explore the woodland walks all the way down to the river and estuary. Complimentary Devon cream tea on arrival.

Tennacott Ln, Bideford,
EX39 4QD
www.oldkeeperscottage.
net

Appledore Qua

Appledore Quay, Torridge Estuary

Launch your kayak or packraft from the steps or jetty into the fast-moving river estuary. Drape your fingers on the tide while looking back to Instow Dunes. Beware strong currents. There are lots of cafes and chippies in which to warm up afterwards.

➤ **Find** Churchfields Long Stay Car Park (The Quay, Appledore, EX39 1RL), and walk 400 yards S with the water on your left to reach the jetty.

51.052862, -4.190476

Grey Sand Hill, Northam

Fish for bass and dogfish at low and high tide. It's desolate yet beautiful here at dawn and dusk. Keep walking round to Westward Ho! and get the bus back.

➤ **Find** parking in Burrows Ln (Appledore, EX39 1NG), then walk 700 yards N along the SWCP to the point.

51.061847, -4.209826

Pully Ridge, Northam

Amazing place at sunset and sunrise. The sand banks are best seen at low tide. Care is needed: watch out for the incoming tide and sinking sand in places.

➤ **Find** Grey Sand Hill (see above) and walk N on to the sand bank.

51.069502, -4.216070

Zulu Bank, Northam

Hard sand bank that's ideal for lonely rambles at low tide. Look for dolphins.

➤ **Find** Grey Sand Hill (see above) and walk NE on to the sand bank.

51.072069, -4.227769

RIVERSIDE RESTAURANT & ROOMS, BIDEFORD

Afternoon teas or lunches outdoors on an undercover terrace with wonderful river views. Self-catering accommodation sleeping up to ten people.

New Rd, Bideford, EX39 5HB
www.riversidebideford.co.uk

THE ROYAL GEORGE, APPLEDORE

Pub food and rooms right beside the sea. Some rooms are family friendly, some are dog friendly, some are both.

Irsha St, Appledore, EX39 1RY
trgpub.co.uk

THE BEAVER INN, APPLEDORE

Pub where the rivers Taw and Torridge join before emptying into the sea. Riverside patio for dining on local fish and organic produce.

Irsha St, Appledore, EX39 1RY
www.beaverinn.co.uk

PIG AND OLIVE, WESTWARD HO!

Home-reared pigs cooked on wood-fired ovens.

1 Pebbleridge Rd, Westward Ho!, EX39 1HN
www.pigandolive.co.uk

Northam Burrows Country Park, Westward Ho!

Feel the space and summer breeze around 253 hectares of grassy coastal plain. Walk down to the sand dunes and marsh of the Taw-Torridge Estuary.

➤ **Find** Northam Burrows Car Park (Westward Ho!, EX39 1HN), and walk N, S, E or W.

51.054924, -4.222487

Sandymere Pool, Westward Ho!

Dunes and brackish pool, peppered with offshore surfers.

➤ **Find** Northam Burrows Car Park (Westward Ho!, EX39 1HN), then walk a few yards N.

51.054804, -4.230100

Pebble Ridge, Westward Ho!

Belly surf or board the main beach and Westward Ho! by hiring boards along the strip. The shops are busy in summer but the surf is sensational.

➤ **Find** Northam Burrows Car Park (Westward Ho!, EX39 1HN), then walk towards the surf.

51.057182, -4.237151

Westward Ho! Sea Pool, Westward Ho!

Low-tide Victorian pool/lido. Rubber shoes needed as the rocks can be troublesome on tired feet after a long walk. Shrimps and crabs in surrounding rock pools.

➤ **Find** Seafield Car Park (Merley Rd, Westward Ho!, EX39 1JU), then walk E along the SWCP ¼ mile to the pool.

51.040785, -4.243102

Westward Ho! Sea Pool

MORANS
RESTAURANT & BAR,
WESTWARD HO!

 Thai and British
restaurant a
few steps
from the beach, with
spectacular views.

Golf Links Rd,
Westward Ho!, EX39 1LH
moransrestaurant.co

Mermaid Pool, Westward Ho!

**Warm-water plunge in a natural rock pool. Access from the cliff
and beach or walk the sewage pipe case from low tide over the
rocks where the S beach of Westward Ho! ends.**

➤ **Find** Seafield Car Park (Merley Rd, Westward Ho!, EX39 1JU),
then walk W 400 yards to find the pool.

51.038688, -4.257443

Rock Nose, Seafield House, Westward Ho!

**Listen to ravens around the point, and particularly over the site
once known locally as the 'Haunted House' or 'Spooky House'
(which will likely be demolished and rebuilt by the time you
read this).**

➤ **Find** Seafield Car Park (Merley Rd, Westward Ho!, EX39 1JU).
Seafield House (51.038058, -4.251561) is directly in front of the
car park, then walk 400 yards W to Rock Nose.

51.038688, -4.257443

Kipling Tors, Westward Ho!

**Estuary and coast views after a steep climb. Only a five-min
diversion from the FP.**

➤ **Find** Seafield Car Park (Merley Rd, Westward Ho!, EX39 1JU),
and with your back to the shore, walk along the SWCP and up
and into the scrub peak.

51.038058, -4.251561

Abbotsham Cliffs, Abbotsham

Listen to mewing buzzards over this sheep field detour from the beach up to cooler, higher ground.
➤ **Find** Rock Nose (see opposite) and walk ⅔ mile to the FP signed R on the SWCP. Take the SWCP 600 yards over farmland.

51.025994, -4.264555

Greencliff, Abbotsham

A small but loud waterfall surrounded by wild flowers in spring.
➤ **Find** Rock Nose (see opposite) and walk 1⅓ miles SW along the SWCP to the cliff.

51.040785, -4.243102

Westacott Cliff, Abbotsham

Paddle in freshwater and seek out driftwood where the FP meets the beach.
➤ **Find** Rock Nose (see opposite) and walk 2 miles SW along the SWCP to the cliff.

51.010796, -4.287117

Babbacombe Cliff, Bideford

Look out for puffins. Lone birds fly all along this coastal area when they stray away from Lundy Island offshore.
➤ **Find** Rock Nose (see opposite) and walk 3 miles SW along the SWCP to the cliff.

51.005138, -4.293957

Peppercombe Beach, Bideford

The dark stones here heat up so much in the summer sun that the sand and beach shimmers into a mirage. Swim later in the afternoon as the cold water will have been warmed on the hot pebbles.
➤ **Find** Rock Nose (see opposite) and walk 3 miles SW along the SWCP to the cliff. Alternatively, walk E along the SWCP 2⅓ miles from Bucks Mills NT car park. For the NT car park, find St Anne's Church (Bucks Mills, EX39 5ND). With the church on your L, continue on the lane another ½ mile to the car park on the R. Make the rest of the way on foot. The beach is ⅓ mile down the lane.

51.005138, -4.293957

HARTLAND

WILD THINGS TO DO BEFORE YOU DIE:

LOOK for fin whales along the shipwreck coast.

BATHE in a waterfall plunge pool.

SMELL a wood of bluebells and take a nap there.

LISTEN to stonechats around a prehistoric burial ground.

WADE at low tide between rock arch, waterfall and wooded cliffs.

FORAGE for winter chanterelles.

GLAMP on a working farm.

EXPLORE an eroding Iron Age fort.

TRAMP around a headland of breeding seals.

LOOK for pods of dolphins at Clovelly before having dinner at the harbour.

Sloo Wood

Sloo Wood, Torridge

Navigate the mud-slide FP in winter mist between centuries-old, twisted sessile oaks cloaked in grey and green lichens.

➤ **Find** Bucks Mills NT car park (see Peppercombe Beach, page 91), then walk to the shore to find the SWCP and follow it E for 1 mile.

50.990081, -4.321352

Worthygate Wood, Bideford

Touch pussy willow snow in late May and early June, along with sweet woodruff and wood millet. Smell around where the butterflies feed on betony, orchids and ragged robin.

➤ **Find** Bucks Mills NT car park (see Peppercombe Beach on page 91), then walk to the shore to find the SWCP and follow it E for ⅔ mile. Sloo Wood (see above) and Worthygate Wood are joined, Sloo being a little furthest E from Bucks Mills.

50.989919, -4.325421

Bucks Mills Beach, Bideford

The waterfall by St Anne's Church (Bucks Mills, EX39 5ND) is best seen at low tide. There's masses of ancient woodland, beach and cliffs to explore in all directions.

➤ **Find** Bucks Mills NT car park (see Peppercombe Beach, page 91). The beach is ⅓ mile down the lane.

50.989498, -4.346500

COACH AND HORSES, HORNS CROSS

Cosy, family-run pub, offering food and B&B.

Horns Cross, Bideford,
EX39 5DH
01237 451214

THE HOOPS INN & COUNTRY HOTEL, HORNS CROSS

Grade II listed, part-thatched, 13th-century inn set in 2.5 acres of landscaped grounds. Restaurant serving locally sourced produce, and 13 en suite bedrooms.

Horns Cross, Bideford,
EX39 5DL
www.hotelsnorthdevon.
co.uk

MELINDA'S COTTAGE, BUCKS MILLS

Period two-bedroom fisherman's cottage just off the SWCP. Sleeps four. Dog friendly.

5 Forest Gardens, Bucks
Mills, EX39 5DY
melindascottage.
business.site

BIDEFORD BAY HOLIDAY PARK, BIDEFORD

Caravans, luxury lodges or chalets in woodland close to the SWCP.

The Lodge, Bucks Cross,
Bideford EX39 5DU
www.parkdeanresorts.
co.uk/location/devon/
bideford-bay

The Gore, Bucks Mills

Look for porpoises on the wooded climb down to the beach and low-tide spit.

➤ **Find** the spit 500 yards W of Bucks Mills Beach (see opposite).

50.991215, -4.352085

Bothy Steps, Buck's Wood, Bideford

This scented tunnel of wild garlic is split by a wooden staircase up and out of the river valley. It's best in late May and early June when the garlic flowers are at their most pungent.

➤ **Find** Peppercombe Beach (see page 91) and follow the SWCP a little way W (L if you are facing the shore or the bothy).

50.993528, -4.307299

The Hobby (Drive), Higher Clovelly

Feel the long and winding road... This woodland walk of substance leads you out of, or into, Clovelly. It can become extremely tiresome if you're already exhausted after a long day's walk, but it's uplifting before lunch, with glimpses through the trees of Bideford Bay and Clovelly harbour.

➤ **For** the NT car park, find St Anne's Church (Bucks Mills, EX39 5ND). With the church on your L, continue on the lane another ½ mile to the car park on the R. Walk 2⅓ miles W to The Hobby. Take care: it's steep.

50.987352, -4.378008

Clovelly Bay, Clovelly

See the waterfall at the bottom of the bay and beach that trundles down from The Hobby above. Look for tree lichens; there are more than 250 species overhead. While looking, try to catch a glimpse of nesting hobbies as they swoop through the tree canopy.

➤ **Find** Clovelly Visitor Centre (see page 96), then walk 500 yards down the steep cobbled FP.

50.997643, -4.393449

Clovelly Bay

EAST DYKE FARMHOUSE B&B, HIGHER CLOVELLY

B&B set above Clovelly on a 500-acre working farm. Clovelly Dykes – a 2,000-year-old Iron Age hill fort – is open for visitors to explore to the rear of the farmhouse. The 19th-century farmhouse is situated on a country road 1½ miles from Clovelly and the coast FP, but is worth the trek.

Higher Clovelly, EX39 5RU
www.bedbreakfast
clovelly.co.uk

THE OLD SMITHY B&B, HIGHER CLOVELLY

B&B set on the higher part of Clovelly, overlooking Bideford Bay and Lundy Island.

147 Slerra Hill, Clovelly, EX39 5ST
www.oldsmithybandb
clovelly.co.uk

Clovelly Harbour, Clovelly

Paddle the harbour rocks after the long walk down, then walk the harbour wall to see pods of dolphins and porpoises in spring and early summer.

➤ **Find** Clovelly Visitor Centre (see below), then walk 500 yards down the steep cobbled FP to the harbour.

50.997643, -4.393449

Clovelly Visitor Centre, Clovelly

Duck playful swallows that nest and feed young in the centre's entrance eaves from March to September.

➤ **Find** Clovelly Visitor Centre Car Park (EX39 5TL).

50.998851, -4.402432

Mount Pleasant, Clovelly

Sunny memorial and shelter surrounded by buttercups and spring flowers in May and June.

➤ **Find** Clovelly Visitor Centre (see above).

50.998773, -4.400457

The Cabin, Clovelly

Sweet-smelling cliffside hut in a moat of garlic, beech, ash and oak woodland. Peer through the gaps in the trees for coastal views over Wood Rock.

➤ **Find** Clovelly Visitor Centre (see above) and walk ½ mile NW on the SWCP.

51.004238, -4.404341

Mount Pleasant

Clovelly Harbour

NEW INN HOTEL, CLOVELLY

 A 15th-century inn for ales and rooms. It features a medieval courtyard and garden. Complimentary Devon cream tea on arrival.

93 High St, Clovelly, EX39 5TQ
www.clovelly.co.uk

THE RED LION HOTEL, CLOVELLY

 An 18th-century four-star inn that stands on the quay alongside the ancient harbour. Check out the local museum to read up on the Clovelly estate, originally owned by William the Conqueror. Until the middle of the 19th century, Clovelly was largely unknown to the outside world. It was partly as a result of Charles Kingsley's novel *Westward Ho!*, set in and around the village, that visitors began to come. There is still a charge to enter Clovelly village, which is perched on a 400ft cliff, with no vehicular access.

48 The Quay, Clovelly, EX39 5TF
www.clovelly.co.uk

YAPHAM COTTAGES, HARTLAND

 Period stone barn conversions on a sloping valley in landscaped gardens. Dog friendly.

Hartland, EX39 6AN
www.yaphamcottages.com

LOWER BROWNSHAM FARM TEA ROOMS, HARTLAND

 Country tea shop for home-made cakes, scones, drinks and locally made ice cream.

Lower Brownsham Farm, Hartland, EX39 6AN
Facebook: @TinaJeffery17

**LOVELAND FARM
ECO-RETREAT,
HARTLAND**

Glamping with a difference on a former working farm. Pitches are available for a minimum of two nights and must be booked in one of the on-site geodesic pods and 'tentipis'.

Hartland, EX39 6AT
loveland.farm

**GAWLISH FARM,
HARTLAND**

Farm B&B on the SWCP.

Hartland,
EX39 6AT
01237 441320

**LOVELAND FARM
ECO-RETREAT,
HARTLAND**

B&B on the Hartland Peninsula, 1½ miles N of Hartland, 4½ miles from Clovelly and less than 1 mile from the SWCP.

Hartland, EX39 6AS
www.bandbhartland.co.uk

Gallantry Bower Tumulus, Clovelly

Listen for stonechats and meadow pipits. Look for peregrines hunting small seabirds.

> **Find** the tumulus ¾ mile NW of The Cabin (see page 96).

51.010321, -4.418097

Blackchurch Rock Arch Woods, Clovelly

Triangular rock arch on a beach of large pebbles and rock. There are many FPs to explore. It's a steep walk down. Walk through Brownsham Woods while picking and chewing sweet grass stems.

> **Find** Lower Brownsham Farm Tea Rooms (see page 97) and the NT car park next door (Lower Brownsham Farm, Hartland, EX39 6AN). With your back to the tearooms and facing the car park, take the FP and then follow it as it curves R towards the shore and beach 1.2 miles away. Walk less than 1 mile E for Brownsham woodlands and Mouthmill Beach on the edge of Hartland. Clovelly is just over 1½ miles W along the shore.

51.013740, -4.425993

Mouthmill Beach Waterfall, Hartland

Woodland, low-tide adventure. It's well worth the walk when combined with Blackchurch Rock Arch.

> **Find** the waterfall ¾ mile E of Blackchurch Rock Arch (see above).

50.013541, -4.436255

Blackchurch Roc

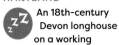
WEST TITCHBERRY
FARM GUEST HOUSE,
HARTLAND

 An 18th-century
Devon longhouse
on a working
sheep and cattle farm,
offering three letting
rooms. Farmhouse
breakfast is included,
and an evening meal is
optional and normally
served at 6.30pm but
can be altered by prior
arrangement. A welcome
tea tray is served on
arrival with home-made
goodies. No dogs.

Hartland, EX39 6AU
westtitchberryfarm.
weebly.com

**THE POINT @
HARTLAND, HARTLAND**

 Small tearoom,
big views. There's
parking, too.

Blagdon Farm, Hartland,
EX39 6AU
www.thepointhartland.
co.uk

**BLACKPOOL MILL
COTTAGE, STOKE**

The SWCP passes
behind the 15th-
century cottage
that sleeps eight. The
place lies beside the
Hartland Abbey stream
about 75 yards from
the beach.

Hartland Abbey, Stoke,
EX39 6DT
www.hartlandabbey.
com/blackpool-mill/

Beckland Bay, Hartland

If you can find a way down, Windbury Head Camp sits 160 yards
overhead at the summit of Beckland Cliffs. The Iron Age hill fort
is being eroded out.
➤ **Find** the bay ½ mile E of Mouthmill Beach Waterfall
(see opposite).

50.015748, -4.451357

Brownsham Cliff, Hartland

After exiting the warm sunshine at the top, rest in the sweet
scent of bluebell woodland, take in the cool saltiness of the cliff
top. Taste the difference in the air.
➤ **Find** the cliff 500 yards E of Beckland Bay (see above).

50.014507, -4.454154

Chapman Rock, Hartland

Look for grey seals that breed in the bays and caves between
here and Hartland Point (see page 100).
➤ **Find** East Titchberry Car Park (Hartland, EX39 6AU), then
walk N on the BW out of the car park 300 yards to the SWCP.
Turn R as you face the sea and walk 2 miles E to the rock.

50.021957, -4.469166

Shipload Bay, Hartland

Look out for dolphins. This rock and shingle bay was once
famous for smuggling and donkey trails but has largely
become inaccessible. Some intrepid climbers do still make
their way down, but it can be dangerous and may be best
seen from the top.
➤ **Find** East Titchberry Car Park (Hartland, EX39 6AU), then
walk 300 yards to the cliffs.

50.019712, -4.501911

PEOPLE OF
THE PATH

**The Long Distance
Walker, Worthygate
Wood, North Devon**
The Hobby Drive in and out
of Clovelly is one of the most
beautiful walks between here
and Land's End. Lots of trees
and birds, and it's relatively flat!

BERRY HOUSE, THE BIG HOUSE COMPANY, HARTLAND

 Large, luxurious house with ten bedrooms that's perfect for large parties, situated just a short walk from stony Berry Beach. Features a games room, BBQ area, sheltered courtyard and hot tub. Dog friendly.

Hartland, EX39 6DA
www.thebighouseco.com/our-big-houses/berry-house

HARTLAND QUAY HOTEL, HARTLAND

Hotel, bar and restaurant serving locally sourced food and ales. Hotel since 1886, with original stables that have now been converted into The Wreckers Retreat bar. Above the stables were the old corn and hay lofts, which are now en suite bedrooms. Perfect stop on the SWCP for walkers, with dramatic Atlantic views and brutal winds. The name is a reference to the number of ships that have been ruined on the shores.

Stoke, Hartland, EX39 6DU
hartlandquayhotel.co.uk

Barley Bay, Hartland

Listen for the constant trill of nightjar song around this super-secluded and wild, rocky bay. There are steps down but the whole area is under constant erosion and it can be tricky to navigate.

➤ **Find** parking at The Point @ Hartland tea shop (see below).

50.021440, -4.520043

Hartland Point, Hartland

Look for fin whales between the spectacular views over Lundy Island and S Wales. There are also varied rock formations between Hartland Point and Hartland Quay.

➤ **Find** The Point @ Hartland and walk 300 yards E to the point.

50.022371, -4.525943

Smoothlands Waterfall, Hartland

This waterfall can run slow in summer. Listen for the sound of water to help you locate it.

➤ **Find** the waterfall 1 mile S of Hartland Point (see above).

50.012014, -4.525386

Blackpool Mill Waterfall, Hartland

Beach and waterfall. From February, look for cleaver stems, which can be used to flavour bottled water (you'll need 5-10 of them).

➤ **Find** the mill 1 mile S of Smoothlands Waterfall (see above).

50.005061, -4.529548

Hartland Quay Museum, Hartland

Visit the museum for photographs, artefacts and documents of shipwrecks, smuggling, geology and coastal industries. Open in the summer.

➤ **Find** Hartland Quay Hotel (Hartland, EX39 6DU).

50.994906, -4.533858

Parish Church of St Nectan and St Nectan's Well, Stoke

Divert inland to the church spire that hangs almost 130ft above the coastline like a beacon - it's the tallest spire in Devon. Look for St Nectan's Well (Stoke) nearby as it has a fascinating story worthy of being kept alive.

➤ Walk the river FP SE from Dyers Lookout (51.002521, -4.530539) where it leaves the SWCP and follow it for 1 mile to the Parish Church of St Nectan (Stoke, EX39 6DU).

50.995486, -4.516411

**SOUTHOLE BARNS
SELF CATERING
COTTAGES,
HARTLAND**

Self-catering barns by the SWCP leading down to Welcombe Mouth Beach (50.933906, -4.545308). Open moorland and woodland down to the coast, waterfalls and rocky shores.

1 Southole Barns, Southole, EX39 6HW
www.southole.co.uk

**STOKE BARTON FARM
AND CAMPSITE,
STOKE**

Camping on 500 acres of working farm. Spectacular night skies on the Hartland Peninsula mean that it's a great place from which to gaze at the Milky Way on a clear night.

Stoke Barton Farm, Stoke, EX39 6DU
www.westcountry-camping.co.uk

St Catherine's Tor, Hartland

Take in the views, look for lone fallow deer, and find the waterfalls N and S of the Tor.

➤ **Find** the car park near Hartland Quay Hotel (see opposite) and follow the SWCP ½ mile S to the tor.

50.989089, -4.530435

Speke's Mill Mouth Waterfall, Hartland Quay Woods

Dramatic waterfall into a plunge pool; sandy bays either side of the falls. Take a short walk S for views. It's a one-hour walk N from here to Hartland Point.

➤ **Find** the car park near Hartland Quay Hotel (see opposite). Facing the sea, walk L along the SWCP ⅓ mile to St Catherine's Tor (see above). Walk on another ⅔ mile for the Mill Mouth and the FP inland to Milford for a cuppa at Docton Mill Gardens & Tea Rooms (Hartland, EX39 6EA). Milford is 1.6 miles from the car park.

50. 984046, -4.528986

Elmscott Beach, Hartland

Look out for dolphins feeding along this section of beach. Access down can be difficult and sporadic, depending on cliff fall and previous access.

➤ **Find** the beach cliff 1½ miles N of Embury Beacon (see page 102) or 1½ miles S of Speke's Mill Mouth Waterfall (see above).

50.965001, -4.536163

PEOPLE OF THE PATH

**The Camper,
Hartland, North Devon**

The Stoke Barton Farm and Campsite, at Hartland, is an excellent place to stop for anyone walking the path. Especially if the weather turns bad like it did yesterday. It rained almost constantly. Our clothes were soaked but we managed to dry everything out in the end.

Embury Beacon, Hartland

Prehistoric mound and beacon. Look out for peregrine falcons.

➤ **Find** the site 1 mile N of Welcombe Mouth (see below).

50.947293, -4.539698

Welcombe Mouth, Welcombe

Magical meadow glades surrounded by woodland and beach. Waterfalls and pool at the N end of the beach just S of Chiselridge Beach (50.93939972, -4.55010087). Discover more waterfalls S at Marsland Mouth (50.92869948, -4.54698536) and the Old Mill Leat stream. Low-tide dark sand and shingle. The stone shelter, Ronald Duncan's Writing Hut, is near the top of the steps on the way down to S beach.

➤ **Find** the NT car park at the end of the lane (Bideford, EX39 6HL – 50.933571, -4.544706)

50.9338, -4.5444

Marsland Water, Hartland

Look for edible winter chanterelles on rotting wood or moss along the wet river valley. The fresh water empties into Marsland Beach with a waterfall. Follow the stream FPs a little inland to forage for hazelnuts in autumn. Rare butterflies and small pearl-bordered fritillaries can be seen in summer. There's a stone shelter on the way down to the low-tide dark sand and shingle beach.

➤ **Find** Old Smithy Inn (see above left). With the pub on your R, follow the road to the three-lane junction. Take the middle lane. At the next crossroads, go straight over following the sign for Welcombe Mouth. There is a small car park on the SWCP looking R over the beach. Walk from here, by turning L as you look out to sea along the SWCP. Keep walking past the stone building, known as Ronald Duncan's Writing Hut, and the small beach below. As the beach ends, the FP hooks inland. Follow this FP all the way inland, ignoring the FP that turns back to the coast. Keep taking the L FP that follows the line of the Old Mill Leat stream and eventually a ford ⅔ mile from the beach.

50.928743, -4.546273

Hartland Quay

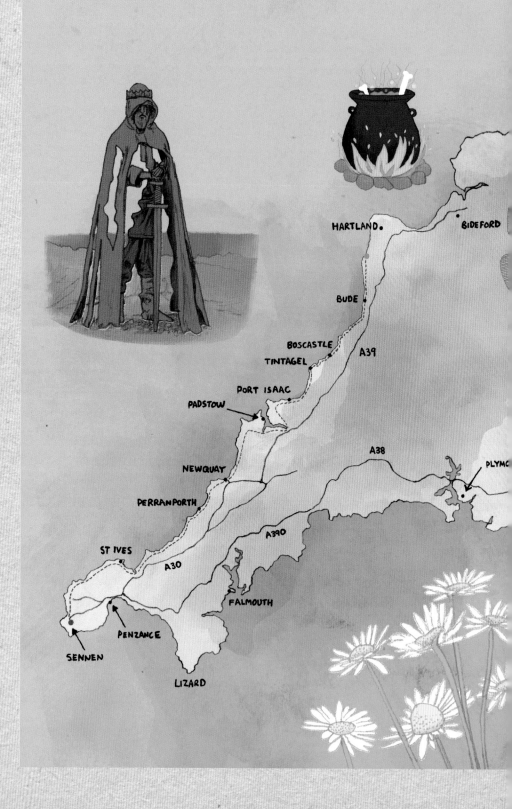

HARTLAND • • BIDEFORD

BUDE

BOSCASTLE
TINTAGEL A39

PORT ISAAC
PADSTOW

A38

NEWQUAY PLYMO

PERRANPORTH

A390

ST IVES
A30 FALMOUTH

PENZANCE

SENNEN

LIZARD

NORTH CORNWALL

TOUCH OF SPRING – the Coloured Cave is beneath Carn Gluze, south of Cape Cornwall. A tomb of shades between the tides and the bats. No rules, nor lifeguards, nor boats, nor guides. Only danger and beauty, in the Cot Valley. One old lady calls it a nursery. 'Some day in spring the bats disappear', she says. 'After a while they come back. Always more of them – some a little smaller.'

Duckpool Beach

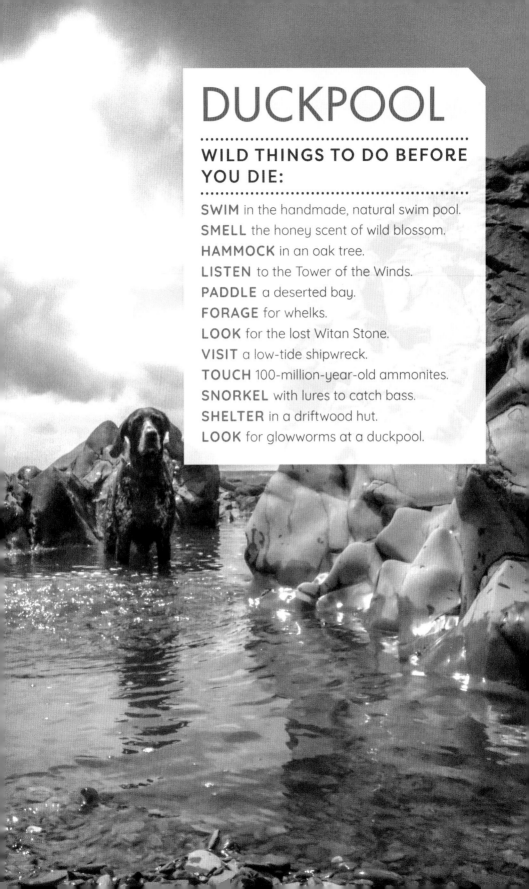

DUCKPOOL

WILD THINGS TO DO BEFORE YOU DIE:

SWIM in the handmade, natural swim pool.
SMELL the honey scent of wild blossom.
HAMMOCK in an oak tree.
LISTEN to the Tower of the Winds.
PADDLE a deserted bay.
FORAGE for whelks.
LOOK for the lost Witan Stone.
VISIT a low-tide shipwreck.
TOUCH 100-million-year-old ammonites.
SNORKEL with lures to catch bass.
SHELTER in a driftwood hut.
LOOK for glowworms at a duckpool.

THE OLD VICARAGE, MORWENSTOW

 B&B next to the medieval Church of St Morwenna and St John the Baptist.

Morwenstow, EX23 9SR
01288 331369

THE BUSH INN, MORWENSTOW

 B&B in a 13th-century country pub. Beer garden and sea views.

Morwenstow, EX23 9SR
www.thebushinnmorwen
stow.com

Marsland Mouth, Welcombe

Taste whelks foraged from the rock pools around the beach and cooked into broth. Look for Alexanders either side of the beach. They were once cultivated as a pot herb, similar to celery, and make a lovely whelk soup cooked over gorse. The first Alexander shoots are found in late autumn and winter. Late-summer seeds can be used to spice your soup.

➤ **Find** the NT car park at the end of the lane for Welcombe Mouth Beach (Bideford, EX39 6HL). Facing the sea, after high tide, walk 600 yards R to the mouth of West Mill Beach. The waterfall can be found up the cliff along the SWCP.

50.929264, -4.544054

Devil's Hole, Morwenstow

Look for fulmars riding the thermals and pink heather along Marsland Cliff (50.92639923,-4.54985801), with views over Gull Rock and Devil's Hole.

➤ **Find** the NT car park at the end of the lane for Welcombe Mouth Beach (Bideford, EX39 6HL). Avoid the beach, and, facing the sea, take the SWCP R (S) for 1 mile to Marsland Cliff. Keep walking another 200 yards to find the footbridge and waterfall at Litter Mouth.

50.926426, -4.556636

Yeolmouth Cliff Waterfall and Springs, Morwenstow

Smell the honey scent of frothy blossomed lady's bedstraw, between Yorkshire fog grass. This is one of the few places along the SWCP where you can find meadow 'Iron Butterfly'.
➤ **Find** parking at The Rectory Tearooms (Rectory Farm, Morwenstow, EX23 9SR), and, keeping the church on your R shoulder, follow the FP W for 600 yards to the SWCP. Facing the sea, turn N (R) and follow the FP 1 mile, past St Morwenna's Well (see below) and footbridge to the waterfall and springs.

50.917208, -4.559510

St Morwenna's Well, Morwenstow

Reopened by Rev Hawker (see Vicarage Cliff page 110), but since lost to time, all that's left is crumbling cliff and vegetation. At various intervals, a FP is cut back down to the well 400ft below, but it's hazardous and best avoided. It's nice to know it's there though.
➤ **Follow** directions for Yeolmouth Cliff (see above), but find the well location after 600 yards. There's a small waterfall close to the footbridge to make up for the well's status as sometimes missing, collapsed or hazardous.

50.910687, -4.563973

Church of St Morwenna and St John the Baptist

Explore the stories in stained glass and the stones in the graveyard of this Saxon church. More than 40 shipwrecked seamen are buried here. The figurehead of the *Caledonia* ship is preserved in the churchyard. The church looks windswept from the outside. The dell around the graveyard is a good place in which to hide from the wind and rain.
➤ **Find** the Church of St Morwenna and St John the Baptist (Morwenstow, EX23 9SR), opposite The Rectory Tearooms (Rectory Farm, Morwenstow, EX23 9SR).

50.909645, -4.553416

PEOPLE OF THE PATH

The Retired Farmer, Morwenstow, North Cornwall

The amount of erosion that has occurred in the last 50 years is incredible. I look down and can't believe how much it has changed over the decades. It's really quite a shock. People need to be wary and take care.

Vicarage Cliff, Morwenstow

Somewhere between the cliff and the edge of the moor is the 'Gauger's Pocket' at Tidnacombe Cross. The pocket is rumoured to be rock crevice, overgrown with moss and lichen, sealed by a moveable piece of rock, where smugglers would leave gold bribes to pay off the customs men. Rev Hawker referred to it as the Witan Stone, and although its location today remains a mystery, it may still be out there, just waiting to be found. It's fun looking.

> **Find** the Church of St Morwenna and St John the Baptist (Morwenstow, EX23 9SR), then follow the FP W for 600 yards to the SWCP and Vicarage Cliff.

50.907900, -4.562592

Hawker's Hut, Morwenstow

Touch the driftwood hut set in the side of a cliff, built by the wonderful and eccentric 19th-century vicar and poet Rev Robert Stephen Hawker, of St Morwenna and St John the Baptist (see page 109). The vicar is worthy of more research. The hut is worth more than a moment … for no other reason than that Hawker wrote and rewrote many poems here, including (perhaps) the anthem 'Trelawny'. It really is quite special.

> **Find** Vicarage Cliff (see above) and, facing the sea, turn S (L) and walk 300 yards to the hut. 50.906964, -4.565208

50.906964, -4.565208

Hawker's Hut

DUCKPOOL COTTAGE, MORWENSTOW

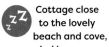

Cottage close to the lovely beach and cove, surrounded by narrow lanes, steep climbs and big views.

Duckpool Beach, Morwenstow, EX23 9JN
01271 882865

HOUNDAPITT COTTAGES, SANDYMOUTH BEACH

Dog-friendly cottages 1 mile from Sandymouth Beach, which is also dog friendly. Free coarse fishing on the onsite lakes, as well as a games room and play area. Sea views from all the cottages.

Houndapitt Farm Cottages, Sandymouth Bay, EX23 9HW
houndapitt.com

SANDYMOUTH CAFE, SANDYMOUTH BEACH

Relaxing family-run cafe serving food and drinks for energetic walkers. Local ingredients. Try the vegan falafels. Surf equipment is available to hire.

Stibb, Bude, EX23 9HW
Facebook:
@sandymouthcafe

Higher Sharpnose Point Cave and Waterfall, Morwenstow

Smell the scent of heavy rain when fresh water from the Tidna falls heaviest over the cliff grass. The area is ablaze in spring with flowering squill.

➤ **Find** Hawker's Hut (see opposite). Walk on another 300 yards for the Tidna Shute footbridge, cave and waterfall, although sadly the entire area is hazardous and falling into the sea. Much care is needed.

50.904571, -4.567707

Steeple Point, Morwenstow

Bat watch around the cliffs and inland towards Duckpool Cottage (see left). Five species, including lesser horseshoe bats, inhabit the nearby derelict mill located 600 yards E.

➤ **Find** NT Duckpool Bay car park (Morwenstow, EX23 9JN). Walk NW a few yards to find the SWCP and follow the FP uphill 400 yards to the point.

50.876248, -4.560818

Duckpool, Morwenstow

Look for glowworms in July at dusk. It's a stony beach, where a freshwater lake forms against a pebble dam. Invariably, there are ducks. Unusual stone stacks at the beach rim have edges worn into bulbous nodules.

➤ **Find** NT Duckpool Bay car park (Morwenstow, EX23 9JN), then walk 200 yards W to the stone beach and pool.

50.874733, -4.560154

Sandymouth Waterfalls, Sandymouth Beach

Smell the unmistakable scent of where waterfall meets saline. This one marks the start of a 2-mile, low-tide stretch of beach and pools from Sandymouth.

➤ **Find** NT Sandymouth Bay car park (Stibb, Bude, EX23 9HW), then walk 300 yards towards the beach. Turn R to find the waterfall, depending on rainfall and season.

50.862098, -4.557343

Sandymouth Beach, Sandymouth

Summer surf hire. There are vast rock pools to explore at low tide – look for mussels. Rocks fall around the foreshore and expose their fossilised contents, mostly plant remains.

➤ **Find** the Sandymouth Cafe and surf school (see left). There's lots of parking to the rear. The beach is a few yards away.

50.861023, -4.557958

Menachurch Point, Northcott Mouth

Find the shipwreck of SS *Belem* at low tide just N of Northcott Mouth. The steamship ran aground in 1917.

➤ **Find** NT Northcott Mouth Car Park (Bude, EX23 9ED), then walk towards the beach to find the SWCP. Turn R and head N along the FP 500 yards to the point. Alternatively, walk along the beach after high tide. Much care is needed as the tide comes in quickly and there is little or no escape up the cliffs to safety.

50.850427, -4.558619

Curtis's Rock, Northcott Mouth

Fish with sand eel lures for bass. Look for remnants of a Bronze Age barrow and burial chambers in and around the collapsed cliffs.

➤ **Find** Northcott Mouth Car Park (Bude, EX23 9ED), then walk along the beach 300 yards N.

50.848818, -4.556857

Northcott Mouth Beach, Northcott Mouth

Fossils of plants and fish scales can be found in the layers of shale.

➤ **Find** NT Northcott Mouth Car Park (Bude, EX23 9ED), then walk to the beach.

50.844693, -4.555032

Northcott Mouth

Bude

POT AND BARREL B&B, BUDE

 Luxury B&B with sea views a few yards from Crooklets Beach (see right). Just a ½ mile walk to the shops in Bude.

Crooklets, Bude,
EX23 8NE
www.potandbarrel.com

THE CLIFF HOTEL, BUDE

 Dog- and family-friendly hotel.

Maer Down Rd,
Bude, EX23 8NG
www.cliffhotel.co.uk

CROOKLETS BEACH CAFE, BUDE

 Coffee and cake, all-day breakfasts and baps on the promenade overlooking Crooklets Beach (see right). Indoor and outdoor seating.

Crooklets, Bude,
EX23 8NE
Facebook:
@CrookletsBeachCafe

LIFE'S A BEACH, BUDE

 Bar and restaurant on Summerleaze Beach in Bude. Everything from Cuban sandwiches and fresh locally caught fish, to Fairtrade coffee and ice-cold beers. Watch the tide come in over the sand to experience the full range of Summerleaze social vibes.

16 Summerleaze Cres,
Bude, EX23 8HN
www.lifesabeach.info

Crooklets Beach, Bude

Look for seaweed to dry or eat around the quieter part of Bude Haven. Farmers used to fertilise their acidic soil with the weed they collected here.

> **Find** Crooklets Car Park (Bude, EX23 8NF), then walk 300 yards W to the shore and sand.

50.835675, -4.556084

Bude Cliffs, Bude

Bude Cliffs are home to an incredibly rare 300-million-year-old goldfish-sized fossilised sea creature – *Cornuboniscus Budensis.* It has never been found anywhere else in the world. Good luck tracking one down... Even if you don't find one, enjoy a river walk out of Bude to the beach and Compass Point (see page 114). It's quite a climb, but worth it if you're staying in Bude.

> There's plenty of parking in Bude, but if you travel just 1½ miles away, you'll find The Rustic Tea Garden (see opposite), just off the SWCP (Bude, EX23 9ED). With the tearoom on the L, follow the road 275 yards to the NT car park. Walk on to the SWCP from here, turning L if you're looking to sea. Walk back to Bude along the cliff tops down to Summerleaze Beach and the River Neet estuary. Cross the river estuary at low tide via the bridges. Take a break at the Life's A Beach cafe (see left), and then return to the start.

50.830533, -4.549466

Bude Sea Pool, Bude

Swim in the handmade, natural swim pool. A reminder of what it is to be human: immersed in nature with a safety line attached to someone else.

> **Find** Summerleaze Long Stay Car Park (Summerleaze Cres, EX23 8HJ), then walk 500 yards NW to the top of Bude Beach and the pool.

50.832666, -4.554240

THE BARGE, BUDE

Sit on a converted barge to sample local Cornish dishes and ingredients on Bude Canal. Cooked breakfasts, main meals and daily specials.

The Lower Wharf, Bude, EX23 8LG
www.thebargebude.co.uk

OLIVE TREE, BUDE

Al fresco drinking and eating in Bude beside the picturesque canal. Mouthwatering burgers, salads, pasta and a variety of vegetarian dishes.

Lower Wharf, Bude, EX23 8LG
www.olivetreebude.co.uk

UPTON CROSS GUEST HOUSE, BUDE

B&B just outside Bude, a few steps from the SWCP.

Bude, EX23 0LY
01288 355310

EFFORD CAMPING, BUDE

Cheap and on the SWCP. No-frills hillside camping for small vehicles and tents. Water, toilets and showers.

Vicarage Rd, Bude, EX23 8LJ
effordcamping.co.uk

Bude Haven River, Bude-Stratton

Seaweed, fresh water and tides. Look for bass and mullet that feed around the deeper still waters. It's just S of rock cliffs that are studded with fish fossils. Much care is needed here if you're swimming, because the currents are treacherous and lives are lost each year.

➤ **Find** Summerleaze Long Stay Car Park (Summerleaze Cres, EX23 8HJ), then walk 300 yards in the opposite direction to the pool over the sands to the river.

50.830646, -4.553295

Compass Point, Bude

Listen to the roll of waves into Bude on the north breeze. The point structure is known as the 'Tower of the Winds'.

➤ **Find** the SWCP next to Bude Quay and walk across the canal and W 400 yards to the point.

50.828609, -4.556728

Efford Beacon View, Bude-Stratton

Magical view inland to the Dartmoor tors.

➤ **Find** Compass Point (see above) and walk S on the SWCP 500 yards.

50.824068, -4.557393

Phillips Point, Bude-Stratton

Cliffs, views N of Hartland Point, and grey seal spotting.

➤ **Find** Efford Beacon View (see above) and walk 1 mile S on the SWCP.

50.810539, -4.559634

Lower Longbeak Tumulus, Marhamchurch

Sit in sea campion and pink thrift and look north to Hartland Point and south to Widemouth Bay.

➤ **Find** Viewing Point North Car Park, Marine Dr, Bude, EX23 0AW, then walk 400 yards W to the cliff edge. Walk 200 yards further to find a way down to the beach, taking care.

50.800766, -4.559514

Widemouth Sand, Widemouth Bay

Best surfing in autumn and winter when waves peak. Rock pool when the tide is out.

➤ **Find** Widemouth Beach Car Park, (Bude, EX23 0AH), then walk 200 yards to the beach.

50.791357, -4.559406

Widemouth Bay

Widemouth Bay, Widemouth

**Find fossilised molluscs and other shells. Stony at high tide
but vast sands as the water goes out to reveal rock pools.
Swimming is possible, but much care is needed around rips.**
➤ **Find** the Freewave Surf Academy off Marine Dr (Widemouth
Bay, EX23 0AD). There's parking all around. Walk R and along
the vast beach.

50.79127, -4.55726

Wanson Mouth, Poundstock

**Find ammonites in the dark stone beneath the sandstone in
the cliffs around the N end of the Widemouth Bay Beach.**
➤ **Find** Widemouth Bay (see above) and walk 300 yards S
at low tide. Care is needed to avoid getting cut off by tides.

50.783361, -4.565062

Foxhole Point, Poundstock

**Paddle deserted bays and beaches at low tide, but take care not
to get cut off when the tide returns.**
➤ **Find** Penhalt Cliff Car Park (Poundstock, EX23 0DF). There
are parking bays and scree FPs either side of the road, but
care is needed.

50.775747, -4.570307

**TRECANE
BEACH HOUSE,
WIDEMOUTH BAY**

Holiday house next to the beach and cafe.

Sleeps ten.

Marine Dr, Widemouth Bay, Bude, EX23 0AH
www.trecane.co.uk

**BLACK ROCK CAFE,
WIDEMOUTH BAY**

Cafe with outside seating next to Widemouth Bay Beach. Perfect for coffee and cakes.

Marine Dr, Widemouth Bay, EX23 0AG
01288 361563

**BARFORD BEACH
HOUSE, POUNDSTOCK**

Sea views and wide balconies, along with an outdoor wood-fired hot tub, and an indoor sauna with a view. There's also a cinema room and underground bunker with a survivalist bar, pool table, arcade games and a vintage pinball machine. Secret doorways, magical features and quirky design touches for groups of up to 12.

Poundstock, Bude, EX23 0DF
www.tregullandandco.
co.uk/barford/

Millook Haven, Poundstock

Low-tide shingle beach fed by streams that push up through the pebbles. The beach is sheltered by cliffs that form the zigzag-shaped Crackington Formation – a rock formation of national importance that can be seen from the beach.

➤ **Find** Foxhole Point (see page 115) and walk 400 yards W on the SWCP to Millook Haven.

50.772551, -4.577474

Dizzard Point, St Gennys

Ancient oak, blackthorn and wild service trees adorn this headland. These woods are believed to be at least 4,000 years old – among the oldest in Cornwall. Shelter from sun and storm in pygmy trees draped in lichens and mosses, stunted by the force of the wind.

➤ **Find** Millook Haven (see above) and walk 2 miles SW on the SWCP.

50.760683, -4.601265

Long Cliff, St Gennys

Feel your thighs slow burn on one of the steepest climbs along the SWCP.

➤ **Find** Dizzard Point (see above) and walk 300 yards SW on the SWCP.

50.760167, -4.607447

Chipman Cliff, St Gennys

Low-tide beach access to Scrade Beach at the bottom of steep cliff, just N of Mot's Hole Waterfall (see below). Look for honeycomb worm reef and water-rippled sandstone exposed by the tide and erosion. Snorkel the waist-high shallows at mid tide. Beware currents, rips and surges.

➤ **Find** Long Cliff (see above) and walk 600 yards SW on the SWCP.

50.757929, -4.615433

Mot's Hole Cave and Waterfall, St Gennys

Known locally for butterflies because so many feed here on the summer flowers. Stand or sit between red admirals, pearl-bordered fritillaries, ringlets and meadow browns.

➤ **Find** Chipman Cliff (see above) and walk 300 yards SW on the SWCP.

50.756187, -4.615904

Foxhole Point

PENHALT FARM, POUNDSTOCK

 Coastal down camping and caravanning, 1 mile south of Widemouth Bay, on a sheep farm. The farmhouse stands on a hill overlooking Widemouth Bay. Part of Penhalt Farmhouse is available for self-catering accommodation.
Widemouth Bay,
EX23 0DG
www.penhaltfarm.co.uk

LOWER TRESMORN FARM B&B AND HOLIDAY COTTAGES, CRACKINGTON HAVEN

 B&B and self-catering accommodation close to Crackington Haven beaches. Medieval farmhouse on a family farm.
Lower Tresmorn Farm,
Crackington Haven,
EX23 0NU
www.lowertresmorn.co.uk

Cleave Strand and Waterfall, St Gennys

Low-tide rock and shingle beach accessed via rope ladder or precarious steep trails. Care is needed. Snorkel the shallows or line fish for bass.

➤ **Find** Mot's Hole (see opposite) and walk 200 yards SW on the SWCP.

50.753169, -4.620362

Castle Point, St Gennys

Celtic fort ruin, thought to be 3,000 years old. Best in summer so you can inhale the fragrance of the purple heather. Much of the ruin has fallen over the cliff, so there's not much fort left to see.

➤ **Find** Crackington car park (Mill Ball Hill, Bude, EX23 0JG). Walk away from the beach to find the SWCP 50 yards back on the L. Follow the FP ⅔ mile to the point.

50.748609, -4.633196

Aller Shute, St Gennys

Listen for the waterfall after rain as it cascades into the Aller Shute inlet, where smugglers once collected and moved goods up a steep climb and into hiding.

➤ **Find** Castle Point (see above). The shute is 200 yards SW towards the cliff. Care is needed as the cliff edge is not safe.

50.747705, -4.634211

Pencannow Point, St Gennys

Star watch and spot bats after dusk. By day, there are views N to Hartland Point and Lundy Island.

➤ **Find** Crackington car park (Mill Ball Hill, Bude, EX23 0JG), then follow the FP towards Castle Point (see above), but take the FP detour after 500 yards towards the point.

50.744526, -4.638567

Rumps Point

RUMPS POINT

WILD THINGS TO DO BEFORE YOU DIE:

TOUCH a prehistoric stone carving.

SNORKEL through kelp-covered reef.

SHELTER in the Museum of Witchcraft and Magic.

LOOK for pottery beside an Arthurian castle.

TRAMP over ancient donkey trails.

CAMP on a grass cliff with a view.

SMELL coconut-scented gorse.

LISTEN to the Devil's Bellows.

WALK under a rock arch.

VISIT a Phoenician-favoured harbour.

Crackington Haven

TREVIGUE,
CRACKINGTON HAVEN

 Cliff top accommodation, a five-min walk above The Strangles beach (see right), between Boscastle and Crackington Haven. The farm has steep valleys and hills, with the highest cliff in Cornwall. Choose between a cottage that sleeps six, or self-catering accommodation for two in a wing of the main house that's entered via a private courtyard. The Strangles beach is accessed via a winding footpath next to the farmhouse, where the family lives.

Trevigue Farm,
Crackington Haven,
EX23 0LQ
www.trevigue.com

Crackington Haven

Smell coconut-scented gorse in spring when the hills are lit up in yellow. The flowers are most fragrant in April and May. Swim and look for fossils. Crackington's sheltered harbour is safer than most, but care is still needed.

➤ **Find** the Haven Beach Shop & Cafe (Mill Ball Hill, Crackington Haven, EX23 0JG). The public car park is opposite. Walk a few yards down to the beach.

50.741340, -4.634358

Little Strand, St Gennys

Look for oxeye daisies - sometimes known as 'moon daisies' because they glow in the dark. The flower buds can be eaten raw or pickled. The beach has a rock arch at its N end.

➤ **Find** Crackington Haven (see above) and walk 1 mile S on the SWCP.

50.728289, -4.649850

The Strangles, St Gennys

Isolated beach. Watch the sands unravel as the tide recedes like a slow-motion tsunami. It comes back in quite slowly, too, so take care. The beach was possibly named by the early Cornish smugglers who, when they saw it from the sea, said that it looked like 'strange-hills'.

➤ **Find** Little Strand (see above) and walk 300 yards S on the SWCP on the beach at low tide.

50.728289, -4.649850

LOWER PENNYCROCKER CAMPING & CARAVAN SITE, BOCASTLE

Farm-based campsite with breathtaking views.

Lower Pennycrocker Farm, Boscastle, PL35 0BY

pennycrocker.com

CLIFFHANGER BAR, BOSCASTLE

Pop-up bar on the SWCP.

SWCP, Boscastle, PL35 0HL
07901 820090

TREBYLA FARM CAMPING AND CARAVANNING SITE, BOSCASTLE

Working farm, run by a family that has a herd of Charolais cattle and Devon Longwool sheep. Toilets, showers and fire pits, and within walking distance of Boscastle via the SWCP.

Trebyla Farm, Boscastle, PL35 0HL
boscastlecampsite.co.uk

High Cliff, St Juliot

Listen for peregrines from the highest point in Cornwall. Look below for the coastal heath where erosion has left an undercliff. Feel the FP beneath your feet ... and stick to it. Closer views of rock formations and beaches are tempting, but not worth the sheer-drop gauntlet to the Atlantic below.

> **Find** The Strangles beach (see opposite) and walk 1 mile S on the SWCP on the beach at low tide.

50.717644, -4.650436

Rusey Beach, St Gennys

Touch the long-distant past at one of the best fossil sites in Cornwall. Look for paths down in between landslips, but much caution is needed as conditions are always changing and hazardous.

> **Find** High Cliff (see above) and walk ½ mile S on the SWCP.

50.715766, -4.655864

Rusey Cliff, St Juliot

Snorkelling is good on the far L of the beach. Look for plant and coral fossils.

> **Find** the car park on the Unnamed Rd (Boscastle, PL35 0HN). Facing the road, turn R and walk 110 yards before turning L on to the greenway FP. Follow the FP a little way down and then veer off to the R and down to the cliffs and SWCP, and FPs down to the beach.

50.715545, -4.651741

Buckator Cliff, Beeny

The imposing black cliff of Buckator towers over the equally impressive Gull Rock. Home to grey-seal colony. Look for pups at low tide.

> **Find** Rusey Beach (see above) and walk 1 mile SW on the SWCP.

50.709854, -4.666249

PEOPLE OF THE PATH

The Holiday Maker, Duckpool Bay, North Cornwall

I come here to walk. I love walking. The views over Duckpool from the cliffs are one of my favourite places on the path. There's a bench up there and it's a lovely place to sit and look down.

Sidebar

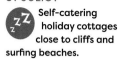

THE OLD FARMHOUSE, ST JULIOT

Self-catering holiday cottages close to cliffs and surfing beaches.

Hayloft Barn Hillsborough, St Juliot, PL35 0HH
cottagesboscastle.co.uk

BOSCASTLE FARM SHOP & CAFE, BOSCASTLE

Home-reared award-winning beef, lamb and pork, and home-made pies and cakes, from a traditional mixed farm surrounded by grazing Devon cattle.

Hillsborough Farm, Boscastle, PL35 0HH
www.boscastlefarmshop.co.uk

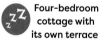

GULL COTTAGE, BOSCASTLE

Four-bedroom cottage with its own terrace overlooking the harbour, and near the end of a small row of old Boscastle Harbour cottages.

Gull Cottage, Boscastle, PL35 0HA
gullcottageboscastle.co.uk

Main

Beeny Cliff, Beeny
Look out for grey seals around the aptly nicknamed 'Seals' Hole'.
➤ **Find** Buckator Cliff (see page 121) and walk 1 mile SW on the SWCP.

50.703123, -4.681088

Pentargon Waterfall, Forrabury and Minster
Find the 100ft waterfall at the end of the stream that falls into the sea at Pentargon.
➤ **Find** Rusey Cliff (see page 121) and walk ⅔ mile SW on the SWCP.

50.696741, -4.679918

Penally Hill, Forrabury and Minster
Watch and listen for mewing buzzards that hunt here. There are kestrels, too..
➤ **Find** Pentargon Waterfall (see above) and walk ⅔ mile SW on the SWCP.

50.693506, -4.697728

Penally Point, Forrabury and Minster
Listen to the Penally blowhole on a high tide, with a rare view over what was the most important and richest harbour in Bronze Age Britain. Known as the 'Devil's Bellows', the blowhole fires water over the harbour with a sound reminiscent of a cannon.
➤ **Find** Penally Hill (see above) and walk 300 yards SW on the SWCP.

50.692227, -4.701249

Boscastle Harbour Settlement, Boscastle
Explore the sheltered harbour on the N coast where Phoenician traders arrived seeking tin 4,000 years ago.
➤ **Find** Cobweb Car Park (2 Penally Hill, Boscastle, PL35 0HG), and walk W ½ mile towards the coast and the SWCP and harbour.

50.689741, -4.704552

The Museum of Witchcraft and Magic, Boscastle
One of most interesting museums in England, and the largest of its kind in the world.
➤ **Find** Cobweb Car Park (see Boscastle Harbour, above) and walk ¼ mile towards the coast.

50.690728, -4.694926

Boscastle

Willapark Lookout, Forrabury and Minster

Ancient settlement headland most recently used as a coast watch station. Walk up to St Symphorian's Church (Forrabury Stitches, Boscastle, PL35 0DJ) to explore the graveyard, before returning to Boscastle and Warren Point on the N side of the harbour. Good for fossils.

➤ **Find** The Riverside restaurant (The Bridge, Boscastle, PL35 0HE), on the River Valency. There's a public car park right next door. Follow the river FP downhill and cross the arched bridge just past The Museum of Witchcraft and Magic (see opposite). After crossing the bridge, turn R and head uphill away from the river. Walk to the cliffs ⅓ mile away, where you'll find the naze that looks over Boscastle Harbour. Walk a little further along the SWCP before finally turning L towards the church.

50.689629, -4.704406

Forrabury Stitches, Forrabury and Minster

Look for the unique, common land markings of strip fields known as 'stitches'. Best seen under the long shadow of dawn and dusk.

➤ **Find** Willapark Lookout (see above) and, facing the coast, turn around and walk back 300 yards to the SWCP for a view of the stitches.

50.688979, -4.701523

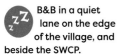

Western Blackapit Cave, Forrabury and Minster

Look for and touch yellow- or brown-stained slates. They are a telltale sign of a period containing rare trilobite fossils. Good places to look for slate tips are where the mines are falling into the sea on the walk W from here.

➤ **Find** Willapark Lookout (see page 123) and, facing the coast, turn L and walk 200 yards to the SWCP for a view.

50.688619, -4.703951

Ladies' Window, Trevalga

Step through the magical rock arch carved into the headland over Short Island. Sea otters have been seen here, but not for some time. Keep looking, while watching guillemots and razorbills.

➤ **Find** Western Blackapit Cave (see above) and walk SW 1 mile on the SWCP.

50.684098, -4.720242

Foot Cove, Trevalga

Listen for peregrine falcons, guillemots, razorbills and other nesting birds along the cliff edges.

➤ **Find** Ladies' Window (see above) and walk 300 yards NW on the SWCP.

50.684949, -4.721014

Firebeacon Hill, Trevalga

Puffins and seabird colonies are found all along this cliff ridge and islands.

➤ **Find** Foot Cove (see above) and walk 200 yards NW on the SWCP.

50.682991, -4.724598

Trevalga Cliff, Trevalga

Look for bottlenose dolphins and basking sharks from late spring.

➤ **Find** Firebeacon Hill (see above) and walk 300 yards NW on the SWCP.

50.680755, -4.72599

Rocky Valley, Tintagel

Inhale the scent of a wet wooded valley. A waterfall meets the coast in a sweeping trough.

➤ **Find** Trevalga Cliff (see above) and walk 1 mile SW on the SWCP.

50.672251, -4.734527

Rocky Valley Mill, Tintagel

Touch the stone carving on the side of an abandoned mill. Historic England describes the work as prehistoric art, possibly more than 3,000 years old, either Neolithic or Bronze Age.

➤ **Find** Rocky Valley (see opposite) and walk 300 yards S on the river FP.

50.671942, -4.729039

Benoath Cove, Tintagel

Snorkel over kelp-covered reef. The track down was once used by farm donkeys to haul sand and seaweed up to fertilise the fields.

➤ **Find** Rocky Valley (see opposite) and walk 600 yards W on the SWCP.

50.672251, -4.734527

Lye Rock, Tintagel

This is a great place from which to look out for puffins.

➤ **Find** The Castle Car Park (5 Atlantic Rd, Tintagel, PL34 0DD), and walk W to the SWCP 600 yards, and then turn R and N on the SWCP and walk 1.3 mile to the rock.

50.676120, -4.741893

The Sisters, Tintagel

Rocky reef around two islets where cormorants, razorbills and guillemots nest.

➤ **Find** Lye Rock (see above) and look out.

50.677317, -4.746141

Tintagel

ST EDWARD'S COTTAGE, TINTAGEL

 Cottage sleeping six to nine in beautiful grounds close to the SWCP.

Back Ln, Tintagel, PL34 0EB
www.stedwardscottage.co.uk

THE HEADLAND CARAVAN & CAMPING, TINTAGEL

 Family-run campsite, a ten-min walk from the ruins of King Arthur's Castle, and 300 yards from the SWCP.

Atlantic Rd, Tintagel, PL34 0DE
www.headlandcaravanpark.co.uk

THE AVALON HOTEL, TINTAGEL

 Boutique hotel a ten-min walk from Tintagel Castle. Room 6 has great sea view. Dog friendly.

Atlantic Rd, Tintagel, PL34 0DD
www.visitcornwall.com/accommodation/bb-guest-houses/north-coast/tintagel/avalon

TREVENNA LODGE, TINTAGEL

Good service and rooms close to pubs and the SWCP.

Castle Heights, Tintagel, PL34 0DE
www.bedandbreakfasttintagel.co.uk

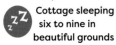

Willapark Settlement, Tintagel

Look down for seals from the Bronze Age tumuli, which are at least 3,000 years old.

➤ **Find** Lye Rock (see page 125), then walk 200 yards W.

50.674862, -4.743625

Barras Nose, Tintagel

Find and touch the prehistoric flint heads that are sometimes found around the rock settlement and burial site. There are superb cliff top views of the reefs below, and flat ledges for fishing.

➤ **Find** Willapark Settlement (see above) and walk 1 mile W on the SWCP.

50.671775, -4.757400

Merlin's Cave, Tintagel

A freshwater well inside a magical cavern under 3 million tonnes of rock. Only an open mind for myths and magic is needed. Dreams are made of this.

➤ **Find** The Castle Car Park (5 Atlantic Rd, Tintagel, PL34 0DD), then walk on to Castle Rd from one of the most epic trails in England. Within less than ⅔ mile, explore the magic of Merlin's Cave, the King Arthur sculpture and Tintagel Castle. Turn L at Tintagel Castle to check out St Materiana's Church, too. Keep walking in either direction for seclusion and rocky views.

50.668236, -4.759280

Tintagel Castle, Tintagel

Look for ancient pottery around one of the most important Celtic settlements in England. Vast amounts of imported post-Roman pottery has been excavated from the headland. It's one of many places that's worthy of more than one day, let alone a walk-through. Best seen at night ... and in winter on a clear day at dawn or dusk.

➤ **Find** Merlin's Cave (see above) and walk 100 yards S.

50.668144, -4.762593

St Materiana's Church, Tintagel

Small church and cemetery with super views of Tintagel Castle (see above).

➤ **Find** Tintagel Castle (see above) and walk 400 yards S on the SWCP.

50.663126, -4.760203

CAMELOT CASTLE HOTEL, TINTAGEL

 Stunning sea views. Dog friendly. Restaurant, bar, tearoom and coffee house.

Castle View, Tintagel, PL34 0DQ
www.camelotcastle.com

YHA TINTAGEL, TINTAGEL

From Camelot to bunk beds: the magic of the YHA. Cliff top hostel set close to the drama and legend of Tintagel Castle and Merlin's Cave (see opposite for both). Private rooms are available.

Dunderhole Point, Tintagel, PL34 0DW
www.yha.org.uk

THE PENALLICK, TINTAGEL

Budget hotel midway between Tintagel and Trebarwith Strand surfing beach, 1 mile from the centre of Tintagel and 300 yards from the SWCP. Ask for a sea view. Dog friendly.

Treknow, Tintagel, PL34 0EJ
www.tintagelbedand breakfast.co.uk

ATLANTIC VIEW HOTEL, TREKNOW

 Victorian house in tiny hamlet of Treknow, 1 mile from Tintagel. The hotel is set 300 yards back from the cliff top.

Treknow, Tintagel, PL34 0EJ
www.atlanticviewhotel tintagel.co.uk

Dunder Hole, Tintagel

Listen to the earth-shattering boom of this vast gaping hole in the cliff face that plummets below; originally called 'Thunder Hole'. Waves surge and bellow up through the rock like an exploding brass organ.

➤ **Find** Glebe Cliff and walk 300 yards S on the SWCP.

50.659929, -4.765554

Hole Beach, Tintagel

Snorkel over seaweed and large rocks beneath the cliffs – beware rips and currents. This coast is renowned for fatalities.

➤ **Find** Trebarwith Car Park (Delabole, Tintagel, PL33 9DF), then walk W to find the SWCP. At the coast, turn R (N) and walk ²/₃ mile on the SWCP.

50.652284, -4.759954

Lill Cove, Trebarwith

Stunning high-tide beach, with access to neighbouring bays and rock pools at low tide. Explore the eroded copper mine workings to the rear of the beach with care.

➤ **Find** Trebarwith Car Park (Delabole, Tintagel, PL33 9DF), then walk W 500 yards to find Trebarwith Strand Beach. Once at the beach, turn R (N) and walk 300 yards to Lill Cove.

50.646449, -4.761725

Trebarwith Strand, Trebarwith

Best in summer at low tide. Not a wide bay and the rocks are slippery, but if you take care, you'll discover lots of interest and wildlife in the pools and seaweed. Gull Rock looks green in spring when it becomes coated entirely in rock samphire.

➤ **Find** Trebarwith Car Park (Delabole, Tintagel, PL33 9DF), then walk W 500 yards.

50.644071, -4.763177

Port William Caves, Trebarwith

Explore the caves at the end of a mile-long low-tide beach walk. All these mines are home to bats, including the rare greater horseshoe bat.

➤ **Find** Trebarwith Car Park (Delabole, Tintagel, PL33 9DF), then walk W 500 yards to the beach and then turn L to the caves.

50.644071, -4.763177

Dennis Point, Tintagel

Feel the pain of a 300ft walk up. The views are glorious.

➤ **Find** Port William Caves (see above) and walk 300 yards SW on the SWCP.

50.636485, -4.765971

Trebarwi

THE PORT WILLIAM INN, TREBARWITH

 Dog-friendly B&B. Sea-facing terrace seats, al fresco dining, contemporary decor and a woodburner.

Tintagel Heights, Trebarwith, Tintagel, PL34 0HB
theportwilliam.co.uk

THE STRAND CAFE, TREBARWITH

 Outdoor benches over the rocky beach. Good place to relax after a morning's rock pooling.

Trebarwith Strand, Tintagel, PL34 0HB
01840 779482

Backways Cove, Tintagel

Hot black slate beneath scented spring flowers peppered with butterflies. Look for the old donkey tracks down around the old slate quarry and buildings now reclaimed by nature.

➤ **Find** Dennis Point (see page 127) and walk 400 yards S on the SWCP.

50.636485, -4.765971

Treligga Cliff Tumuli, Tintagel

Look for and taste wild chives around the ancient burial site and cliffs. The chives are rare in other parts of the UK.

➤ **Find** Backways Cove (see above) and walk 600 yards S on the SWCP.

50.636485, -4.765971

Tregardock Beach Fall, St Teath

Low-tide beach for waterfalls, caves and paddling. Best to the S but avoid tides as they come in quickly

➤ **Find** Treligga Cliff Tumuli (see above) and walk 1 mile S on the SWCP.

50.625485, -4.770259

THE CHAPEL, DELABOLE

 Beach house with coastline views to Port Isaac and Rock. The Chapel sits in 1½ acres of private gardens, with a FP to a secluded beach.

Treligga, Delabole, PL33 9EE
www.treliggachapel.com

CARADOC OF TREGARDOCK, DELABOLE

 Holiday home that sleeps eight with a sea-facing upstairs suite and a log-burning fire.

Treligga, Delabole, PL33 9ED
caradocoftregardock.com

PORT GAVERNE RESTAURANT & HOTEL, PORT GAVERNE

 This five-star restaurant and hotel is nestled in a secluded cove near Port Isaac.

Port Gaverne, Port Isaac, PL29 3SQ
portgavernehotel.co.uk

Bounds Cliff, St Endellion

Listen for peregrine falcons and nesting guillemots and kittewakes in the summer.

➤ **Find** St Endellion Car Park (Port Gaverne, PL29 3SG), then walk W to the SWCP. Facing the water, turn R and walk 2 miles E to the cliff.

50.597816, -4.794193

Port Gaverne

Follow the freshwater stream down over the stones and into the sea at low tide with bare feet. It's the perfect place from which to launch a kayak. Find the cob-walled fishing cellars, which once traded more than a million fish each week.

➤ **Find** St Endellion Car Park (Port Gaverne, PL29 3SG), then walk W 200 yards on the SWCP to the port.

50.594034, -4.824118

Port Gaverne

PEOPLE OF THE PATH

The Bude Lifeguard, North Cornwall

Swimmers must be aware of currents. They tend to be strongest where the canal enters the bay, so it's safer to swim away from there. Still water is sometimes an indicator of a current. We look at where the waves break and know that is where there is a shallow sand bar. If you get caught in a current, try not to panic. Swim sideways to try to get out of it and then swim back inland.

Port Quin

The Alleys, Port Isaac

Explore Port Isaac's famous narrow alleyways that connect up the village. The smallest is called Squeeze Belly Alley or 'Squeeze-ee-belly' and runs between Fore St and Dolphin St.

➤ **Find** Port Gaverne (see page 129) and walk S on the SWCP ⅔ mile.

50.59194961474088, -4.83129967125621

Lobber Point, St Endellion

Star watch or head to the point in order to look back, when it's light, over Tintagel Church and Castle, Port Isaac and even further on a clear day.

➤ **Find** The Alleys (see above) and walk N 300 yards on the SWCP.

50.595778, -4.835341

Pine Haven, St Endellion

Remote, rocky inlet and small beach.

➤ **Find** The Alleys (see above) and walk N 300 yards on the SWCP.

50.593194, -4.841600

Scarnor Point Tumuli, St Endellion

Look for ancient relics around Downgate Cove that have eroded out. Dartmoor ponies graze here.

➤ **Find** Pine Haven (see above) and walk SW 1½ miles on the SWCP.

50.594732, -4.855261

Port Quin, St Minver Highlands

Smell squill flowers in spring around the edges of the pebbled natural harbour. There is a cave and tunnel beside Quay Cottage that was once used by smugglers.

➤ **Find** Scarnor Point Tumuli (see above) and walk W 1 mile on the SWCP.

50.589674, -4.868727

THE OLD SCHOOL HOTEL, PORT ISAAC

 Dramatic cliff top hotel, with 12 en suite rooms, a licensed bar and a seafood restaurant.

Fore St, Port Isaac, PL29 3RD
www.theoldschoolhotel.co.uk

THE GOLDEN LION, PORT ISAAC

 This 18th-century pub overlooks Port Isaac. The 'Bloody Bones Bar' has a smuggling tunnel down on to a causeway on the beach. Cask ale in front of open fires.

10 Fore St, Port Isaac, PL29 3RB
www.thegoldenlion portisaac.co.uk

CHAPEL CAFE, PORT ISAAC

 Cafe in a restored 19th-century Methodist chapel on Roscarrock Hill, serving up locally roasted coffee.

Roscarrock Hill, Port Isaac, PL29 3RG
www.chapelcafe.co.uk

DOYDEN CASTLE, ST MINVER HIGHLANDS

Folly built on Doyden Point that's rented out by the NT.

Doyden, Port Quin, Port Isaac PL29 3SU
www.nationaltrust.org.uk/holidays/doyden-castle-cornwall

Gilson's Cove, St Minver Highlands

The old antimony mines at Gilson's Cove once produced a silver crystal that has been used since ancient times as powdered medicine for eyes and for cosmetic purposes. It is sometimes known by the Arabic name kohl, and is the origin of charcoal mascara, used in the East to protect infants' eyes. Currently rated as one of the rarest elements on earth, it may be toxic...
➤ **Find** Doyden Castle (see below left) and walk 400 yards S on the SWCP to the cove.

50.587017, -4.875915

Lundy Hole, St Minver Highlands

Paddle three sandy beaches in a row at low tide and explore the collapsed cave and stack.
➤ **Find** Gilson's Cove (see above) and walk ⅔ mile S and W on the SWCP to the hole.

50.583134, -4.886687

Carnweather Point, St Minver Highlands

Headland views above Port Quin Bay to The Rumps, and The Mouls (see below).
➤ **Find** Lundy Hole (see above) and walk ½ mile W on the SWCP to the point.

50.585897, -4.896397

The Mouls, St Minver Highlands

This small offshore island is a puffin breeding site. Bring binoculars. Watch gannet, too, from the time when they come in to feed on shoals of sardine and mackerel.
➤ **Find** farmhouse parking (Pentireglaze, Polzeath, PL27 6QY), and walk W on the FP for ⅔ mile to the SWCP. Turn R (E) and walk ½ mile to the fort point.

50.596729, -4.914071

The Rumps Entrance, Pentire Head

Burrow your nose into the gentle sway of wild thyme and dog violets, and inhale, while listening to the roar of the rocky headland and angry gulls. Beauty and beast.
➤ **Find** The Mouls (see above) and walk 300 yards S.

50.592856, -4.920311

The Rumps Fort, Pentire Head

Walk to this Iron Age fort just off the trail. Evidence of prehistoric trade with Mediterranean peoples has been discovered here. The fort once had stone ramparts and circular houses. Pottery found here was made from clay sourced at the Lizard.

➤ **Find** The Rumps Entrance (see page 131) and walk 200 yards W.

50.592856, -4.920311

The Rumps Path, Pentire Head

This area is a swallows' playground. Birds bank silently and playfully on walls of grass either side of the track on this inland detour when the weather turns foul … which it invariably does.

➤ **Find** The Rumps Fort (see above) and walk 300 yards S.

50.586002, -4.920767

Pentire Point

Taste golden samphire and rock sea lavender growing in between the rocks. Trace the line of pillow lava in the rock leading to The Rumps behind you. There are great views from here of Padstow Bay.

➤ **Find** The Rumps Fort (see above) and walk ⅔ mile SW.

50.587172, -4.934244

Hayle Bay, Polzeath

Surfers' bay. Watching them skim around the ragged surface of the chaotic waves is as hypnotic as staring into a campfire.

➤ **Find** New Polzeath Long Stay Car Park (Bishop's Hill Rd, Polzeath, PL27 6UF), then walk 300 yards W to the beach.

50.577924, -4.920140

PEOPLE OF THE PATH

The Mum, Bude, North Cornwall

Our children are out there surfing and we've got dry robes waiting for them when they come in. It's important to wear the right clothes and to stay warm on the path. Even in June. And whatever you're doing.

Broadagogue Cove, St Minver Lowlands

The shipwreck coast. Explore the rocks and low water either side of the small cove for wreck evidence and maybe, just maybe, treasure lost and trapped E on the bay's currents.

➤ **Find** Hayle Bay (see opposite) and walk 500 yards S on the SWCP.

50.570055, -4.925729

Trebetherick Point, Daymer Bay

Warm the hands and fingers on a hot day against multicoloured rocks that include green-and-purple striped slates.

➤ **Find** Daymer Bay Car Park (SWCP, Wadebridge, PL27 6SA), and walk 600 yards NW on the SWCP.

50.564185, -4.931395

Daymer Bay

Walk over soft mud and dry dunes between creeks and streams. The sand at low tide is breathtaking. Bass feed on the flood tide. The shallow water is good for swimming but beware rip tides and currents. The bay is the entrance to Cornwall's second longest river, which trails 30 miles into Bodmin Moor.

➤ **Find** Trebetherick Point (see above) and walk 300 yards along the beach.

50.559742, -4.928946

Daymer Bay

THE MARINERS AT ROCK, ROCK

 Pub overlooking the Camel Estuary. Cream teas and an all-day menu.

The Slipway,
Rock, PL27 6LD
www.paul-ainsworth.
co.uk/the-mariners/
about/

TRISTRAM CAMPING PARK, POLZEATH

 Camping on a grassy cliff overlooking Polzeath Beach. Cracking Crab Cafe is handily situated next door, for breakfast and lunch.

Tristram Cliff,
Polzeath, PL27 6TD
www.polzeathcamping.
co.uk

St Enodoc Church, Trebetherick

Explore the graveyard of this 12th-century church bunkered between sand dunes and the golf course. Until the 19th century, the church was completely buried by sand and was known as 'Sinking Neddy'.

➤ **Find** Trebetherick Point (see page 133) and walk ⅔ mile SE over the beach and dunes, keeping Brea Hill Tumuli (see below) on your right shoulder.

50.558107, -4.921694

Brea Hill Tumuli, Trebetherick

Somewhere to sit still while watching the estuary drift by below.

➤ **Find** St Enodoc Church (see above) and walk 200 yards E to the top of the hill.

50.557302, -4.926264

BLUE TOMATO CAFE, ROCK

Beachside eatery, for burgers and sandwiches as well as salads, pasta and daily specials.

Rock Rd, Ferry Point, Rock, PL27 6LD
www.bluetomatocafe.co.uk

THE ROCK INN, ROCK

Restaurant in Rock beside the Camel Estuary with an elevated dining deck. Specials include the mussels.

6 Beachside, Rock, Wadebridge, PL27 6FD
www.therockinnrock.co.uk

St Michael's Church churchyard cross, Porthilly

Sandy cove marked by an ancient cross in the churchyard situated on the banks of the Camel Estuary, in Porthilly Cove. It's a short walk from the village of Rock, or a ferry ride from Padstow. Nice views from the churchyard benches.

➤ **Find** Rock Quarry Car Park, on the SWCP (Rock, PL27 6LD). Looking across the river at Padstow, turn L and walk up the beach past the Rock Sailing & Waterski Club. At low tide only, walk around the hard-sand cove ⅓ mile to the church. Alternatively, turn R at Rock Quarry Car Park and walk 1.1 miles to the stunning views over Daymer Bay (see page 133) at low or high tide from Brea Hill (50.557152, -4.926245) – one of the most sacred sites in England.

50.540992, -4.91289

Little Petherick Creek & Saints Way, St Issey

Schools of bass feed on the surface of the creek on a calm day. The wooded cliffs are somewhere to find plant fossils.

➤ **Find** the bridge at The Old Mill House on the A389 (Little Petherick, Padstow, PL27 7QT). Opposite the Mill is a small blue parking sign. Follow the sign and walk past the church, through the car park and on to the creek FP. Follow the FP for ⅓ mile to the woodland or keep walking 1⅓ miles to Padstow on the Camel Trail, beside the River Camel.

50.515744, -4.939682

Crantock Beach

CRANTOCK

CLIMB the highest dunes in Britain.

SEARCH for sea holly.

SMELL summer orchids.

EXPLORE low-tide islets.

LOOK for flint arrowheads.

FORAGE marsh samphire.

WATCH dolphins off a beacon point.

SWIM a chapel pool.

VISIT the UK's oldest deer park.

TOUCH the remains of a tin mine.

TRAVEL back in time at Droskyn Point Sundial.

DENNIS COVE CAMPSITE, PADSTOW

 The closest campsite to Padstow, situated on a gentle hill looking over the harbour.

Dennis Ln,
Padstow, PL28 8DR
www.denniscove
campsite.co.uk

GREENS OF PADSTOW, PADSTOW

 Licensed restaurant and mini golf garden perched high above Padstow Harbour, with panoramic views over the Camel Estuary and town.

North Quay,
Padstow, PL28 8AF
greenspadstow.co.uk

THE FORESHORE – DENNIS FARM, PADSTOW

 The camping field lies between the River Camel and the Camel Trail FP and cycle track. There are 25 campsite pitches for tents.

Dennis Ln,
Padstow, PL28 8DR
www.theforeshore
padstow.co.uk

Padstow, River Camel

Suck in the morning view over one the most stunning estuaries in Cornwall.
> **Find** Padstow Harbour car park (Riverside, Padstow, PL28 8BY), then walk 1 mile S to Dennis Hill and the view over the estuary.

50.529513, -4.936193

Prideaux Place, Padstow

Listen for the bark of mating deer in autumn around the ancient park, thought to be the UK's oldest: it dates back to AD440.
> **Find** Padstow Harbour car park (Riverside, Padstow, PL28 8BY), then walk N on the SWCP 600 yards to the war memorial. Just past the memorial, take the 2nd FP L and follow it ½ mile to the deer park.

50.543086, -4.944964

The Doom Bar, Padstow

Vast sand bank where many ships have run aground once the wind was lost from their sails in the harbour. It's best explored on foot at low tide when the sands are vast, or before low tide on a kayak or paddleboard.
> **Find** Padstow Harbour car park (Riverside, Padstow, PL28 8BY), then walk N on the SWCP 2 miles, past the war memorial, towards Stepper Point (see opposite) with Doom Bar on your R shoulder as the estuary opens up.

50.558716, -4.938652

Gun Point, Padstow

Touch the ground and remains of fortifications thought to date back to the Spanish Armada.
> **Find** Doom Bar walk (see above). The point is 1 mile N of the car park, just N of St George's Cove and Well.

50.553543, -4.938485

CAFFÈ ROJANO BY PAUL AINSWORTH, PADSTOW

Seasonal small plates, deli sandwiches, beautiful sourdough pizzas and fresh pasta dishes.

9 Mill Square, Padstow, PL28 8AE
www.paul-ainsworth.co.uk

TREVERBYN HOUSE, PADSTOW

B&B overlooking Padstow's Camel Estuary, with views to Rock and Daymer Bay. Two-min walk from Padstow Harbour.

Treverbyn, Station Rd, Padstow, PL28 8DA
treverbynhouse.com

PADSTOW HARBOUR HOTEL, PADSTOW

Victorian hotel with harbour views. Afternoon teas with pastries, home-made scones, finger sandwiches and savoury snacks.

Station Rd, Padstow, PL28 8DB
www.harbourhotels.co.uk

Harbour Cove Dunes, Padstow

Smell summer orchids and listen to reed buntings in the marshes around the edges of Harbour Cove.

➤ **Find** Gun Point (see opposite) and walk ½ mile W along the SWCP to the dunes.

50.554722, -4.948244

Hawkers Cove, Padstow

Watch bass feed on the still surface of this sheltered beach on a calm windless day. The fish are protected since the Camel Estuary is a breeding ground.

➤ **Find** Harbour Cove Dunes (see above) and walk 600 yards N to the cove.

50.554722, -4.948244

Stepper Point, Padstow

Good views. Listen for the nesting birds in spring and early summer on the limestone rock.

➤ **Find** Hawkers Cove (see above) and walk N ½ mile on the SWCP.

50.569412, -4.945005

Roundhole Point, Trevone

Find the collapsed sea cave and cliff around the N edge of Trevone Bay. Visit just before low tide, but take great care of incoming water.

➤ **Find** Trevone Beach Car Park (Padstow, PL28 8QY), then walk 400 yards NW to the beach at low tide.

50.548195, -4.979444

PEOPLE OF THE PATH

The Cottage Maid, Hayle Bay, North Cornwalll

There's a lovely little beach in the northern corner of Hayle Bay that I like. My favourite things to do around the path are paddleboard and swim.

PUFFINS B&B, TREVONE

B&B overlooking Trevone Bay.

Trevone Rd, Trevone, PL28 8QX
www.cornwall-online.co.uk/puffinsbandb-trevone/

WELL PARC HOTEL, TREVONE

Hotel in 2 acres of grounds overlooking the coast, with Trevose Head (see right) to the L and Round Hole of Trevone (50.5482, -4.9794) to the R.

Dobbin Ln, Trevone, PL28 8QN
www.wellparc.co.uk

HARLYN BEACH HOUSE, HARLYN

Beach house, 200m above Harlyn Bay, with private FP to the beach.

Harlyn Place, Harlyn, PL28 8SQ
www.harlynbeachhouse.co.uk

POLMARK BEACH COTTAGES, HARLYN

These self-catering cottages are a two-min walk from the beach in Harlyn Bay. Two of them have a sea view.

Harlyn Bay, PL28 8SB
www.polmarkbeachcottages.co.uk

Harlyn Bay, Harlyn

Smell wild flowers around the edges of the sandy bay. Swim at low tide in the shallows.

➤ **Find** the small car park in Harlyn (Padstow, PL28 8SB), and walk 100 yards W to the bay.

50.542809, -4.997976

Harlyn Burial Ground, Harlyn

This N-facing bay and beach was used for thousands of years as a Celtic burial site. There's something in the air. Cliff erosion continues to give up trinkets, burial items and other clues, including hundreds of Bronze Age graves with bodies facing north and links to Egyptian ritual and afterlife gifts. Good for surfers and seals.

➤ **Find** Harlyn Bay (see above) and walk off the beach from its centre to reach the burial ground.

50.539728, -4.999259

Trevose Head, Trevose

A scented heathland of wild meadows and 360-degree views. Great in a storm when the black clouds rear up and funnel down the valley from Padstow. Many grey seals fish here. The lighthouse is available for holiday hire.

➤ **Find** the NT car park (Padstow, PL28 8SH), then walk 500 yards N to the head and lighthouse.

50.549268, -5.036605

Stinking Cove Tumulus, Dinas Head

Ancient burial ground a few yards N of Dinas Head. Find and feel history in the hand: look for 6,000-year-old flint arrowheads around the coast between Booby's Bay (see below) and Trevose Head (see above). If stone is not your thing, the best-tasting wild asparagus grows about the cliffs. Fulmars and guillemots nest overhead. It's an incredible place.

➤ **Find** the NT car park (Padstow, PL28 8SH), then walk 200 yards W to the cliff over the cove. Walk on 200 yards to Dinas Head with views across to The Bull.

50.546942, -5.036831

Booby's Bay

Explore the shipwrecked SV *Carl* while it is still visible above the sand at low tide.

➤ **Find** Dinas Head (see above) and walk 1 mile S on the SWCP.

50.538416, -5.027108

St Constantine Dunes, Constantine Bay

Quiet surf beach but beware low reef and rocks. Walk N to the neighbouring beach at low tide to explore rocks and paddle pools.

➤ **Find** Booby's Bay (see opposite) and walk the beach at low tide 400 yards S to the dunes.

50.532775, -5.021915

Treyarnon Point, Treyarnon Bay

Natural low-tide rock pool for safer swims. This coast can be treacherous for both sea craft and swimmers. Much care is needed.

➤ **Find** Treyarnon Bay car park (Treyarnon Bay, PL28 8JP), and walk 500 yards NW to the point.

50.530198, -5.027580

Trethias Island, Treyarnon Bay

Feel the rush of cold water all year round. Explore the island and vast cave at low tide. Swim the deeper rock pools beneath the castle ruins of Pepper Cove Settlement (see page 142) overhead.

➤ **Find** Treyarnon Point (see above) and walk ⅔ mile S along the SWCP or 400 yards at low tide across the bay.

50.525315, -5.028696

Harlyn Bay

YHA TREYARNON BAY

Youth hostel by the beach.

Treyarnon Bay, PL28 8JP
www.yha.org.uk

THE STABLE CAFE, TREYARNON BAY

Cafe 500 yards from Treyarnon Bay (see page 141).

Trethias Farm, Treyarnon Bay, PL28 8PL
www.trethiasfarm.co.uk/
stablecafe.php

TREDREA INN, PORTHCOTHAN BAY

Pub with views of Porthcothan Bay.

Porthcothan Bay, PL28 8LN
Facebook: @tredreapub

PORTHCOTHAN BAY STORES, PORTHCOTHAN BAY

Home-made food to go, great coffee, beach equipment and surf hire.

Porthcothan Bay, PL28 8LW
www.porthcothanbay
stores.co.uk

LANTHORN HOUSE, PORTHCOTHAN BAY

Luxury holiday home that sleeps ten, a five-min walk from the beach.

Porthcothan Bay, PL28 8LW
www.lanthornhouse.co.uk

Pepper Cove Settlement, Treyarnon Bay

One of the UK's most unique and mysterious castle ruins, spanning three separate headlands. The surrounding caves made the site an ideal smuggling spot for priceless spices, including pepper, from which the cove below the castle ruin now takes its name.

➤ **Find** Trethias Island (see page 141) and walk 500 yards S on the SWCP.

50.522736, -5.027279

Porthcothan Bay

Vast bay backed by dunes. Explore rock stacks and collapsed caves at low tide. Good crabbing and rock pools for blennies and shrimps. Loos and shop behind the dunes.

➤ **Find** Porthcothan Bay Car Park (Padstow, PL28 8LP), then walk W 200 yards to the dunes.

50.510347, -5.029597

Trescore Islands, St Eval

Fancy playing at being Robinson Crusoe for an hour or more? Explore islets at low tide by wading through the shallows from the shore. Look for dolphins. Don't get stranded.

➤ **Find** Porthcothan Bay (see above) and walk 300 yards S on the SWCP.

50.507631, -5.034562

Park Head, St Eval

Stunning views from the ramparts of an Iron Age fort on a greenstone headland.

➤ **Find** Trescore Islands (see above) and walk 1¼ miles S to the head.

50.498026, -5.047557

Trevose Head

BEACH HEAD BUNKHOUSE, ST EVAL

 NT barn conversion that sleeps 14. **Minimum stay of three nights.**

Park Head,
St Eval, PL27 7UU
www.nationaltrust.org.uk/
holidays/beach-head-
bunkhouse-cornwall

EFFLINS FARMHOUSE B&B, BEDRUTHAN

 B&B in a traditional Cornish farmhouse. Sea views from the Florentine-style dining table.

Efflins at Bedruthan
Steps, Porthcothan,
PL27 7UU
www.efflins.com

Bedruthan Steps, Bedruthan

Feel the rush of beauty and danger – irresistibly attractive to mortals. Perhaps the wildest and best beach in Cornwall, reclaimed by nature to create a human-free zone since it has eroded out all the steps. Take care if you try to gain access from the north at low tide as people lose their lives here each year doing exactly that. It's tempting, but... Instead, why not explore rock stacks at low tide from a distance, ideally with binoculars, until the steps are reinstalled. For now, let nature have it.
➤ Find Carnewas car park off the B3276 (Bedruthan, PL27 7UW). Facing the beach, walk along the cliff top to the N end of the beach ⅔ mile away.

50.486319, -5.033223

Redcliffe Castle Ruin, Bedruthan

Explore prehistoric rampart remains on the cliff and below.
➤ Find Carnewas car park off the B3276 (Bedruthan, PL27 7UW), then walk E to the SWCP and then N on the FP 300 yards to the ruin.

50.487351, -5.032108

CARNEWAS FARM HOLIDAYS, MAWGAN PORTH

 Small campsite with big views. There are two static caravans for self-catering, a touring caravan site, and a large field with electric hook-ups for camping.

Unnamed Rd, Mawgan Porth, PL27 7UW
www.carnewasfarm holidays.co.uk

BLUE BAY HOUSE, MAWGAN PORTH

 B&B and self-catering lodge accommodation in Mawgan Porth, halfway between Padstow and Newquay.

Mawgan Porth, TR8 4DA
www.bluebaycornwall.co.uk

BEDRUTHAN HOTEL AND SPA, MAWGAN PORTH

 Self-catering villas and apartments. Wild Cafe, bar and terrace, sensory spa garden and more.

Bedruthan Hotel and Spa, Mawgan Porth, TR8 4BU
www.bedruthan.com

DIMORA B&B, MAWGAN PORTH

 B&B in Mawgan Porth, close to Watergate Bay, Padstow and Newquay.

Gwel-An-Mor, Mawgan Porth, TR8 4DW
www.dimora-bed-breakfast.co.uk

Mawgan Porth Beach, Mawgan Porth

Sandy swims, trapped between the headland and warm, scented August sea breezes.

➤ **Find** Bedruthan Steps (see page 143) and walk 1 mile S on the SWCP to the beach.

50.468165, -5.037484

Beacon Cove, Mawgan-in-Pydar

Great views. No FP down, so access is by boat only, unless you can find the ropes that sometimes hang to the beach. Much care is needed. Griffin's Point Fort is overhead.

➤ **Find** Catch Seafood Bar & Grill (see page 146). Cross the footbridge across the River Menalhyl and turn R following the course of the SWCP at the hairpin bend. Walk 1 mile around the coastline to Beacon Cove.

50.460273, -5.038122

Griffin's Point Fort, Mawgan-in-Pydar

Iron Age fort at the N point of Watergate Bay and the main surf beach in the area.

➤ **Find** Beacon Cove (see above) and walk 300 yards S on the SWCP to the point.

50.458440, -5.042055

Mawgan Porth Beach

SCARLET HOTEL, MAWGAN PORTH

 Hotel and restaurant that serves breakfast, lunch, afternoon tea and dinner on a sea-view terrace from which you can watch surfers on the beach below. There's also a cliff top hot tub and an outdoor pool designed to look like a wild swimming spot.

Tredragon Rd, Mawgan Porth, TR8 4DQ
www.scarlethotel.co.uk

MERRYMOOR INN, MAWGAN PORTH

 B&B serving pub food, situated between Newquay and Padstow, run by three generations of the same family. There are dramatic beach and cliff views over the River Menalhyl.

Mawgan Porth, TR8 4BA
www.merrymoorinn.com

MARVER CAMPSITE, MAWGAN PORTH

 Camping 150 yards from the beach in Lanherne valley.

Mawgan Porth, TR8 4BB
marverholidaypark-cornwall.co.uk/camping/

BEACH BOX MAWGAN PORTH, MAWGAN PORTH

 Cafe by the waterside.

Mawgan Porth, TR8 4BA
beachboxcornwall.co.uk/mawgan-porth/

Watergate Bay

Fox Hole, Mawgan-in-Pydar

Surf beach backed by cliffs that stretches 2 miles S. At its best and roughest in an easterly wind. Look for starfish in rock pools at low tide.

➤ **Find** Griffin's Point Fort (see opposite) and walk 300 yards S on the SWCP.

50.454411, -5.041347

Watergate Bay

The N gateway to Newquay is flushed in June and July with a rainbow of blue sea, yellow sand and emerald-gorsed cliffs, peppered with seabirds and occasional humans.

➤ **Find** car park (The Phoenix, Newquay, TR8 4AY), and walk 20 yards W to the beach.

50.446194, -5.044631

Fruitful Cove Tumuli, Newquay

Look at and touch prehistoric relics washed up from eroded cliffs. Stone Age hammers and Bronze Age artefacts linked to the surrounding barrows have been found here.

➤ **Find** car park (The Phoenix, Newquay, TR8 4AY), and from the beach, walk ⅔ mile along the shore after high tide to the cove. Beware getting cut off by the incoming tide.

50.434768, -5.051453

Whipsiderry Beach, Porth

Feel the cold air of caves at low tide; smell the lemony scent of rock samphire around the cliff steps.

➤ **Find** car park (Alexandra Rd, Porth, Newquay, TR7 3NB), then walk 400 yards N of Trevelgue Head (see page 146) to the beach.

50.429595, -5.057316

CATCH SEAFOOD BAR & GRILL, MAWGAN PORTH

 All-day breakfasts, brunches, coffees, lunches, cream teas and dinners in a beach house restaurant next to Mawgan Porth Beach.

4 B3276, Mawgan Porth, TR8 4BJ
www.catchmawgan porthbeach.co.uk

Porth Beach

WAX WATERGATE BAY, WATERGATE BAY

 From small plates of olives and squid to pizzas, burgers and fish.

Watergate Bay, TR8 4AB
waxwatergate.co.uk

BEACH RETREATS, MILL HOUSE, WATERGATE BAY

 Self-catering luxury cottages, on the beach!

On the Beach, Watergate Bay, TR8 4AA
www.beachretreats.co.uk

PORTH BEACH HOTEL, NEWQUAY

 Breakfasts, dinners and rooms. The hotel has a wellness garden that can be used as a coastal yogic space.

Alexandra Rd, Newquay, TR7 3NB
www.porthbeachhotel.co.uk

Trevelgue Head, Porth

Iron Age earthworks under erosion. Look for flint arrowheads around the prehistoric and Bronze Age settlement and barrows. The site is flanked by more caves, tunnels, rock pillars and stacks. It's worthy of at least several hours of your time at low tide, and also at high tide, when you can listen to the sound of blowholes where water is trapped in caves and blasts to the surface. 'Concert Cavern' below once hosted a low-tide concert.
➤ **Find** car park (Alexandra Rd, Porth, Newquay, TR7 3NB), then walk 400 yards N of Trevelgue Head to the beach.

50.427452, -5.065374

Porth Beach, Porth

Suck up a historic view: a sandy bay framed in a prehistoric N rim that reaches out into the sea. There's a sheltered strip for sea swims next to the fort, with a river running along the top edge where you can wash off the salt. Storm tides sometimes expose a sunken prehistoric forest 20ft below the surface: evidence of when the sea level was lower, more than 7,000 years ago.
➤ **Find** Trevelgue Head (see above) and walk S 200 yards to the beach.

50.252208, -5.032268

Wine Cove, Newquay

Stone and flint tools dating back more than 6,000 years have been found in and around the cove and head to the N.
➤ **Find** Porth Beach (see above) and walk 300 yards S on the SWCP to the cove.

50.423699, -5.066324

WHIPSIDERRY HOTEL,
NEWQUAY

 Family-run hotel surrounded by rolling cliffs and sand, set in 2 acres overlooking Porth Beach and Bay. There's a swimming pool and restaurant.

Trevelgue Rd,
Newquay, TR7 3LY
www.whipsiderry.co.uk

PORTH BEACH
HOLIDAY PARK,
PORTH

 Camping in Porth village, just over a mile from Newquay.

Alexandra Rd, Porth,
Newquay, TR7 3NH
porthbeach.co.uk

THE MERMAID INN,
PORTH

 Sandwiches served in bread from The Chough Bakery.

Alexandra Ct, Porth,
Newquay, TR7 3NB
www.themermaidinn.co.uk

CAFE COAST PORTH,
NEWQUAY

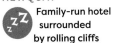 Cafe overlooking Porth Beach, for hot drinks and snacks.

Porth Beach Rd, Porth,
Newquay, TR7 3LN
01637 871962

Barrowfields, Newquay

Sacred burial site that's riddled with barrows, tumuli and erosion. See what you can find to touch.

> **Find** Wine Cove (see opposite) and walk 500 yards SW on the SWCP.

50.419570, -5.069584

Tolcarne Beach, Newquay

Explore the N beach area beside rocks and Lusty Glaze Beach (50.422134, -5.067130) for prehistoric relics eroded out of the burial mounds and cliffs above. More than 15 burial mounds have been identified overhead near the conical mound, some of which are almost 4,000 years old.

> **Find** Barrowfields (see above) and walk 200 yards SW to the beach.

50.418762, -5.073782

Towan Head, Newquay

Listen for the kittiwake colony on the cliffs out to Towan Head.

> **Find** Towan Headland Car Park (Headland Rd, Newquay, TR7 1HN), and walk 300 yards NW to the head.

50.425716, -5.098389

Fistral Beach, Newquay

Surfers' paradise. Taste salty marsh samphire around the wet, shady areas at the N and S edges of the beach.

> **Find** Towan Head (see above) and walk 300 yards SW to the beach.

50.415427, -5.100913

PEOPLE OF THE PATH

The Swimmer, Morwenstow, North Cornwall

We learnt to swim at Crackington Haven as children. I think it's my favourite place on the path. I don't live here any more but I have wonderful memories. The bay is sheltered and quite small so it's a bit safer than other places along the coast.

LEGACY HOTEL VICTORIA, NEWQUAY

 Hotel on the cliffs above Newquay's Great Western Beach. Hotel includes a gym, an indoor heated pool, a sauna and a spa.

Hotel Victoria, East St, Newquay, TR7 1DB
www.legacy-hotels.co.uk/
hotels/hotel-victoria-
newquay-cornwall

CLIFF HOUSE, NEWQUAY

 B&B with sea views over Towan Beach.

61 Fore St,
Newquay, TR7 1HA
cliffhousenewquay.com

THE HARBOUR, NEWQUAY

 Hotel built into the cliff overlooking the harbour. Every bedroom has its own balcony overlooking the sea. The restaurant, conservatory and terrace have views over seven of Newquay's beaches. The Harbour Fish and Grill was a grain store that was converted in the 1930s to a house and then in the 1950s to a hotel and restaurant.

N Quay Hill,
Newquay, TR7 1HF
www.harbourhotel.co.uk

Swimming Cove, Newquay

The slopes above Polly Joke put on an incredible display of wild flowers in spring – perhaps the best round the FP.
➤ **Find** Fistral Beach (see page 147) and walk ½ mile SW to the cove.

50.412800, -5.114564

Crantock Beach, Crantock

Probably the sandy remains of a settlement lost to sand and dunes. The Gannel River empties its freshwater into the N edge of the tide at Salt Cove, beneath a prehistoric burial site and a pub (Lewinnick Lodge, see opposite). Check out Piper's Hole cave (49.96667,-6.34968) and its antique carvings. Perfect at low tide for paddleboard lessons and practice.
➤ **Find** Crantock Beach car park (Newquay, TR8 5RN), then walk 400 yards N to the beach.

50.409327, -5.121044

Rushy Green, Crantock

Fine, hot sand in which to wallow or roll or walk through. The dunes are peppered with sea holly and marram grass.
➤ **Find** Crantock Beach car park (Newquay, TR8 5RN), then walk W along the SWCP (R facing the sea) 200 yards and look for the FP on the R over the green.

50.405639, -5.117981

PEOPLE OF THE PATH

The Campsite Owner, Bedruthan, North Cornwall

The stairs have washed away at Bedruthan Steps. People try to walk in from the north at low tide, but it's so easy to get caught out by the tides. It's extremely dangerous so people must take care. I still think this is the best beach in Cornwall; the views are stunning.

Pentire Point West, Crantock

There's an impressive field of red poppies over the E flank of this sandy beach in June and July. The red blanket is decorated by the odd yellow corn marigold, which has an unusual odour. The shoots are edible.

➤ **Find** Crantock Beach (see opposite) and walk ½ mile on the SWCP to the point.

50.408125, -5.135699

Porth Joke, Cubert

This is as good as a summer beach can get: sheltered, north facing, and with its own freshwater stream and no shops. Ringed plover, greenshank, dunlin, curlew and teal are in residence.

➤ **Find** Pentire Point West (see above) and walk 300 yards S to the beach.

50.401866, -5.136572

Tumulus Head, Cubert

Look for dolphins from the head of this ancient burial site.

➤ **Find** Porth Joke car park (Newquay, TR8 5QS) and take the BW on the N edge of the car park 600 yards to Porth Joke (see above). Walk on, keeping the beach on your R shoulder, another ⅔ mile to the head.

50.402313, -5.145999

Holywell Dunes and Beach, Holywell

Taste the fresh air of a well-watered place. It's unmistakable, and our nostrils are attuned to pick up the scent. Of the wells, the best is the spring inside the cave on the N side of the beach, where water settles in a series of basins. The waters here are renowned for curing a variety of ills. If wells aren't your thing, go and find the shipwreck that can be seen at low tide.

➤ **Find** Tumulus Head (see above) and walk ⅔ mile SW to the beach on the SWCP.

50.391055, -5.141965

Penhale Point Settlement, Perranzabuloe

Iron Age defences are still visible but are eroding out. There are views over St Agnes Head, Godrevy Point and St Ives beyond.

➤ **Find** Holywell Bay Car Park (Holywell Rd, Newquay, TR8 5DD), then walk N 200 yards to find the SWCP. Follow the SWCP L and N and W ⅔ mile to reach the point.

50.388259, -5.153386

C-BAY. CAFE. BAR. BISTRO., CRANTOCK

Cafe/bar/bistro and holiday apartments with views over Crantock Beach (see page 148). Breakfasts, home-baked cakes, fresh 'Olfactory Coffee' and iced smoothies.

C-Bay, West Pentire, Crantock, TR8 5SE
www.crantockbay.co.uk/c-bay-cafe-bar-bistro/

BOWGIE INN, WEST PENTIRE

Pub perched on the West Pentire Headland, overlooking Crantock Beach (see page 148), near Newquay. The 'Bowgie' is Cornish for 'cowshed' and has one of the most incredible beer gardens in the whole country. The pub's owner used to grow potatoes in the field on the cliff edge to make the pub chips. Catch some rays on the sun terrace.

W Pentire Rd, West Pentire, TR8 5SE
www.bowgie.com

HOLYWELL BAY B&B, HOLYWELL

B&B in Holywell Bay with views of the sand dunes.

Inshallah, Rhubarb Hill, Holywell, TR8 5PT
www.holywellbaybandb.co.uk

Penhale Point, Perranzabuloe

Look for two offshore rocks in the shape of fish tails, known locally as 'Fish Tail Rocks'. Fulmars glide on the thermals and nest here.

➤ **Find** Penhale Point Settlement (see page 149) and walk 100 yards to the cliff.

50.388259, -5.153386

Ligger Point Tumuli, Perranzabuloe

The tumuli provide a 2-mile view over Perran Sands (50.364154, -5.153448). They are ancient, and were once sacred to our ancestors.

➤ **Find** Penhale Point (see above) and walk ⅔ mile S on the SWCP. Steer clear of the danger area of shafts and collapsed mines 200 yards E of the point.

50.379449, -5.153469

Penhale Sands and Lake, Perranzabuloe

Climb the highest dunes in Britain, which rise more than 100 yards and are more than 55 yards deep. Rare plants live here around the lake, which is rain dependent and can often be mostly dry.

➤ **Find** Ligger Point Tumuli (above) and walk 1 mile SE across the beach at low tide.

50.369240, -5.136260

St Piran's Church remains, Perranzabuloe

Look for human bones and skeletons that can be found when sand is blown or moved from the remnant of a lost cemetery. The church ruin and oratory is close to St Piran's Cross, one of two three-holed crosses in Cornwall; the other is at Wadebridge. St Piran's is the oldest Christian site in Cornwall, founded in the 5th or 6th century.

➤ **Find** Penhale Sands and Lake (see above) and walk S across the dunes 200 yards to find the church wall remains.

50.366174, -5.134458

Chapel Rock Dunes, Perranzabuloe

Site of an old chapel that is better known for a natural rock pool that has become a tidal swimming pool with a wall.

➤ **Find** Droskyn Car Park (Cliff Rd, Perranporth, TR6 0DR), then walk 300 yards N to the dunes.

50.350608, -5.151415

HAVEN PERRAN SANDS HOLIDAY PARK, PERRANPORTH

 Beachside resort, with bells and whistles: lazy river, indoor pool with a slide, tat and pasty shops, a bar, and its own surf school.

Perran Sands Holiday Park, Perranporth, TR6 0AQ
www.haven.com

THE WATERING HOLE, PERRANPORTH

 This joint claims to be the 'ONLY' bar in the UK that is truly on the beach. Whether or not this is true, it is definitely situated on a 3-mile stretch of sand shadowed by dunes and sea between Holywell and St Agnes. The bar was founded in the late 1970s. It's come on a way, serving up live music, food and drink.

Beach, 19 St Pirans Rd, Perranporth, TR6 0BH
www.thewateringhole.co.uk

THE SEINERS ARMS, PERRANPORTH

 Family-run B&B and restaurant on Perranporth seafront.

Beach Rd,
Perranporth TR6 0JL
www.seiners.co.uk

Perran Sands, Perranzabuloe

Watch out for where lifeguards pull swimmers from the water – not to gloat but to identify the rips, currents and backwashes. Take advice on when it's best to swim. People drown here each year. Forage for seaweed in the quieter shallows.

➤ **Find** Droskyn Car Park (Cliff Rd, Perranporth, TR6 0DR), then walk 200 yards N to the beach.

50.350609, -5.156126

Droskyn Point, Perranporth

Touch the remains of the tin mine, which is visible at various gaps and holes in the rocks at low tide. Avoid exploring the tunnels and gaps as invisible shafts can collapse and lead to death or injury. Instead, go for a wonderful sand walk over 2 miles between Droskyn and Ligger Point to the N, or low-tide swims in warm rock pools.

➤ **Find** Droskyn Car Park (Cliff Rd, Perranporth, TR6 0DR) and walk 100 yards W to the point.

50.346733, -5.162294

Droskyn Point Sundial, Perranporth

This Millennium sundial is located on the point of the Droskyn mine overlooking Perran Bay. The dial shows 'Cornish times', which are 20 mins behind GMT.

➤ **Find** Droskyn Point (see above).

50.346733, -5.162294

Perran Sands

YHA PERRANPORTH, PERRAN BAY

 A cliff top hostel, 2½ miles from the nearest beach – perfect for surfing, body boarding, kayaking or coasteering. Perhaps the best-value accommodation around the SWCP.

Droskyn Point, Perranporth, TR6 0GS
www.yha.org.uk

CLIGGA CLIFF FARM CAMPING, PERRANPORTH

 Back-to-basics coastal campsite on a working farm. No frills, but it's on the SWCP, with Perranporth Beach a ten-min walk away. Campfires and BBQs are allowed, and there are compost loos, hot showers and a washing-up area. Check out the farm's ethos and methods with regards to livestock, which are impressive and interesting.

St George's Hill, Perranporth, TR6 0EQ
cliggacliffcornwall.co.uk

ST GEORGE'S COUNTRY HOUSE HOTEL, PERRANPORTH

 Converted mine captain's home, built in the 19th century, with walled garden, panoramic views and English breakfast.

St George's Hill, Perranporth, TR6 0ED
www.stgeorgescountry househotel.com

Cligga Head

Shag Rock, Perranzabuloe

Listen for the high-tide blowhole. Great place for bat watching in the early evening. Also good for watching the shags and cormorants that fish here.

➤ **Find** Droskyn Point (see page 151) and walk 300 yards W on the SWCP.

50.344377, -5.168543

Cligga Head, Perranzabuloe

Smell flowering summer heather and coconut gorse over dark mysterious caves along the headland. Minerals and ores can be seen in the rock formations below, including tin, silver, tungsten and copper. The concrete cap over the mineshaft can be seen on the headland, and there are occasional gaps that open up in the cliff face, where the shaft can still be seen before another collapse obscures the view.

➤ **Find** Shag Rock (see opposite) and walk 1 mile W on the SWCP.

50.339962, -5.181531

Mulgram Hill

ST AGNES

WILD THINGS TO DO BEFORE YOU DIE:

TASTE line-caught bass cooked on an open fire.

VISIT a colony of breeding seals.

TOUCH an ancient harbour wall.

TRAMP around a fossil forest.

LOOK for the flapping fin of a giant sunfish.

CATCH a glimpse of bats while star watching.

HAMMOCK over the perfume of bluebells.

LISTEN for nesting birds around a rock of puffins.

FORAGE for shore crabs.

EXPLORE a tin mine.

Hanover Cove, St Agnes

Forage and taste salty rock samphire, while looking for gold. Literally. The remains of the *Hanover* shipwreck, from 1763, may still shed its cargo of gold bullion and coins. Most was recovered, but… If gold is not your thing, go look for seaweed and shore crabs.

➤ **Find** Trevellas Cove Car Park (St Agnes, TR5 0XP), then walk NE 1 mile on the SWCP to the cove.

50.334638, -5.180959

Trevellas Mine, St Agnes

A stone tower and mine embedded in the mineral and metal formed a million years ago, surrounded by green bracken that is rooted to ancient leaf peat.

➤ **Find** Trevellas Cove Car Park (St Agnes, TR5 0XP), then walk S 500 yards to the tower.

50.321435, -5.192975

Blue Hills, St Agnes

Listen to the song of blackbirds after 4pm in March on rocky paths linking the river valley, tin mines and coast.

➤ **Find** Trevellas Cove Car Park (St Agnes, TR5 0XP), then walk NE 500 yards to the cliff top via the FP.

50.321969, -5.193232

Trevellas Porth Cove, St Agnes

From this rocky bay, you can climb into neighbouring Trevaunance Cove (see opposite) at low tide. The sound of bees over heather is slightly drowned by the breeze and wash of waves on rock below. Sit above the beach bays in the grass next to gorse seeds crackling and popping in hot July sunshine.

➤ **Find** Blue Hills (see above) and walk NW and then SW on the SWCP 100 yards to the cove.

50.323553, -5.197609

Blue Hills

Trevaunance Cove, St Agnes

Find the ancient harbour wall on the W edge of the cove. Keep walking at low tide (but beware the tide on your return journey) to look at caves, stacks and rock arches. Surf the shingle beach at high tide, dig in the sand at low. People-watch around the bay, or paddle about the river and shoreline.

➤ **Find** Trevellas Porth Cove (see opposite) and walk 500 yards W on the SWCP.

50.320813, -5.201669

Newdowns Head, St Agnes

Star watch on the small headland out of St Agnes between the silent flight of horseshoe bats and the smooth wash of moonlit waves. Look out for seals.

➤ **Find** Trevaunance Cove (see above) and walk 1 mile W on the SWCP.

50.322032, -5.220573

St Agnes Head, St Agnes

Listen for nesting razorbills, guillemots and kittiwakes. Also look across to Bawden Rocks offshore for puffins.

➤ **Find** St Agnes Head car park (Beacon Dr, St Agnes, TR5 0NU), and walk 300 yards N to the head.

50.318768, -5.234718

Carn Gowla, St Agnes

Take some time to explore - from a distance - disused tin mines. The remains of the cliff top tin mining industry are one of the highlights along this section. Look out for bats after dusk.

➤ **Find** St Agnes Head (see above) and walk 300 yards S on the SWCP.

50.316175, -5.234790

Tubby's Head Settlement, St Agnes

Prehistoric settlement enclosed inside a 1-yard-thick bank. Listen for the blowhole that spews a fabulous plume of spray during high tide and swells.

➤ **Find** Carn Gowla (see above) and walk ½ mile S on the SWCP.

50.308826, -5.234207

Natural Arch Cave, St Agnes

Fabulous for bats, thanks in part to the many mine shafts and natural caves along this stretch of coast.

➤ **Find** Tubby's Head Settlement (see above) and walk 400 yards S on the SWCP.

50.303667, -5.235083

CHAPEL PORTH
NT BEACH CAFE, ST AGNES

 This little stone cabin that leads out on to vast sandy beaches has served teas since the 1920s.

Chapel Porth, St Agnes, TR5 0NR
www.nationaltrust.org.uk

BLUE BAR, PORTHTOWAN

 Barista coffees and food wrapped in shabby-chic decor on Porthtowan Beach dunes. Dog friendly.

Beach Rd, Eastcliff, Porthtowan, TR4 8AW
www.blue-bar.co.uk

THE UNICORN ON THE BEACH, PORTHTOWAN

Pub by Porthtowan Beach for seasonal dishes or crafted cocktails. There are also five beachside en suite rooms.

W Beach Rd, Porthtowan, TR4 8AD
www.theunicornon thebeach.com

Tubby's Hea

Chapel Remains at Chapel Porth, St Agnes

Feel the magic of an old, sacred site. Find the foundation of the raised chapel, before taking a low-tide walk on the white sands to Porthtowan from Chapel Porth. Great surf.
➤ **Find** Natural Arch Cave (see page 157) and walk 200 yards S on the SWCP.

50.301382, -5.234454

Chapel Porth, St Agnes

Fresh water meets sea at sacred Chapel Porth. Follow the line of the stream up from the beach along the bridleway to Chapel Coombe. There are tin mine tunnels to be explored at low tide on the beach. Walk along the beach to see the remains of the Towanroath Shaft.
➤ **Find** the NT Chapel Porth car park (St Agnes, TR5 0NS). The beach is a few yards from here.

50.300946, -5.236374

Porthtowan Cliffs, Porthtowan

Smell the perfumed scent of purple heather from June. Sit awhile, blue sky above and white horses below.
➤ **Find** Porthtowan Beach Car Park (1 Beach Rd, Porthtowan, TR4 8AA), then walk NE on the SWCP 600 yards to the cliff.

50.291807, -5.240765

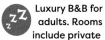

Porthtowan Pool, Porthtowan

Sense the descents of fellow travellers who preceded you in the
last month, and think about how many have gone this way in the
past. The pool architects carved a safe place in nature out of
stone. That alone is perhaps too wonderful for words, although
the water is pretty good, too.

➤ **Find** Porthtowan Beach Car Park (1 Beach Rd, Porthtowan,
TR4 8AA), then walk NE on the SWCP 300 yards to the cliff
and look for stairs down to the pool.

50.290245, -5.243147

Porthtowan Beach, Porthtowan

Surf or swim but take care. Stay warm in a full, thick wetsuit.

➤ **Find** Porthtowan Beach Car Park (1 Beach Rd, Porthtowan,
TR4 8AA), then walk 200 yards E to the beach.

50.288490, -5.246259

Tobban Horse, Porthtowan

Star watch on the small headland, ideally on a low tide.
Lushington Beach below is beautiful for midnight swims but
beware incoming tides..

➤ **Find** Porthtowan Beach (see above) and walk 300 yards
SW on the SWCP.

50.283478, -5.250723

Porthtowan Beach

Sally's Bottom, Portreath

Granite steps carry you down to the cove.

> **Find** Tobban Horse (see page 159) and walk 300 yards SW on the SWCP.

50.276855, -5.261430

Portreath Submerged Forest, Portreath

Submerged forest that gets exposed after winter storms at low tide. Surfing and body boarding on the N shore beside the pier.

> **Find** The Atlantic Cafe Bar (see left). Walk though the public car park down on to the beach a few yards away. Walk out at low tide.

50.262520, -5.292734

Western Hill, Portreath

Look for primroses in spring. Perhaps pick the odd flower to chew. Look for the rocks off the N shore of the bay, where seabirds fish all year.

> **Find** Portreath Beach and walk W 100 yards on the SWCP.

50.261412, -5.300312

Portreath

BASSET ARMS, PORTREATH

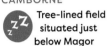 An old seafarers' and miners' pub in a fishing village, 200 yards from the beach. Sit at outdoor benches for ploughman's lunches and baguettes.

Tregea Hill, Portreath, TR16 4NG

Facebook: @bassetarms

MAGOR FARM CAMPSITE, CAMBORNE

Tree-lined field situated just below Magor Farm, a short walk from Godrevy and its famous lighthouse. No reception, just pitch and pay later ... when the owners arrive.

Magor Farm, Magor Hill, Camborne, TR14 0JF
www.magorfarm.co.uk

Ralph's Cupboard, Portreath

Smugglers' rocky cove that was once renowned as a place for stashing and hiding booty.

➤ **Find** Western Hill (see opposite) and walk 300 yards E on the SWCP.

50.259569, -5.306027

North Cliff Plantation, Basset's Cove

Smell the bluebells of the wood in late April and May before walking down to the beach at Basset's Cove.

➤ **Find** Basset's Cove Car Park (Camborne, TR14 0HE), then walk SE 400 yards into woodland.

50.246211, -5.307585

Crane Island, Basset's Cove

Look for sunfish – sometimes seen here in summer. There may be basking sharks, too.

➤ **Find** Basset's Cove (see above) and walk out to Crane Island at low tide.

50.248516, -5.318465

Crane Castle, Basset's Cove

Search at low tide for castle relics as the Iron Age fort ruin continues to fall into the sea because of erosion. On land, ditches and 6ft-high banks are all that's left of the ramparts.

➤ **Find** Basset's Cove Car Park (Camborne, TR14 0HE), then walk SW 200 yards to the castle ruin site.

50.248516, -5.318465

PEOPLE OF THE PATH

The Holiday Maker, Perranporth, North Cornwall

Perranporth is one of my favourite beaches because the disabled access is good. We hired this beach wheelchair. They are available at beaches all along the coast, so are well worth checking out.

HELL'S MOUTH KITCHEN AND BAR, GWITHIAN

A roadside takeaway cafe without a view. But cross the road and ... suck in the scenery of the Hell's Mouth cliffs (see right).

B3301, Gwithian, TR27 5EG
Facebook:
@hellsmouthcornwall

THE ROCKPOOL, GWITHIAN

Beach bar food and a sandy back garden. Enjoy seafood surrounded by cliffs and dunes.

1 Godrevy Towans, Gwithian, TR27 5ED
therockpoolbeach cafe.co.uk

Deadman's Cove, Gwithian

Narrow, steep path down to the cove and neighbouring sands at Greenbank Cove (50.244835, -5.325010).

➤ **Find** NT North Cliffs car park (B3301, Camborne, TR27 5EG), then walk ½ mile W on the SWCP.

50.241720, -5.333290

Hell's Mouth, Gwithian

Listen for the cave blowhole on the E side of the beach. There are great views from these 300ft-high cliffs where fulmars and kittiwakes nest. Beware the sheer drop.

➤ **Find** Deadman's Cove (see above) and walk 500 yards E on the SWCP.

50.238128, -5.363268

Fishing Cove, Navax Point

Taste line-caught bass cooked on a beach BBQ. The headland is backed by orderly fields of green and the chaotic swim of waves over rock. It's a breathtaking rocky point that opens up into a cove for swimming, and sometimes grey seals. If you see seals, go fishing somewhere else. It's a steep walk down. Naturists favour the cove. Walk to Hell's Mouth Kitchen and Bar for a cuppa if the cafe is open and the fishing fails.

➤ **Find** Hell's Mouth Kitchen and Bar (see left). With the cafe on the L and the sea to the R, continue on ¼ mile to the public car park over the cliffs. From here, looking to the sea, walk L along the path, ⅓ mile to the cove. The point is 0.8 miles from the car park.

50.237166, -5.372332

PEOPLE OF THE PATH

The Coastguard, Perran Sands, North Cornwall

No beach is the same, so if you're going to swim anywhere around the coast you must first find out if it's safe, and when and where it's best to swim. The safest place to swim here is between the flags when the lifeguards are on duty.

Navax Point

Fishing Cove, Gwithian

Look out for seals and dolphins when fish shoals come in from July.

➤ **Find** NT North Cliffs car park (B3301, Camborne, TR27 5EG), then walk N to the SWCP and then R and continue 200 yards W to the cove.

50.237112, -5.372366

The Knavocks, Navax Point

Get down to smell the earthy musk of heather on the N-facing headland of Navax Point. The heathland area is known as 'The Knavocks' and is best for butterflies. Look for ponies.

➤ **Find** Hell's Mouth Kitchen and Bar (see opposite). With the cafe on the L and the sea to the R, continue on ¼ mile to the public car park over the cliffs. From here, looking to the sea, walk L along the path, ⅓ mile to the cove. The point is 0.8 miles from the car park.

50.243006, -5.379076

Mutton Cove, Gwithian

Look for the large colony of almost 100 grey seals that breed and fish here.

➤ **Find** The Knavocks (see above) and walk ⅔ mile W on the SWCP.

50.240409, -5.388582

Sennen Cove

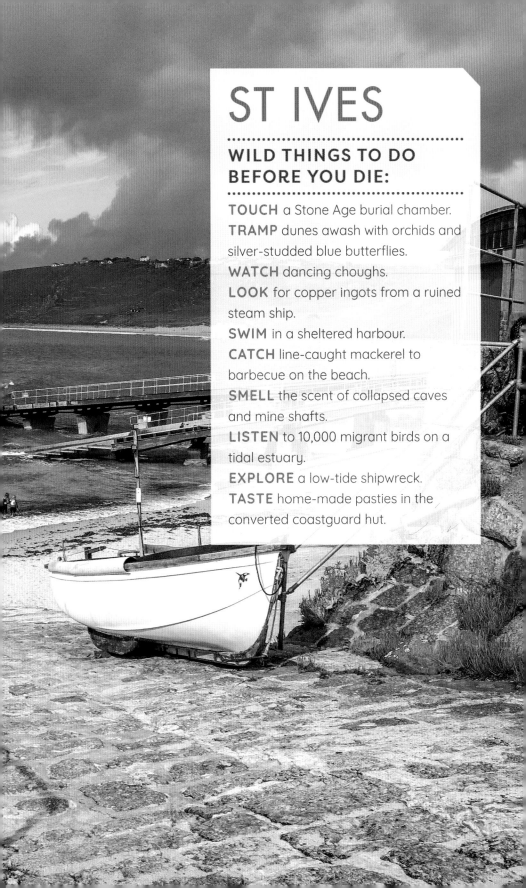

ST IVES

WILD THINGS TO DO BEFORE YOU DIE:

TOUCH a Stone Age burial chamber.

TRAMP dunes awash with orchids and silver-studded blue butterflies.

WATCH dancing choughs.

LOOK for copper ingots from a ruined steam ship.

SWIM in a sheltered harbour.

CATCH line-caught mackerel to barbecue on the beach.

SMELL the scent of collapsed caves and mine shafts.

LISTEN to 10,000 migrant birds on a tidal estuary.

EXPLORE a low-tide shipwreck.

TASTE home-made pasties in the converted coastguard hut.

HUNGRY HORSEBOX CO., GWITHIAN

 Mobile cafe serving drinks and locally sourced food on Gwithian Beach.

St Gothian Sands, Gwithian, Hayle, TR27 5BX
www.hungryhorsebox.co.uk

THE JAM POT CAFE, GWITHIAN

 Home-made cakes, pasties, and cream teas in the converted coastguard lookout over St Ives Bay and Godrevy.

113 Gwithian Towans, Gwithian, Hayle, TR27 5BU
Facebook: @thejampotcafe

Godrevy Rocks Tumulus, Godrevy

Feel cool air and the lighthouse glow after dark. By day, watch the white horses and waves ripple and roar over Stones reef, just offshore. Many lives were lost here until the lighthouse was built in 1859.

➤ **Find** NT Godrevy Car Park (Hayle, TR27 5ED), then walk W 300 yards to the tumulus.

50.240068, -5.393489

Godrevy Rocks, Godrevy

Paddle rock pools. On a good day, basking sharks can be seen. Godrevy Beach is a mating site for seals, who give birth to their pups here. Best from May to September.

➤ **Find** NT Godrevy Car Park (Hayle, TR27 5ED). Facing the sea, with the toilets at the car park to your back, turn R along the FP and walk 330 yards to the point.

50.234839, -5.392760

Red River, Godrevy

Fresh water meets the sea. The river was once red with iron oxide residue from the tin mines.

➤ **Find** NT Godrevy Car Park (Hayle, TR27 5ED), then walk W 200 yards to the river as it enters the beach and sea. The level of the river depends on rainfall.

50.230717, -5.391435

PROSPER HOUSE CAMPING, GWITHIAN

 No-frills campsite in Gwithian village, close to the 3-mile-long beach and dunes between Godrevy and Hayle.

Prosper House, Gwithian, TR27 5BW
prosperhousecamping.co.uk

COVE CAFE, PHILLACK

 Cornish cream teas and Cove afternoon teas for two.

80 Riviere Towans, Phillack, Hayle, TR27 5AF
01736 754889

THE BLUFF INN, PHILLACK

Resort cafe, bar and grill for breakfast, lunch or dinner. Somewhere from which to spot dolphins surfing in the bay.
18 Riviere Towans, Phillack, Hayle, TR27 5AF
www.haven.com/parks/cornwall/riviere-sands/facilities

Gwithian Towans, Gwithian
Smell orchids and look for silver-studded blue butterflies in the dunes in late spring and early summer. Rabbits bound about all year.
➤ **Find** Gwithian Towans Long Stay Car Park (Gwithian Towans, Gwithian, Hayle, TR27 5BT), then walk 200 yards W to the dunes and beach.

50.219816, -5.395412

Upton Towans Dunes, Gwithian
Visit after dark to see the incredible light of glowworms. There are also adders in this vast dune system, to which St Gothian's Chapel has been lost three times.
➤ **Find** Gwithian Towans (see above) and walk 400 yards S along the beach.

50.211920, -5.403375

Black Cliff, Phillack
Look for fin whales and dolphins. Two whales were seen here in December 2020.
➤ **Find** Upton Towans Dunes (see above) and walk 600 yards S along the beach.

50.199147, -5.428952

Hayle Estuary, Hayle
Listen in winter to the call of more than 10,000 migrant birds that feed here.
➤ **Find** Black Cliff (see above) and walk 3 miles around the estuary edge.

50.189114, -5.423532

PEOPLE OF THE PATH

The Dog Owner, Perran Sands, North Cornwall

My favourite part of the coast is walking just south of here because I like looking round the old tin mines. They are incredible. I love the history.

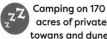

SANDY ACRES CAMPSITE, HAYLE

 Camping on 170 acres of private towans and dunes with direct access to the beach. Toilets, hot showers, a washing-up area and fresh drinking water.

Hayle, TR27 5BA
www.sandy-acres.co.uk

SANDY ACRES BEACHSIDE CAFE, HAYLE

Camping, surf school, lodges and cuppas.

Sandy Acres, Hayle, TR27 5BA
sandy-acres.co.uk/cafe/

St Uny Church, Lelant

Church with a tearoom next door. The old church FP leads down to the sea, across the golf course and railway line to dunes, caves and the river estuary at Hayle. The churchyard is built on the site of a prehistoric burial ground and Roman fort. It's also the starting point of St Michael's Way. Pilgrims travelled from Lelant to Marazion, near Penzance, and then on to the Cathedral of St James in Santiago de Compostela, Spain.

> **Find** Lelant Heritage Centre & Cafe (Church Ln, St Ives, TR26 3DY). The church is next door.

50.188702, -5.435953

Porthkidney Sands Caves, St Ives

Visit in winter to see and listen to the thousands of birds that migrate for the warm air; the dunes never freeze on Britain's most south-westerly estuary. It's often quiet because parking is limited.

> **Find** St Ives railway station (TR26 2BH), then walk S on to the SWCP and 2½ miles E to the caves.

50.193538, -5.437093

St Gothian Sands

THE BADGER INN, LELANT

Food and rooms. Once the haunt of Virginia Woolf.

Fore St, Lelant,
St Ives, TR26 3JT
thebadgerinn.co.uk

THE OLD QUAY HOUSE, HAYLE

A traditional inn on a tidal estuary, with lodges. Breakfast is served in the estuary-view restaurant. Dog and child friendly, with a playground.

Griggs Quay,
Hayle, TR27 6JG
www.quayhousehayle.co.uk

CARBIS BAY HOTEL BEACH CLUB RESTAURANT, CARBIS BAY

Beach houses or the ultra-chic beach lodges. Posh.

Carbis Bay,
St Ives, TR26 2NP
www.carbisbayhotel.co.uk

TREGENNA CASTLE, CARBIS BAY

More than 50 self-catering properties or hotel rooms overlooking St Ives, on a 72-acre resort near the beach. Sunday roast and brasserie open for non-residents.

Trelyon Ave, Carbis Bay,
St Ives, TR26 2DE
www.tregenna-castle.co.uk

Carrack Gladden, Carbis Bay

Human remains found around the dunes between the shore and golf course indicate that the area may have once been an ancient burial site. Also, the lost chapel of St Antra may have been based here. Visit at low tide when the sands E of this point stretch more than 1 mile out to the shoreline.

➤ **Find** Porthkidney Sands Caves (see opposite) and walk 1 mile W along the beach at low tide to the point. If the tide is in, walk the SWCP along the railway FP.

50.198208, -5.455204

Carbis Bay

Find the shipwreck of the SS *Vulture* at very low tide on the E side of the bay.

➤ **Find** Carrack Gladden (see above) and walk 200 yards W to the bay.

50.198860, -5.458251

Porthminster Beach, Porthminster

Taste the magic of rod-caught mackerel and wrasse. It's worth the queue for the boat trip offshore in search of fish shoals. If fishing isn't your thing, try seal watching from the harbour a ½-mile walk N along the low-tide sand – it's a fun way to pass the time.

➤ **Find** St Ives railway station (TR26 2BH), then walk E 200 yards on to the beach.

50.208684, -5.474646

St Ives Cross, St Ives

This beachside town church overlooking St Ives hosts a sacred and historic cross.

➤ **Find** Barnoon Long Stay Car Park (Clodgy View W, St Ives, TR26 1JF), then walk to the top of the car park for views over the graveyard. Leave the car park at the bottom entrance and walk down to the beach. Turn R towards the pier. The St Ives Parish Church (15 St Andrew's St, St Ives, TR26 1AH) and Celtic cross are just past the W Pier behind the lifeboat station.

50.212428, -5.479926

St Nicholas Chapel, St Ives

If you like a story … this chapel has a special one. The Atlantic views are awe-inspiring. There are beaches on either side of the church for swimming.

➤ **Find** the mount next to The Island Car Park (Burrow Rd, St Ives, TR26 1SY). The chapel is 110 yards away.

50.218266, -5.477870

QUEENS HOTEL, ST IVES

 Georgian listed pub close to the beach and harbour. Gastropub grub (gastrogrub!) and rooms.

High St, St Ives, TR26 1RR
www.queenshotelstives.com

ZENNOR CHAPEL GUESTHOUSE, ZENNOR

 Cafe and backpackers' hostel near the SWCP. There's internet access, an onsite restaurant, a garden and laundry facilities.

Zennor, TR26 3BY
www.zennorchapelguest house.com

BOSWEDNACK MANOR B&B AND CAMPION COTTAGE, ZENNOR

This Edwardian farmhouse is a special place, set in 3 acres of organic meadows and garden, which are a haven for wildlife and home to more than 200 species of native plants. Watch the sun set over Gurnard's Head (see opposite). There are field or sea views from all bedrooms.

Zennor, St Ives, TR26 3DD
www.boswednackmanor. co.uk

Three Brothers, St Ives

Feel the energy of stone set over water - especially around a graveyard. The cemetery beside the water's edge continues to hold the sea at bay. Rock pooling and paddles are to be had at low tide.

➤ **Find** The Island Car Park (Burrow Rd, St Ives, TR26 1SY), and walk 400 yards W to the beach and cemetery.

50.217335, -5.480534

Brea Cove, Zennor

Look out for seals that come in to fish around Carn Naun Point just to the N of cove. There are sometimes dolphins, too.

➤ **Find** NT Rosewall Hill Car Park (B3306, St Ives, TR26 3BB). Cross the road and walk L 100 yards, and then turn R into the lane. Follow the lane ⅔ mile until you reach the BW on the L. Follow the BW ⅔ mile N to the SWCP, turn R on the FP a few yards to find the FP off the SWCP leading to the cliff edge.

50.214124, -5.534558

Wicca Pool, Zennor

Paddle the stream. Look out for giant granite fingers above the pool.

➤ **Find** Brea Cove and walk 1½ miles W on the SWCP.

50.205838, -5.555074

Zennor Head, Zennor

Wild, rugged, lonely. Dolphins. The area has been farmed since the Bronze Age.

➤ **Find** Wicca Pool (see above) and walk 1½ miles W on the SWCP to the head.

50.200646, -5.575330

PEOPLE OF THE PATH

The Campsite Wardens, Sennen, North Cornwall

Gwynver Beach is a special place. You must explore the tin mines along there too.

TREVOSE HARBOUR HOUSE, ST IVES

Boutique guest house; beautiful breakfasts. There are also self-catering studio apartments close to Porthgwidden Beach.

22 Warren, St Ives, TR26 2EA

www.trevosehouse.co.uk

THE BEACHCOMBER CAFE, ST IVES

Cream teas, crab sandwiches, breakfasts, lunches, cakes and coffees.

Seagull House, The Wharf, St Ives, TR26 1PU

Facebook: @The Beachcomber Cafe

THE MERMAID, ST IVES

A converted sail loft steeped in smuggler and pirate tales, the pub was once linked to the harbour by one of the many tunnels that criss-crossed the town. It's in the old fishing quarter, less than 100 yards from the harbour and in the older part of St Ives, known as 'Down-A-Long'. Visit the narrow cobbled streets in the spring and summer months when they are ablaze with flowers.

21 Fish St, St Ives, TR26 1LT

mermaidstives.co.uk

Pendour Cove, Zennor

This legendary spot is better known as 'Mermaid's Cove'. Visit at summer dusk and strain your ears to see if you can hear the singing man who fell in love with a mermaid and followed her out to sea. Super views.

➤ **Find** Zennor Head (see opposite) and walk 1 mile W on the SWCP to the cove.

50.194877, -5.581509

Veor Cove, Zennor

Porpoises bring their young into this cove from late June to feed around the shallows. It's best to sit and wait a while on a calm day.

➤ **Find** Pendour Cove (see above) and walk 300 yards W on the SWCP to the cove.

50.194877, -5.581509

Gurnard's Head, Zennor

Touch the earth bank, ditches and ramparts of this Iron Age fort. Look for Roman and Iron Age relics about the rocky cliffs. It's one of the wildest and most magnificent promontories in Cornwall.

➤ **Find** Veor Cove (see above) and walk 1½ miles W on the SWCP to the head.

50.192047, -5.599255

Bosigran Castle, Zennor

Feel the weight of history and time around this cliff fort at Castle Rock, above Halldrine and Porthmoina coves. No turrets, just a spectacle of ancient time. Walk to Gurnard's Head (as in the headland, not the pub, though you could go there afterwards!). Proper wild. Climbers like it here.

➤ **Find** Carn Galver Engine House public car park on the B3306 (Zennor, TR20 8YX). Walk past the R side of the engine house (keeping it to your L) along the FP. Keep going for ⅓ mile until you reach the cliff edge.

50.177403, -5.621953

Portheras Cove, St Just

Secluded cove from which to listen for nesting choughs and look for feeding dolphins.

➤ **Find** Bosigran Castle (see above) and walk 2½ miles W on the SWCP to the cove.

50.164495, -5.658021

GURNARD'S HEAD (PUB), ZENNOR

 In front of the fire by the bar during winter; in the garden for gentle south-westerlies and afternoon siestas in the summer. Eat, drink, sleep. Historians suggest that Jesus spent some time in the West Penwith community a couple of millennia ago. That may or may not be the case, but the area does lay claim to some remarkable anthropological finds, including Chysauster Ancient Village, one of the earliest known pre-Roman settlements in the country.

Zennor, St Ives, TR26 3DE
Facebook:
@gurnardshead

WHEAL ROSE HOLIDAY COTTAGE, MORVAH

 300-year-old stone farmhouse for hire. Sleeps eight. Look out for seals around the beach along what is one of the wildest stretches of the SWCP.

Wheal Rose, Morvah,
Pendeen, TR19 7TU
www.whealrose.co.uk

PENDEEN OLD CLIFF AND SHAFT, ST JUST

 Lighthouse opened in 1900 on what was considered Britain's most dangerous coast. Part of the lighthouse is rented out for holidays.

St Just, Penzance, TR19 7ED
www.trinityhouse.co.uk/
lighthouse-cottage-rental/
pendeen-holiday-cottages

Pendeen New Cliff, St Just

Look for seals. Listen for the peregrine falcons that feed here.
> **Find** Portheras Cove (see page 171) and walk ½ W on the SWCP to the cliff and lighthouse.

50.166324, -5.672097

NT Levant Mine and Beam Engine, Trewellard

A spectacular cliff top, where peregrine falcons nest. Book ahead for a guided tour. There's a restored 1840s beam engine running on steam.
> **Find** the car park at Trewellard, Pendeen, TR19 7SX.

50.152130, -5.685031

Carn Vellan Natural Arch and Waterfalls, St Just

Freshwater falls and dancing choughs. It's an isolated place worthy of a few hours of your time.
> **Find** Levant Mine and Beam Engine (see above) and walk ½ mile S to the arch and waterfalls.

50.147668, -5.691698

Botallack Mine, St Just

Look for copper ingots that wash up here and, to the S, remnants of cargo from the steamship *Malta* that ran aground in 1889. The ruined engine houses on the cliff once extracted copper and tin. Tunnels extend under the sea.
> **Find** Carn Vellan Natural Arch and Waterfalls (see above) and walk ½ mile S on the SWCP.

50.140531, -5.693227

Kenidjack Cliff Castle, St Just

Better than Land's End, and there are fewer people. Promontory fort on the edge of a cairn circle (see opposite). Walk 1 mile S to Cape Cornwall (see opposite) for lovely bay views or walk N to swim the tiny sand beach at Portheras Cove (see page 171).
> **Find** NT Cape Cornwall Car Park at Priest's Cove, at the end of the Cape Cornwall Rd (St Just, Penzance, TR19 7NN). Walk away from the sea along the road, turn L on to the FP and walk just under 1 mile to the old castle cliff.

50.134368, -5.702680

THE QUEEN'S ARMS, BOTALLACK

Olde worlde pub 700 yards from the SWCP with a beer garden. Serves steak and good pints.

Botallack Ln, St Just, TR19 7QG
www.queensarms
cornwall.co.uk

CHY LOWENA HOLIDAY COTTAGE, BOSCASWELL

Granite cottage that sleeps six, with gardens and sea views, a few steps away from the SWCP.

25 Boscaswell Rd, Lower Boscaswell, Pendeen, TR19 7EP
www.chylowenacornwall.
com

COUNT HOUSE CAFÉ, PENDEEN

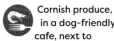
Cornish produce, in a dog-friendly cafe, next to Geevor Tin Mine and museum.

Pendeen, TR19 7EW
www.counthousecafe.com

TREWELLARD ARMS, TREWELLARD

Restored pub between St Just and Pendeen on the Land's End-St Ives coast road. Traditional pub games, such as darts, Shut the Box, shove ha'penny etc. Cream teas are available until 6pm every day.

Trewellard Rd, Trewellard, Pendeen, TR19 7TA
goodpubfoodlands
end.com

Cairn Circle and Caves, St Just

Bronze Age cairn circle. This place is riddled with collapsed caves, mine shafts and mines so take care, but have fun.
➤ **Find** Kenidjack Cliff Castle (see opposite) and walk 300 yards S to the circle and caves.

50.132870, -5.701209

Porth Ledden Pools, St Just

Feel the tingle of cold water and history. Marvel at a row of three man-made tidal pools blasted out by miners into the rock platforms. The central and largest is known as Pullandase Pool and can be seen at mid and low tide.
➤ **Find** NT Cape Cornwall Car Park (St Just, TR19 7NN), then walk ⅓ mile around the cape to the pools on the N side.

50.129130, -5.708135

St Helen's Chapel, St Just

Star watch from one of the most exposed edges of the N Cornwall coast. Look out for bats shortly before dusk on the headland. Choughs gather to feed here in groups.
➤ **Find** Porth Ledden Pools (see above) and walk 200 yards S.

50.128427, -5.708547

Cape Cornwall, St Just

A geographic wonder: the point at which the Atlantic currents split and flow S along the English Channel or N into the Bristol Channel and Irish Sea. Star watch on the former tin mine. Touch the chimney that once marked the spot.
➤ **Find** St Helen's Chapel (see above) and walk W 100 yards to the cape edge.

50.127141, -5.709985

Cape Cornwall

TREMORRAN, TRUTHWALL

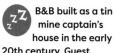 B&B built as a tin mine captain's house in the early 20th century. Guest rooms are named after local mines. Explore Annie's Angel sculptures in the garden. The Queen's Arms (see page 173) is only a few mins' walk away.

Truthwall, St Just, TR19 7QJ
www.tremorran.co.uk

PARKNOWETH FARM CAMPING AND GLAMPING, BOTALLACK

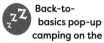 Back-to-basics camping pop-up on the former 18th-century Parknoweth Mine between the hamlets of Botallack and Truthwall. There are showers, and campfires, BBQs and dogs are all allowed.

Parknoweth Farm, Botallack, TR19 7QJ
www.parknowethfarm.com

TREVAYLOR CARAVAN & CAMPING PARK, BOTALLACK

 Family-run campsite for caravans, motorhomes and tents 550 yards from the SWCP, 5 miles away from Land's End, 3 miles from Sennen Cove.

Botallack, TR19 7PU
www.cornishcamping.co.uk

Priest's Cove, St Just

Paddle in relative safety in the large rock pool left at low tide and dammed to trap water. There are many more pools for fishing and fun around the vast reef, which is divided by water currents and the moon's gravitational pull.

> **Find** Cape Cornwall (see page 173) and walk 200 yards S to the cove.

50.125155, -5.707400

Ballowball Barrow, St Just

Ancient site that has given up artefacts dating from Stone Age to Roman, indicating it has been in use for many thousands of years. The burial chamber has two concentric inner walls. The barrow faces W towards the setting sun, and is also known as Carn Gluze or Carn Gloose.

> **Find** parking at the end of the lane (Carn Gloose Rd, St Just, TR19 7NR; 50.118807, -5.699239), then locate the SWCP and walk 1 mile E (away from coast) and then NW to the barrow.

50.121398, -5.702904

Porth Nanven, Cot Valley

Sand and shingle cove that's best swum and explored at low tide. There's an annual swim from Priest's Cove to the Brisons islets. It's known as 'Dinosaur Egg Beach' because of the round granite boulders found there.

> **Find** Porth Nanven car park on the SWCP (Penzance, TR19 7NP). The beach is a few yards away. There are some tricky climbs in places, so care is needed.

50.119240, -5.700679

Natural Arch, Progo Beach, St Just

Watch gannets when they come in to feed on inshore shoals of sardines and mackerel.

> **Find** Porth Nanven car park (see above) and walk 500 yards S on the SWCP to the cliff over the arch.

50.115110, -5.700844

Aire Point, St Just

Big views over a sandy bay. Look and listen for peregrine falcons.

> **Find** Sennen Top Car Park (18 Mayon Green Cres, Penzance, TR19 7BT), and walk 1½ miles N on the SWCP to the point.

50.094503, -5.694243

TRUTHWALL FARM AND THE HONEYPOT, TRUTHWALL

 Two houses close to the shops, cafes, pubs and galleries of St Just.

Truthwall Ln, Penzance, TR19 7QN
truthwall.info

BOSWEDDEN HOUSE, ST JUST

 B&B combined with retreats between Land's End and St Ives, 600 yards from the SWCP.

Cape Cornwall Rd, St Just, TR19 7NJ
boswedden.org.uk

WHEAL CALL HOLIDAY COTTAGE, ST JUST

 Cottage with exposed beams, granite walls and wood-burning stoves. There's a cliff top garden to the front and side. The cottage is almost 200 years old and was a count house – where the work-force would get paid – for the Boswedden group of mines, many of which were worked under the sea. A pony used to trot across the wooden 'bridge' at Wheal Call and into its stabling, which is possibly now the cottage bathroom.

Cape Cornwall, St Just, TR19 7NN
whealcall.co.uk

Gwynver Beach

Tregiffian Vean Cliff, St Just

Taste line-caught mackerel cooked on a beach BBQ. They are best caught from June on a still, calm day when there are no waves at the top of the beach.
➤ **Find** Aire Point (see opposite) and walk ½ mile S and down to the beach from the SWCP.

50.092487, -5.690393

Gwynver Beach, St Just

Beach in Whitesand Bay possibly named after Guinevere of Arthurian legend. You can see the Isles of Scilly from here on a clear day. It's also a surfer's paradise that provides the perfect combination of a wave on occasion thanks to the right wind, the perfect tide and the angle and width of the bay mouth.
➤ **Find** Aire Point (see opposite) and walk ½ mile on the SWCP to the beach.

50.090780, -5.690251

Carn Barges, Sennen

Forage for seaweed to dry or chew raw. Look out for dolphins. Paddle at low tide when white beach merges with the better surf beach, Gwynver Bay, next door. There's more than 1 mile of beach to paddle.
➤ **Find** Gwynver Beach (see above) and walk 400 yards S on the SWCP to the point.

50.083790, -5.692155

PHOENIX BARN HOLIDAYS, ST JUST

Self-catering accommodation set back 60 yards from the cliffs of West Penwith, at the end of a quiet lane.

Phoenix Barn, Bosorne Rd, St Just, TR19 7NR
www.phoenixbarn.com

BOSORNE BARN HOLIDAY COTTAGE, COT VALLEY

Cottage accommodation in a conversion from a 19th-century granite barn.

Cot Valley, St Just, TR19 7NR
www.atlanticcottage
holidays.com/cottage/
bosorne-barn-holiday-
cottage/

SURF BEACH BAR, SENNEN COVE

Restaurant with views over Sennen Cove (see right). Family and dog friendly at the rear.

Sennen Cove, TR19 7BT
surfbeachbar.co.uk

Sennen Cove, Sennen

A working harbour around which it's good to feel lazy. Swim in relative safety inside the harbour. It's cold all year. Roll and warm your bare skin in sun-dried sand from June to September.

➤ **Find** Sennen Cove Harbour Car Park (Sennen Cove, TR19 7DA), and walk N 100 yards.

50.083790, -5.692155

Irish Lady, Sennen

Look for basking sharks and dolphins around the island from this section of the SWCP, which is known as 'Mayon Cliff'. Also look for prehistoric burial remains around animals' holes and areas of erosion.

➤ **Find** Sennen Cove (see above) and walk W and then S on SWCP ½ mile to the cliffs and a view of the island S.

50.076871, -5.708367

Maen Castle Fort, Sennen

Look for pottery and arrowheads around this Neolithic and Iron Age site. Stone Age flints dating back more than 15,000 years have been found all along this stretch of coast. Two earthwork 'ditches' are still visible across the headland, although their purpose is unknown: ceremonial, defence or sacred.

➤ **Find** Irish Lady (see above) and walk 400 yards S on the SWCP to the fort

50.072758, -5.708507

PEOPLE OF THE PATH

The Lifeguard, Gwynver Beach, North Cornwall

I love to swim at Sennen Cove harbour. It's much safer. I've see too many casualties of people who swim where it's not safe.

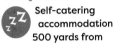

Dr Syntax's Head, Land's End

Dr Syntax's Head, at Land's End, is the last place the sun sets in mainland England. Dolphins, basking sharks and orcas can be seen from here. At low tide, try to spot the offshore reef that has sunk the 37 ships that remain … sunk. On a clear evening, look for the light from the Seven Stones Lightship 16 miles to the W that warns sailors of the notorious Seven Stones, Kettle's Bottom and Shark's Fin reefs, which can be seen at low tide.
> **Find** Land's End Car Park (Penzance, TR19 7AA), and walk 200 yards W to the coast edge. Find the SWCP and walk N 400 yards to the head.

50.069007, -5.717132

Meineke, Land's End

Feel the 'otherworldly' nature of this place. It's unmistakable – much like the Lizard. The offshore beacon is a reminder that wild places come with a safety warning, which is perhaps why the magic is partly obscured by too many people and the trinket shops behind. Walk for 30 mins in either direction to find fewer people and more nature.
> **Find** Dr Syntax's Head (see above) and walk S 400 yards to the hotel, where there is a telescope and view of Meineke.

50.069007, -5.717132

Carn Greeb, Land's End

Crouch down to smell sea campion, thrift and red fescue grass. Feel the still air that sits in the shallow cliff valley beneath the westerly winds.
> **Find** Land's End Car Park (Penzance, TR19 7AA), and walk E 200 yards and then S 100 yards to the farm edge. Take the steps down behind the fenced fields, where the salt-hardy wild flowers grow.

50.069007, -5.717132

Enys Dodnan, Land's End

An island and cave where you can watch fulmars, shags, rock pipits and the occasional peregrine falcon.
> **Find** Carn Greeb (see above) and walk 200 yards SW to the coast edge.

50.061064, -5.712873

Lion's Den, Land's End

Smell bell heather and cross-leaved heather along this section. Stay alert to catch a glimpse of an adder in spring and summer.
> **Find** Enys Dodnan (see above) and walk 500 yards S to the cliff.

50.057633, -5.708220

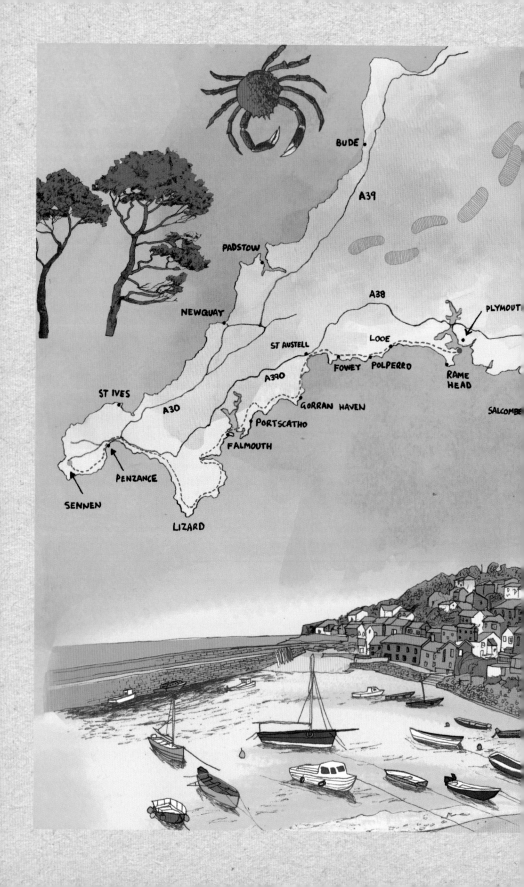

SOUTH CORNWALL

LISTEN TO SUMMER – he was a poor man, which meant too many sounds were out of his reach. The silence of disordered stones at Church Cove. Dolphins breaching Minack Point. Moonlight above a pine tree at Prussia Cove. Shallow waves lapping against Gillan Harbour. But to hear again, he needed to change only one thing. His use of time.

Carn Scathe

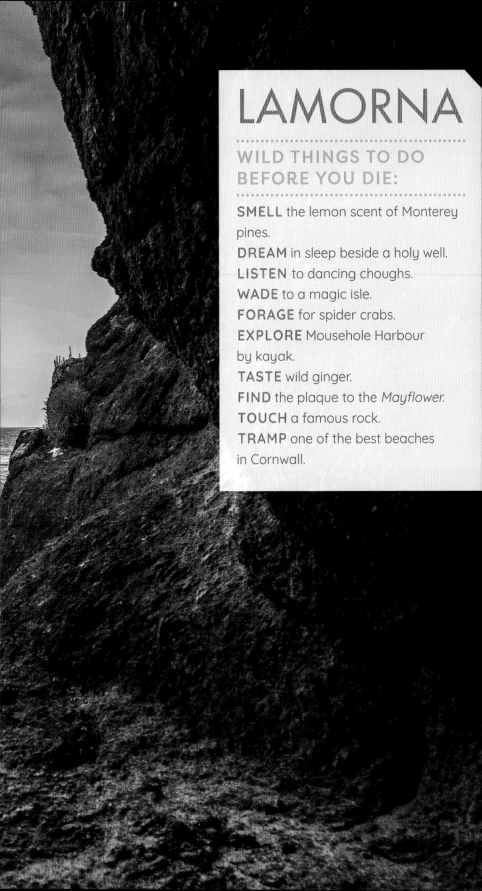

LAMORNA

WILD THINGS TO DO BEFORE YOU DIE:

SMELL the lemon scent of Monterey pines.

DREAM in sleep beside a holy well.

LISTEN to dancing choughs.

WADE to a magic isle.

FORAGE for spider crabs.

EXPLORE Mousehole Harbour by kayak.

TASTE wild ginger.

FIND the plaque to the *Mayflower*.

TOUCH a famous rock.

TRAMP one of the best beaches in Cornwall.

Higher Bosistow Cliff Fort and Tumulus, St Levan

Watch dolphins from a sweet-scented platform of heather and fort.

➤ **Find** the car park at Porthgwarra Cove (Penzance, TR19 6JR), then walk NW 2 miles on the SWCP.

50.050633, -5.692851

Gwennap Head, St Levan

Natural land bridge and cliff castle, that's now a National Coastwatch station.

➤ **Find** the car park at Porthgwarra Cove (Penzance, TR19 6JR), then walk NW 600 yards on the SWCP.

50.035143, -5.677916

Hella Point, St Levan

Listen for the choughs that feed and dance in large groups here. Sit beside sea campion and suck in the sea views.

➤ **Find** the car park at Porthgwarra Cove (Penzance, TR19 6JR), then walk NW 300 yards on the SWCP.

50.034939, -5.672970

Porthgwarra Cove, St Levan

Snorkel a bay full of seaweed and sea life: seals, spider crabs and sand eels. At low tide, look for caves. Also explore the wooden remains of crates that fishermen once used to keep fish fresh for market before taking them by horse and cart to Newlyn. The crates, known as 'ullies', were covered by the high tide and can still be seen on the E side of the cove.

➤ **Find** the car park at Porthgwarra Cove (Penzance, TR19 6JR), then walk SE 100 yards on the SWCP.

50.034939, -5.672970

PEOPLE OF THE PATH

The Holiday Makers, Porthgwarra, South Cornwall

We come here because we love the walks. I was snorkelling in the bay earlier with a seal. You can see choughs a very short walk north of here on the path.

Porthgwarra Cove

Carn Scathe, St Levan

This is a rocky headland with a dark, haunting, natural rock amphitheatre.

➤ **Find** the car park at Porthgwarra Cove (Penzance, TR19 6JR), then walk SE 300 yards on the SWCP and on the FP, keeping Porthgwarra Cove on your R shoulder.

50.034939, -5.672970

Porthchapel Beach, St Levan

Climb down to one of the best beaches in Cornwall, topped only by the Holy Well of St Levan overhead and the views. The well water is still used in baptisms, but was once used to cure various ailments. The efficacy was supposed to be maximised by a night's sleep next to the well.

➤ **Find** the car park in St Levan (Penzance, TR19 6JT), then walk 400 yards S to the beach.

50.039140, -5.657789

Minack Point, St Levan

Smell the wild flowers and rocks that bridge the bays either side of this headland. Look for dolphins and orcas; two were seen here in 2021. There's also a world-famous open-air theatre carved into the rock.

➤ **Find** Porthchapel Beach (see above) and walk 700 yards E on the SWCP.

50.041069, -5.650384

Porthcurno Beach

CABLE STATION INN, PORTHCURNO

 Pub food and drink in a large location. For if you have a big appetite.

Porthcurno, TR19 6JX
Facebook:
@cablestationinn

PORTHCURNO BEACH CAFE, PORTHCURNO

 Locally caught seafood, burgers and drinks just off the beach, with farmland and forest gardens to the rear.

Porthcurno, TR19 6JU
www.porthcurno
beachcafe.co.uk

SEA VIEW HOUSE, PORTHCURNO

 B&B 400 yards from Porthcurno Beach (see right).

The Valley,
Porthcurno, TR19 6JX
www.seaviewhouse
porthcurno.com

TRENDRENNEN FARM B&B, PORTHCURNO

 B&B between the hamlet of St Buryan and Porthcurno, set into 1,000 acres of countryside. Visit nearby open-air Minack Theatre on the cliff top at the bottom of the farmhouse meadow. The Logan Rock Inn pub (see opposite) is within walking distance.

Porthcurno, TR19 6LH
www.trendrennen.com

Porthcurno Beach, Porthcurno

Blue sea and white wash, surrounded by green bracken, sand and breeze. Look for basking sharks from late spring.
➤ **Find** Minack Point (see page 183), then walk N 200 yards to the beach.

50.042606, -5.650390

Treryn Dinas, Treen

Cliffs drenched in the scent of wild ginger provide views of beaches from Logan Rock, and of Porthcurno from the cliff fort. Climb down to Pedn Vounder Beach at low tide for views and access to a magical sand island and salt pools.
➤ **Find** the car park next to Treen Local Produce Cafe and Shop (Treen Hill, St Buryan, TR19 6LF). Follow the signposts to Treen Farm Campsite, 220 yards away along the BW, then bear L and carry on 330 yards down the FP to the beach and cliffs.

50.041983, -5.636885

Logan Rock, Treen

This 80-ton granite boulder on the edge of the cliffs once rocked back and forth merely in response to hand pressure. A group of sailors under Lt Goldsmith dislodged it in 1824 and it fell crashing to the sea below. The sailors were ordered to replace it at their own cost, which took nearly seven months. Happily, it's more secure now.
➤ **Find** the car park next to Treen Local Produce Cafe and Shop (Treen Hill, St Buryan, TR19 6LF). Follow the signposts to Treen Farm Campsite (see above right), 220 yards away along the BW, then bear L and carry on 330 yards down the FP to the beach and cliffs.

50.041983, -5.636885

Cribba Head, St Levan

Fulmars, shags, rock pipits and occasional peregrine falcons can be seen along this stretch of the SWCP.

➤ **Find** the car park next to Treen Local Produce Cafe and Shop (Treen Hill, St Buryan, TR19 6LF), then walk 700 yards S to the SWCP, turn L and continue 200 yards E to the head.

50.045893, -5.630366

Penberth Cove, St Levan

Stunning, quiet cove. Look for basking sharks.

➤ **Find** Cribba Head (see above), then walk E 500 yards on the SWCP.

50.047408, -5.629020

St Loy's Cove, St Buryan

Woodland-backed beach – a rare treasure of shade and smells.

➤ **Find** Penberth Cove (see above) and walk 1½ miles E on the SWCP.

50.051980, -5.599048

Lamorna Cove Quay, Lamorna

A natural rock quarry that has been borrowed by humans and more recently claimed back by nature. Artists, including potters and writers, like it here – John le Carré among them.

➤ **Find** the car park in Lamorna Cove (Lamorna, TR19 6XJ), then walk 30 yards S to the quay.

50.061826, -5.563545

Logan Rock

TREGIFFIAN FARM, LAMORNA

 Working farm for bed, breakfast and sea views.

Penzance, TR19 6BG
www.tregiffianfarm.co.uk

TREGURNOW FARMHOUSE, LAMORNA

 Victorian farmhouse B&B and self-catering accommodation, set in ½ acre of walled garden with sea views.

Lamorna, TR19 6BL
www.lamorna.biz

LAMORNA COTTAGES, LAMORNA

Luxury cottage hideaways, with sea views and hot tubs.

Kymaurah, Kemyel Wartha, Lamorna, TR19 6NR
www.2lamorna.co.uk

Little Heaver, Lamorna

Headland from which to watch seals. On the 400-yard walk E to Kemyell Point (50.070462, -5.542078), smell the lemon scent of Monterey pines and cypress trees. The area is also rich in fungi, and if you are walking in the summer or autumn months, you may see the unusual earth star fungus.

➤ **Find** Lamorna Cove Quay (see page 185), then walk SE ½ mile on the SWCP.

50.059994, -5.554901

Point Spaniard, Lamorna

Where the Spanish landed before ransacking Mousehole.
➤ **Find** Little Heaver (see above), then walk NE 1½ miles on the SWCP.

50.076108, -5.539176

LAMORNA COVE CAFE, LAMORNA

 Cold drink and ice cream stop.
Lamorna Cove, Lamorna, TR19 6XJ
Facebook: @lamorna.cove.3

THE OLD PILCHARD PRESS CAFE, MOUSEHOLE

 Traditional cream teas beside the wharf slipway. Try the pork pie or mackerel.
8 Old Quay, Portland Pl, Mousehole, TR19 6RY
Facebook: @theoldpilchardpresscafe

OLD COASTGUARD, MOUSEHOLE

Hotel rooms with sea views as far as St Michael's Mount and the Lizard Peninsula.
The Pde, Mousehole, TR19 6PR
oldcoastguardhotel.co.uk

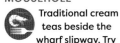

Kemyel Cliff, Kemyel

Sacred high grounds extending from Point Spaniard to Kemyel Rock down to Lamorna Cove, indicated by several standing stones. Freshwater springs riddle the area and leach into the sea. A small conifer plantation (50.064453, -5.550536) slopes down to the sea. Forage for fungi in summer and autumn, or head to Lamorna Cove Beach for snorkelling and kayak launch.

➤ **Find** Lamorna Cove Cafe (see left), then walk across the beach and up to the SW on the SWCP. Continue on for ⅔ mile past Kemyel and another 1 mile to the Swingate Standing Stone.

50.066911, -5.552535; 50.074541, -5.544292

Lamorna Cove

St Clement Isle

FOUR TEAS CAFE, MOUSEHOLE

 Fry-ups, fruit bowls, sarnies and ploughman's from a family-run village cafe.

3 Mill Ln, Mousehole, TR19 6RP
Facebook: @4TeasMousehole

ROCK POOL CAFE, MOUSEHOLE

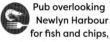 Sip coffee and suck in wonderful views from the rocks over the Mousehole sea pool and coast.

www.rockpoolmousehole.co.uk

RED LION, NEWLYN

 Pub overlooking Newlyn Harbour for fish and chips, steak and ale pie and more.

36 Fore St, Newlyn, TR18 5JP
Facebook: @Red Lion Newlyn

THE SMUGGLERS, NEWLYN

Restaurant and four bedrooms overlooking Newlyn Harbour, with views over Mount's Bay and St Michael's Mount on a clear day.

12–14 Fore St, Newlyn, TR18 5JN
www.smugglersnewlyn.co.uk

St Clement Isle, Mousehole

Bring binoculars so you can watch seabirds and seals over rooftops, look on to the rocky St Clement Isle ... or else take a kayak out from the harbour.

➤ **Find** Mousehole car park (Penzance, TR19 6PS), then walk SW up the hill away from the harbour to look over the isle.

50.081820, -5.532773

Mousehole Harbour, Mousehole

Small quay, narrow streets, granite cottages. Wander among harbour smells and St Michael's Mount views. The scent gets sweeter as you come down to the water. Feral pigeons have the best of it as peregrine falcons and cats tend not to venture here to keep them in check.

➤ **Find** Mousehole car park (Penzance, TR19 6PS), then walk 50 yards E to the harbour.

50.082855, -5.537421

Newlyn Quay, Newlyn

Find the plaque to the *Mayflower* at the entrance to the old quay in Newlyn Harbour. The harbour may have been the last port of call for the ship, before the Founding Fathers arrived in the USA. It's a calm, traditional harbour that mostly tames the most violent storms, but is still best seen in a winter fury.

➤ **Find** The Smugglers (see left), then walk down to the harbour entrance to find the plaque.

50.104297, -5.549282

Jubilee Pool, Penzance

Art deco pool that was built into rocks in 1935. It's Britain's largest seawater lido.

➤ **Find** the car park (New Rd, Penzance, TR18 4NP), then walk ½ mile E on the SWCP to the lido.

50.114433, -5.531666

COCKLESHELL COTTAGE, MARAZION

A beach hideaway with spectacular sea views to St Michael's Mount.

5 Cliff Cottages, Chapel St, Marazion, TR17 0AE
www.cockleshell
cottage.co.uk

CHAPEL ROCK CAFE, MARAZION

Greek salads, falafel sandwiches, breakfast baps and cream teas.

Kings Rd, Marazion, TR17 0EJ
Facebook:
@ChapelRockCafe

THE GODOLPHIN, MARAZION

Hotel, restaurant and bar looking out over iconic St Michael's Mount.

West End, Marazion, TR17 0EN
www.thegodolphin.com

ROSARIO B&B, MARAZION

Victorian house with views of St Michael's Mount. Pet friendly and 30 yards from the beach. Enjoy an English cream tea in Rosario's tea gardens.

The Square, Marazion, TR17 0BH
www.rosario-marazion.co.uk

South Pier Dock, Penzance

Touch the water and the stone moat that surrounds it: the 18th-century granite pier. Penzance is peppered with historic buildings and artefacts to see and feel. The rail journey (the station is just 600 yards N of the pier) along the combined SWCP and St Michael's Way is a visual treat.

> **Find** Harbour Long Stay Car Park (Penzance, TR18 2JX), then explore on foot.

50.117281, -5.529367

Long Rock, Penzance

This is an offshore landmark on Penzance Beach. Keep walking E for the most secluded parts.

> **Find** Long Rock Car Park (Penzance, TR20 9BJ), then walk S 300 yards at low tide to the rock.

50.125884, -5.501075

St Michael's Mount, Mount's Bay

A low-tide walk you'll never forget. The castle and island form the setting for the Cornish legend of *Jack the Giant Killer*. In winter, walk to the R along the beach to Marazion Marshes to watch flocks of starlings roosting at dusk.

> **Find** St Michael's Mount Slipway Car Park (Kings Rd, Marazion, TR17 0EQ). If the tide is in, wait a while at The Godolphin (see left) while looking across the sea.

50.117122, -5.477102

Perran Sands, Perranuthnoe

Beach surrounded by mining history and land scars to explore.

> **Find** the car park (Perranuthnoe, TR20 9NE), then walk 300 yards S to the beach.

50.111363, -5.441609

PEOPLE OF THE PATH

The Dancer, Newlyn Harbour, South Cornwall

I was a professional dance teacher, now I dance around the path. I do it every day and still feel fit at 81. I'm going to join a tap dancing club. There's nothing better than dance for fitness!

Lizard RNLI lifeboat station ramp

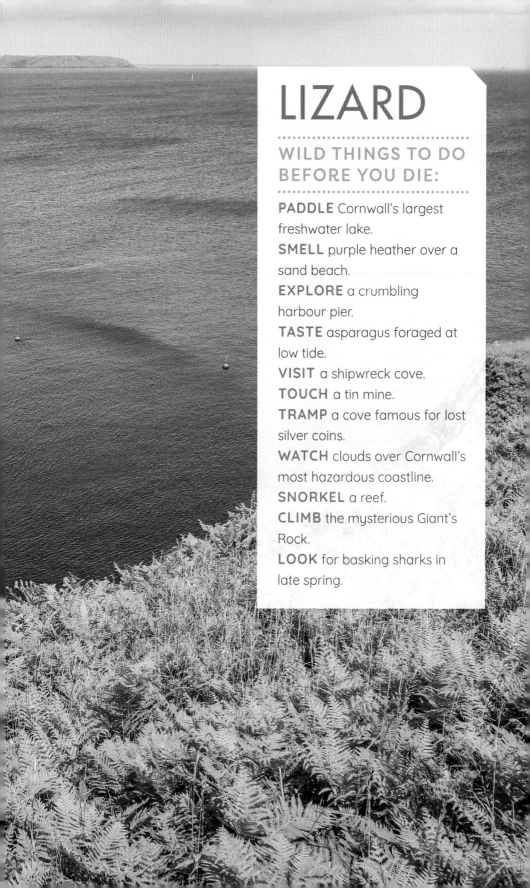

LIZARD

WILD THINGS TO DO BEFORE YOU DIE:

PADDLE Cornwall's largest freshwater lake.

SMELL purple heather over a sand beach.

EXPLORE a crumbling harbour pier.

TASTE asparagus foraged at low tide.

VISIT a shipwreck cove.

TOUCH a tin mine.

TRAMP a cove famous for lost silver coins.

WATCH clouds over Cornwall's most hazardous coastline.

SNORKEL a reef.

CLIMB the mysterious Giant's Rock.

LOOK for basking sharks in late spring.

THE WORKSHOP, PRUSSIA COVE

Sleeps two in an open-plan, studio-style room, two sides of which are entirely glazed and overlook the sea.

Porth-en-Alls, Prussia Cove, TR20 9BA
prussiacove.co.uk/list_of_
properties/the-workshop/

Trevean Cove, Perranuthnoe

Swim the low-tide shingle cove. Paddle when the wind whips up. An ancient slipway leads down to the pebbles.

> **Find** the car park (The Old Chapel, Perranuthnoe, TR20 9NE), then walk ½ mile E on the SWCP.

50.107945, -5.435376

Stackhouse Cliff, Perranuthnoe

Snorkel over reef and stone from the shingle and sand beach. It's best explored at low tide when there's access to neighbouring coves and pools.

> **Find** Trevean Cove (see above), then walk 400 yards E on the SWCP.

50.105033, -5.428381

COASTGUARD COTTAGES, PRUSSIA COVE

Available by the week for four to six people, but worth a punt for bucket-loads of mini adventures in autumn when the prices drop.

4 Coastguard Cottages, Prussia Cove, Rosudgeon, TR20 9BB

prussiacove.co.uk/list_of_ properties/coast-guards-cottages/

NABLUS B&B, PRAA SANDS

B&B on the SWCP, serving good food.

Castle Dr, Praa Sands, TR20 9TG

01736 761889

BEACON CRAG, PORTHLEVEN

B&B on 5 acres of private cliff top with access to coves below via a terraced garden. The house was built in 1887 for a local artist.

West End, Porthleven, TR13 9LA

beaconcrag.com

THE LOOKOUT B&B, PORTHLEVEN

Cottage base from which to explore the harbour.

Mount Pleasant Rd, Porthleven, TR13 9JS

www.porthlevenholiday cottages.co.uk/ properties/the-lookout/

Cudden Point, St Hilary

Look out for basking sharks and dolphins from late spring.

➤ **Find** the car park (St Hilary, Penzance, TR20 9BA), then walk 30 yards SW to the SWCP and then ⅔ mile W on the SWCP.

50.097585, -5.429167

Piskies Cove, St Hilary

Smell purple heather and listen to bees over foxgloves along the cliffs. The sandy beaches are known as 'piskies'.

➤ **Find** the car park (St Hilary, Penzance, TR20 9BA), then walk 30 yards SW to the SWCP and then 600 yards W on the SWCP.

50.099365, -5.422154

Bessy's Cove, St Hilary

Find the harbour and cart wheel track cut into the rocks of this renowned smuggling bay with historic links to Prussia Cove. Nowadays, it's just a fun place to explore.

➤ **Find** Piskies Cove (see above), then walk 600 yards E on the SWCP.

50.099365, -5.422154

Praa Sands, Sydney Cove

Stunning beach wedged between castle remains and rocky headlands at the NW, and best, end of Praa Sands.

➤ **Find** Praa Sands Beach Car Park (Penzance, TR20 9TG), then walk 200 yards SW to the cove.

50.103451, -5.392621

Porthcew, Breage

Touch the tin mine ruins that tower impressively over the cliff edge. Tough climbs. There's a low-tide beach below, but care is needed. This place is isolated. It's also known as Rinsey Cove.

➤ **Find** Rinsey Car Park (Helston, TR13 9TS), then walk SE on the SWCP 300 yards to the beach.

50.093319, -5.367331

Rinsey East Cliff, Breage

Rugged scenery: granite to slate with vertical cliffs to take on after a dip at Porthcew Bay.

➤ **Find** Porthcew (see above), then walk 300 yards SE to the cliff.

50.092149, -5.364466

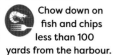

Tregear Point, Porthleven

Monument near Tregear Point to the many seamen who drowned and were buried on the cliffs prior to the passing of the Grylls Act in 1808. Burials thereafter took place in consecrated ground.

➤ **Find** Rinsey East Cliff (see page 193), then walk 2 miles E on the SWCP.

50.084752, -5.327321

Giant's Rock, Porthleven

Sit on the mysterious Giant's Rock at low tide, just near the entrance of Porthleven Harbour. Also known as the 'Moonstone', this type of garnet-gneiss rock isn't found anywhere else in the UK, and no one knows how it arrived in Cornwall. Although some claim it to be a glacial erratic, the ice sheets never reached Cornwall, hence the folklore and name, Giant's Rock – as in, 'A giant must have carried it there.'

➤ **Find** Tregear Point (see above) and walk 400 yards SE on the SWCP.

50.081641, -5.321502

Porthleven Sands, Porthleven

Sandy beach flanked by cliffs and wild flowers.

➤ **Find** the car park (Cooper's Ln, Porthleven, TR13 9EU), then walk 400 yards W to the beach. Facing the water, turn R and walk NW 500 yards either along the beach or the SWCP.

50.081491, -5.317478

Carminowe Creek, Porthleven

Smell the odour of wet beech and oak on the walk from the dunes to the N edge of the Loe lake. The creek is one of the outstanding natural wonders of Cornwall. Look for heronries around the Loe.

➤ **Find** the car park (Cooper's Ln, Porthleven, TR13 9EU), then walk 400 yards W to the beach. Facing the water, turn L and walk SE ⅔ mile either along the beach or the SWCP.

50.071837, -5.295127

Porthleven Sands

THE ATLANTIC INN, PORTHLEVEN

 Family-run pub that boasts a terrace with uninterrupted views from the Lizard to Mousehole.

Peverell Tce, Porthleven, TR13 9DZ
www.theatlanticinn.co.uk

BAR LODGE, PENROSE

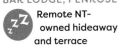 Remote NT-owned hideaway and terrace above Loe Bar Beach. Minimum stay of three nights.

Penrose, TR13 0RD
www.nationaltrust.org.uk/holidays/bar-lodge-cornwall

THE HALZEPHRON INN, GUNWALLOE

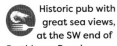 Historic pub with great sea views, at the SW end of Porthleven Beach.

Gunwalloe, TR12 7QB
halzephron-inn.co.uk

CHURCH COVE CAFE, GUNWALLOE

 NT-owned takeaway kiosk that serves up hot drinks, ice cream and sandwiches during the summer months.

Gunwalloe, TR12 7QE
www.cornwall-beaches.co.uk/helston-lizard-falmouth/gunwalloe.htm

Loe Bar

The Loe, Porthleven

Paddle Cornwall's largest freshwater lake. This was once part of the River Cover Estuary – a bar of shingle severed the water from the tide to create a loch-like lagoon.

> **Find** Carminowe Creek (see opposite), then walk 500 yards E and then N on the BW that tracks the water's west edge.

50.071176, -5.293982

Loe Bar, Porthleven

Notorious as a site to avoid even for paddling, as currents, swells and waves combined with shingle collapse have been known to carry people to their deaths. Instead, just take in the views and savour the moment with a camera and memories.

> **Find** Carminowe Creek (see opposite), then walk 300 yards SE across the bar on the SWCP.

50.071176, -5.293982

Halzephron Cliff Cove, Gunwalloe

Myth that mirrors matter: 'Halzephron' is Cornish for 'Cliff of Hell'. Folklore warns of a tide from Porthleven Sands that causes a death by drowning every seven years. It's a tale worth considering, judging from the amount of deaths that occur each year around the South West coast.

> **Find** the car park at Gunwalloe (Helston, TR12 7QE), then cross the road to join the SWCP and walk NW 1 mile to the cove.

50.049940, -5.275836

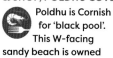

Halzephron Cliff, Gunwalloe

Shipwreck hot spot where many bodies have been buried over the centuries, until unconsecrated burials were outlawed in the 19th century.

➤ **Find** the car park at Gunwalloe (Helston, TR12 7QE), then cross the road to join the SWCP and walk NW ²⁄₃ mile to the cliffs.

50.044607, -5.279141

Dollar Cove, Gunwalloe

A touch of gold? Well no … silver, actually. This place is named after 2½ tonnes of Spanish silver coins that were being transferred to the Bank of England for safety during the Spanish-French war and were shipwrecked in the cove in 1787.

➤ **Find** the car park at Gunwalloe (Helston, TR12 7QE), then cross the road to join the SWCP and walk SE 300 yards to the cove.

50.040432, -5.270359

Church Cove, Gunwalloe

Ancient church cut into the Lizard cliff perfectly positioned over the W-facing beach. It's sheltered by rocks, with coves to either side. Look for the Celtic cross in the churchyard.

➤ **Find** the public car park at Gunwalloe Church Cove Beach (Helston, TR12 7QG). Facing the sea, walk L towards the church, looking over the bay. It's best seen at low tide. There are various FPs down to the sand next to the golf course.

50.03788, -5.26700

Poldhu Cove, Mullion

Look for more booty from the *San Salvador* that was wrecked here in 1669. Thousands of Spanish silver coins were lost. The beach is rimmed by a road and by sea and severed down the middle by a shallow, freshwater stream.

➤ **Find** Church Cove (see above), then walk 700 yards S on the SWCP.

50.033610, -5.263112

Church Cove

Poldhu Cove

POLURRIAN ON THE LIZARD, MULLION

 Hotel and restaurant, serving up Mediterranean-inspired meals cooked in a wood-fired oven. Produce is sourced from within a 20-mile radius. Afternoon teas are available for visitors.

Polurrian Rd, Mullion, TR12 7EN
www.polurrianhotel.com

MULLION COVE HOTEL, MULLION

 Awe-inspiring views during stormy winters and sunny summers. Watch the sun go down from the cliff top outdoor hot tub.

Mullion Cove Hotel, Mullion, TR12 7EP
www.mullion-cove.co.uk/the-hotel

Polbream Point, Mullion

Study the beach at Polurrian to decide whether to wait for the tide to go out to reveal golden sands or to take the plunge in the surf with a board.

➤ **Find** Poldhu Cove car park (Mullion, TR12 7JB), then maybe take a dip before heading N on the SWCP 1 mile to Polbream Point.

50.023892, -5.258627

Mullion

Cloud watch around the stormiest, most hazardous stretch of coast in England. During a six-year period in the 19th century, nine ships were wrecked and 69 lives lost. Walk S from the edge of Polurrian Cove.

➤ **Find** Polbream Point (see above), then walk 400 yards S on the SWCP.

50.021984, -5.256152

Mullion Cove, Mullion

Walk the crumbling breakwater harbour pier, which will surely be gone in less than 50 years. It was most famously painted by JMW Turner's maternal relation, Louis Burleigh Bruhl, in 1923. The harbour has been repaired beyond recognition at least twice since its construction in 1898 to help struggling pilchard fishermen land more catch. By the time the NT took ownership in 1945, the harbour walls (made from faulty Victorian blocks and soft serpentine rock) needed replacing. Mullion storms buffeted and damaged the pier, costing the NT more than £1 million in repairs. The NT states that repairs cannot go on forever. Walk it now before it's all gone. Only Bruhl's iconic painting will live on.

➤ **Find** Porthmellin car park (Coastal Retreat, Mullion, TR12 7EU), then walk 500 yards W along the road to the harbour.

50.014792, -5.258583

Mullion Cliff, Mullion

Providing one of the best sunsets in Cornwall, these deceptively high cliffs are draped in a blanket of silver rock and green, velvety gorse. Look out for dolphins off Mullion Island. There are caves to explore along the W-facing shoreline. Snorkel and swim. The area is rich in tumuli and sacred sites - see them before the tide washes them away.

➤ **Find** Mullion Cove (see page 197), then walk 500 yards S on the SWCP.

50.012379, -5.258315

The Vro, Mullion

This is a headland from which to see breeding colonies of kittiwakes, cormorants and guillemots off Mullion Island.

➤ **Find** Mullion Cove (see page 197), then walk 200 yards S on the SWCP.

50.011731, -5.265015

Predannack Head, Mullion

Wild and isolated. Wild flowers grow in unusual serpentine bedrock.

➤ **Find** the car park, just S of Teneriffe Farm Campsite (Predannack, TR12 7EZ), then walk E and then S on the FP 500 yards to the SWCP. At the coast, turn R and walk NW ⅔ mile to the head.

50.000616, -5.266662

(see right)

ATLANTIC HOUSE B&B, LIZARD

 Complimentary cream tea for three-nighters. One-night stays are an option in the off-season only. The B&B is a 5-min walk from the SWCP, 40 mins to/from Kynance Cove (see right).

Pentreath Ln,
Lizard, TR12 7NY
atlantichouselizard.co.uk

HAELARCHER FARMHOUSE B&B, LIZARD

 Wake up to the smell of fresh bread and one of the most southerly views in Britain.

Lizard Head Ln,
Lizard, TR12 7NN
haelarcher.co.uk

HENRY'S CAMPSITE, LIZARD

The most southerly campsite in Britain is a 10-min walk from the SWCP. It's family run and has sea views.

Lizard, TR12 7NX
www.henryscampsite.co.uk

Vellan Head, Mullion

Look for grazing Soay sheep so you can pick up spare wool caught on bushes, to use for kindling and tinder.
> **Find** Predannack Head (see opposite), then walk 1½ miles S on the SWCP.

49.988351, -5.255475

Asparagus Island, Kynance Cove

Stack from which to look out for gliding fulmars and basking sharks in summer.
> **Find** Kynance Cove NT Car Park (Landewednack, TR12 7PJ), then walk N 400 yards on the SWCP.

49.974068, -5.234060

Kynance Cove

White sand and turquoise sea. It's dramatic at high tide, and even more so on a windy day. The rock arches are the largest outcrop of serpentine in Britain.
> **Find** Kynance Cove NT Car Park (Landewednack, TR12 7PJ), then walk 100 yards S on the SWCP.

49.973990, -5.228752

Kynance Cove Caves, Kynance Cove

Explore the caves and rock stacks at low tide, or walk to the aptly named Asparagus Island (see above) to see … wild asparagus.
> **Find** Kynance Cove (see above), then walk around the W edge of the beach.

50.215723, -3.690348

PEOPLE OF THE PATH

The Family, Mullion Cove, South Cornwall

Mullion Cove is a lovely place to swim. The water is cold, but we don't always need wetsuits and it's relatively safe.

COAST COFFEE BAR & BISTRO, LIZARD

 Enjoy breakfast or a cuppa on the sunny patio area or go for a takeaway.

Lighthouse Rd,
Lizard, TR12 7NJ
www.coastthelizard.co.uk

TREGULLAS FARM SHOP, LIZARD

 Cafe and shop on Lighthouse Rd for meat, veg, fish, ice cream or coffee. The hungriest walkers can purchase a grass-fed half-a-lamb to go, for the BBQ!

www.tregullasfarm.co.uk

WAVECREST, LIZARD

 Cafe over Lizard Point that's been serving food and drink since the 1930s.

Lizard Point,
Lizard, TR12 7NU
wavecrestcornwall.co.uk

POLPEOR CAFE, LIZARD

 Home-made doughnuts, cream tea, fresh air and sea views are up for grabs here.

Lizard Point,
Lizard, TR12 7NU
Facebook: @Polpeor Cafe

Lizard Point, Lizard

A unique place on a calm day, with banks of grass and pink-purple (and yellow) ice plant (Hottentot-fig) flowers. The figs are sweet and some say the leaf sap was once used to stem bleeding. Look for green-veined serpentine granite, and listen for choughs.

➤ **Find** NT Lizard Point Car Park (Landewednack, TR12 7NT), then walk ½ mile W on the SWCP.

49.959516, -5.215869

Bass Point, Lizard

Rocky headland of wild flowers, sea views and gorse.

➤ **Find** NT Lizard Point Car Park (Landewednack, TR12 7NT), then walk 1½ miles E on the SWCP.

49.963262, -5.185282

HOUSEL BAY HOTEL, LIZARD

This hotel is inspired by nature. Tuck into the freshest seasonal dishes and enjoy breakfast on the terrace with endless sea views.

Lizard, TR12 7PG
www.houselbay.com

Lizard RNLI, Lizard

An unusually powerful totem of order around the chaos of the magic Lizard when the wind blows up. Nature always wins in the end, but above the Gulliver-like boat ramp is a good place to sit.

➤ **Find** Bass Point (see opposite), then walk ²/₃ mile N on the SWCP.

49.969667, -5.186741

Lizard Point

GILLAN HARBOUR

TRAMP around a Celtic fortress.
WATCH water 'boil' in a collapsed sea cave.
SIT in the pilchard spotters' chair.
CLIMB rope, down to a white sand beach.
SWIM from a dive centre.
HAMMOCK in a wooded cove.
FORAGE for seaweed.
EXPLORE a natural harbour by kayak.
TASTE hand-caught wrasse.
VISIT a bay to watch ospreys.
TOUCH prehistoric stone flints.

Church Cove Hill, Lizard

A special place: it feels like intruding into a private cottage garden.

➤ **Find** St Wynwallow's Church (see below), then walk E 300 yards to the hill.

49.970539, -5.190459

 # St Wynwallow's Church, Lizard

Listening to the bells ring, this otherwise sleepy place fills with the sense of purpose. It's best on a Sunday morning, but you can get lucky during practice sessions on a Thursday, too. The cemetery is awash with the scent of wild flowers and grasses.

➤ **Find** St Wynwallow's Church (Church Cove Rd, Landewednack, TR12 7PH).

49.970363, -5.193053

 # Church Cove, Lizard

Find the waterfall on the east side of the harbour.

➤ **Find** Church Cove Hill (see above), then walk 200 yards E to the cove.

49.971446, -5.187569

 # Parn Voose Cove, Lizard

Listen to the wind in grassy meadow and gorse and to crickets while looking over the rocks and sea licks.

➤ **Find** Church Cove (see above), then walk N 300 yards on the SWCP.

49.973950, -5.187794

Church Cove

Parn Voose Cove

The Chair, Lizard

Sit back in the Chair – a rocky platform that has been used as a
lookout point by pilchard spotters, customs officials and birders
for centuries.

➤ **Find** Parn Voose Cove (see opposite), then walk 300 yards N
on the SWCP.

49.974880, -5.187666

Devil's Frying Pan, Cadgwith

Look for the 100-yard-wide dish formed by a collapsed sea
cave, with an 'egg' rock centre that appears to be boiled by
water in rough weather.

➤ **Find** Cadgwith Car Park (Ledra Cl, Ruan Minor, TR12 7LD),
then walk 300 yards E to Little Cove and the SWCP. Turn R at
the FP and walk S 200 yards.

49.984697, -5.180156

Kildown Cove, Ruan Minor

Isolated cove with access that changes depending on the tides
and the rockfall. If you can make it down, it's one of the best
fishing sites around the coast, with mackerel and wrasse coming
in from June.

➤ **Find** Devil's Frying Pan (see above), then walk N ²/₃ mile on
the SWCP.

49.990699, -5.171766

St Wynwallow's Church

NAMPARRA CAMPSITE, KENNACK SANDS

 This campsite is a 20-min walk from the beach, on the Lizard Peninsula. There are toilets, showers and farm animals, and campfires are allowed.

Kennack Sands, Kuggar, TR12 7LY
www.namparracampsite. co.uk

TURBO'S KENNACK SANDS BEACH CAFE, KENNACK SANDS

Treat yourself to beer and brunch on the beach.

Kennack Sands, Kuggar, TR12 7LZ
Facebook: @Turbo's Kennack Sands Beach Cafe

Kennack Sands

Swim, sunbathe and touch history. Stone tools have been collected from here that date back more than 10,000 years. Gold coins have also been found in and around the beach, thanks to the many shipwrecks that occurred here. The layered cliffs reveal their own secrets, with veins of talc. In the spring and summer, there are many wild flowers. Watch surfers.

➤ **Find** the car park (Helston, TR12 7LT), then walk S 100 yards to the beach.

50.004539, -5.163645

Caerverracks, Kennack Sands

The rocky reef exposed at low tide can be navigated by foot (wear suitable footwear) between the beaches of East and West Kennack Sands.

➤ **Find** Kennack Sands (see above), then walk 300 yards NW to the rocks.

50.005227, -5.158480

Eastern Cliff, Grade-Ruan

Watch kestrels and buzzards over Eastern Cliffs. The kestrels nest here.

➤ **Find** Caerverracks (see above), then walk ½ mile E on the SWCP.

50.007808, -5.147505

YHA COVERACK, COVERACK

 Stay in this Victorian country house with panoramic sea views.

Parc Behan,
SWCP, TR12 6SA
www.yha.org.uk

BOAK HOUSE, COVERACK

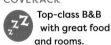 Top-class B&B with great food and rooms.

Coverack, TR12 6SY
01326 280329

PARIS HOTEL, COVERACK

 This hotel is named after the SS *Paris* liner that ran aground on the headland on Whit Monday 1899. The pub serves local seafood, meats and vegetarian dishes, which are best eaten on the outdoor benches looking out to sea on a warm summer's day.

The Cove,
Coverack, TR12 6SX
www.pariscoverack.com

THE LIFEBOAT HOUSE RESTAURANT, COVERACK

 Takeaway, restaurant and bar with a unique sea view.

The Cove,
Coverack, TR12 6SX
thelifeboathouse.co.uk

Hut Circle, St Keverne

This prehistoric habitation has been dated back thousands of years. Ancient flint tools and a hut circle were found here, and a hazelnut was radiocarbon-dated to 5400BC. It's worth exploring.

➤ **Find** Eastern Cliff (see opposite), then walk 100 yards N to the hut circle.

50.010056, -5.145102

Lankidden Fort, St Keverne

Touch the mounds and ditches over 1 hectare of headland that make up this Iron Age cliff castle.

➤ **Find** Eastern Cliff (see opposite), then walk 600 yards E to the fort.

50.006470, -5.133870

Lankidden Cove, St Keverne

Navigate down a steep path with a rope on to a low-tide white sand beach.

➤ **Find** Lankidden Fort (see above), then walk E 100 yards on to the cove.

50.007483, -5.131991

Downas Cove, St Keverne

Look out for the black dorsal fin of basking sharks – most likely to be seen from late spring.

➤ **Find** Lankidden Cove (see above), then walk ⅔ mile E on the SWCP.

50.008856, -5.122132

Beagles Point, St Keverne

Fulmars and kittiwakes soar about the point, and there may be seals and dolphins offshore.

➤ **Find** Downas Cove (see above), then walk SE 400 yards on the SWCP.

50.007167, -5.118106

Treleaver Cliff, St Keverne

Listen for peregrine falcons screeching while they hunt small seabirds.

➤ **Find** Beagles Point (see above), then walk 60 yards SE on the SWCP.

50.003753, -5.110567

ARCHIES LOFT, COVERACK

Cafe for ice creams, cakes, hot drinks and views over Coverack Harbour.

The Cove,
Coverack, TR12 6SX
01326 281440

BAY HOTEL, COVERACK

Hotel overlooking the white beach and fishing village of Coverack, on the Lizard Peninsula. Dog friendly.

Coverack,
TR12 6TE
www.thebayhotel.co.uk

PORTHKERRIS DIVERS BEACH CAFE, PORTHKERRIS

A family-run dive centre with a cafe for cream teas and sandwiches. They also have some areas for camping. Watch out for rocky reef offshore. It's also a great place in which travellers can share stories from the depths to the trail.

Porthkerris, TR12 6QJ
Facebook: @Porthkerris Divers Beach Cafe

Chynhalls Point Promontory Fort, St Keverne

Touch and walk the cliff castle fort. There are several banks to explore and a ditch that may have acted as a defence is still visible across the rocky headland. Birdwatch by day, star watch at night.

➤ **Find** St Keverne Parish Council Charity Car Park (Coverack, TR12 6TF), then walk 1 mile S on the SWCP.

50.015722, -5.092388

Dolor Point, St Keverne

Look for porpoises and dolphins from June until autumn.

➤ **Find** St Keverne Parish Council Charity Car Park (Coverack, TR12 6TF), then walk ½ mile S on the SWCP.

50.022283, -5.092731

Great Wrea, St Keverne

Shelter in the wooded cliff side around prehistoric salt works where water was boiled. Hut circles and pottery have been found in the area. Look for Stone Age tools, which date from the Mesolithic period.

➤ **Find** Dolor Point (see above), then walk 2 miles E on the SWCP.

50.034536, -5.074819

Lowland Point, St Keverne

Look out for remnants of Bronze Age field systems at dusk.

➤ **Find** Great Wrea (see above), then walk 300 yards E on the SWCP.

50.035575, -5.067404

Godrevy Cove, St Keverne

Use binoculars to spy on cormorants and shags that nest on Shag Rock to the south of the bay. The granite reef, known as 'the Manacles', can be seen a mile offshore on a clear day when the waves run over it. Hundreds of shipwrecks attract scuba divers.

➤ **Find** Porthoustock Village Hall car park (Helston, TR12 6QW), then walk S 1 mile on the SWCP.

50.047878, -5.066073

Porthoustock Beach, St Keverne

A quiet beach for relaxing and seaweed foraging. Seals come in with the fish in June and July.

➤ **Find** Porthoustock Village Hall car park (Helston, TR12 6QW), then walk E 200 yards.

50.055889, -5.063857

GALLEN-TREATH
GUEST HOUSE,
PORTHALLOW

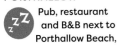

This place has a sea view and is dog friendly. Full English breakfast, vegetarian and vegan food, and two or three-course evening meals are on offer.

Porthallow, TR12 6PL
www.gallen-treath.com

THE FIVE PILCHARDS,
PORTHALLOW

Pub, restaurant and B&B next to Porthallow Beach, on the Lizard Peninsula. Walkers will receive a uniquely special welcome as The Five Pilchards stands at the midpoint of the SWCP. The official halfway point is marked by a granite sculpture on the beach at Porthallow.

Porthallow, TR12 6PP
thefivepilchards.com

Batty's Point, St Keverne

Taste mackerel and wrasse that have been line caught and beach barbecued. The fishing tends to be best in late July.
➤ **Find** Porthoustock Beach (see opposite), then walk N over the beach 300 yards to the point.

50.056769, -5.063431

Porthallow Cove, Porthallow

Swim the cove at high tide. Explore the rock pools at low tide.
➤ **Find** The Five Pilchards (see left), then walk 200 yards N to the beach.

50.068906, -5.078792

Nare Point, St Keverne

Look for dolphins and porpoises from June.
➤ **Find** Porthallow Cove (see above), then walk 1½ miles N on the SWCP.

50.085807, -5.074824

Gillan Harbour, Manaccan

Natural harbour that can be navigated by kayak or walked by path. Sit awhile and listen to waders. A ferry is sometimes available.
➤ **Find** Nare Point (see above), then walk 1 mile W on the SWCP.

50.086789, -5.103587

Gillan Harbour

SPINNEYWOOD, ST ANTHONY-IN-MENEAGE

 Holiday cottages situated at the mouth of Gillan Creek.

St Anthony-in-Meneage, TR12 6HL
www.purecornwall.co.uk/property/spinneywood/

FERRY BOAT INN, HELFORD PASSAGE

 This pub is perfectly positioned on the river below wooded banks of the North Helford Passage waterfront. It's a short walk from Frenchman's Creek, the inspiration for Daphne du Maurier's novel. There's beachside seating in summer and an open fire in winter.

Helford Passage, TR11 5LB
ferryboatcornwall.co.uk

St Anthony Church, St Anthony-in-Meneage

A 13th-century church on the SWCP that's worth exploring.
➤ **Find** the church car park (St Anthony-in-Meneage, Manaccan, TR12 6JW).

50.089405, -5.100840

Dennis Head/Little Dennis, St Anthony-in-Meneage

Touch the prehistoric earthworks – remnants of an early Celtic fortress.
➤ **Find** St Anthony Church (see above), then walk 600 yards E on the SWCP.

50.089382, -5.092954

Ponsence Cove, St Anthony-in-Meneage

This isolated wooded cove provides views of the Helford Estuary. Look for herons, kingfishers and even ospreys.
➤ **Find** Dennis Head (see above), then walk 1 mile W on the SWCP.

50.094049, -5.109626

SHIPWRIGHTS ARMS, HELFORD

 A hidden pub on the banks of the Helford River from which to watch the high tide lap the sea wall or wading birds on the ebb.

Helford, TR12 6JX
www.shipwrightshelford.
co.uk

SEASHELLS COTTAGE, HELFORD PASSAGE

This is a one-bedroom cottage by the beach at Helford Passage and the Ferry Boat Inn (see opposite) overlooking Helford River. Bring your own boat or hire one from the beach, or take a trip across the river on the ferry to walk to Frenchman's Creek.

Helford Passage,
TR11 5LB
www.helfordpassage
cottage.co.uk

GLENDURGAN TEAHOUSE, MAWNAN SMITH

Cakes, cream teas and Cornish service. Dog friendly inside and outside, and you (and they!) can warm up near the log burner.

Mawnan Smith, TR11 5JZ
www.nationaltrust.org.
uk/glendurgan-garden
/features/eating-at-
glendurgan

Helford Point, St Anthony-in-Meneage

Shaded woodland on the river an hour's walk out of Helford for hot summer days when you want to keep out of the sun while watching fish feed on the surface at high tide. There's a shingle beach at Bosahan Cove with rock pools to explore. Daily ferry trips from April to October. Out of season, the options are a bus or a 13-mile walk around the estuary.

➤ **Find** the Holy Mackerel Cafe car park (Helston, TR12 6JU). Take the path opposite the cafe and follow it 0.8 miles to the woodbine-lined shore.

50.096026, -5.121677

The Bar, Mawnan Smith

Join kingfishers and fulmars to fish the tidal waters. Best for bass on lures, especially around nearby Frenchman's and Porthnavas creeks on opposite sides of the river.

➤ **Find** the Church of St Mawnan and St Stephen (SWCP, Falmouth, TR11 5HY), then walk E 2 miles on the SWCP.

50.099610, -5.134670

Glendurgan, Mawnan Smith

This wooded cove is perfect for snorkelling over seaweed-laden rocks in crystal-clear water. It's a jungle of colour.

➤ **Find** Bosveal car park (Mawnan Smith, TR11 5JR), then walk S 500 yards to the SWCP. Turn R at the FP and walk E 200 yards.

50.104193, -5.116259

PEOPLE OF THE PATH

The Shop Owner, Mullion Cove, South Cornwall

I came here because people are friendly. Everyone helps each other out and I like that.

Batty's Point

PENDOWER BEACH

WILD THINGS TO DO BEFORE YOU DIE:

KAYAK the deepest natural harbour in western Europe.

TASTE chestnuts roasted on a beach fire.

SMELL magnolias around castle gardens.

WALK barefoot through a freshwater stream.

VISIT a cemetery with sea views.

TOUCH a sunken forest.

TRAMP with Dartmoor ponies.

FORAGE for samphire.

SWIM a rock reef.

EXPLORE a flooded bar of shingle.

THE RED LION, MAWNAN SMITH

This traditional pub is a few mins away from the SWCP and just a short stroll through the woods to Maenporth Beach.

The Square, Carwinion Rd, Mawnan Smith, TR11 5EP
redlioncornwall.com

HOTEL MEUDON, MAWNAN SMITH

Secluded hotel set in 8½ acres of subtropical gardens.

Maenporth Rd, Mawnan Smith, TR11 5HT
www.meudon.co.uk

TRELAWNE HOTEL, MAWNAN SMITH

Family-run hotel, restaurant and bar with views over Falmouth Bay over to Rosemullion Headland.

Maenporth Rd, Mawnan Smith, TR11 5HT
www.trelawnehotel.co.uk

Helford Passage, Mawnan

Hear the silence at the green rump over Helford's estuary entrance at Toll Point.

➤ **Find** the Church of St Mawnan and St Stephen (see below), then walk ½ mile W to Toll Point for super estuary views.

50.100739, -5.103023

Church of St Mawnan and St Stephen, Mawnan

Seafarers' beacon ... a cemetery with sea views though the cracks in the trees. The 13th-century church FP leads down to the Helford Estuary, for river swims.

➤ **Find** the car park on the SWCP (Falmouth, TR11 5HY). You have arrived. Turn R while looking out to sea and walk ⅓ mile to Toll Point for views over the estuary.

50.103953, -5.095100

Rosemullion Head, Mawnan

Snorkel safari over a jungle of multicoloured, fluorescent seaweeds.

➤ **Find** the Church of St Mawnan and St Stephen (see above), then walk NE ⅔ mile on the SWCP.

50.110276, -5.082399

Rosemullion Head

THE COVE RESTAURANT & BAR, MAENPORTH

 Restaurant on the shoreline of Maenporth Beach with views across Falmouth Bay. Breakfast, lunch and dinner by the sea, with glass-fronted and open-air terrace views across the Roseland Peninsula, and to, Pendennis Castle and St Anthony Lighthouse.

Maenporth Beach, TR11 5HN
www.thecovemaen porth.co.uk

MAENPORTH BEACH CAFE, MAENPORTH

 Cafe on the beach serving up freshly ground coffee, cream teas and Cornish ice creams. Watersports add to the chilled atmosphere in this wooded valley a few miles W of Falmouth.

Maenporth Rd, Maenporth, TR11 5HN
lifesabeachcafe.co.uk

HOOKED ON THE ROCKS, SWANPOOL

 Seafood restaurant overlooking Swanpool Beach for Falmouth lobsters, mussels and crabs. There's an outdoor terrace.

Swanpool Rd, Swanpool, TR11 5BG
www.hookedontherocks falmouth.com

Falmouth Bay

Maenporth Beach, Maenporth

Busy in summer. Best on a cold, sunny day around Christmas when the days are short and the sun is low.

➤ **Find** the car park (Maenporth Beach, TR11 5HN), then walk E 200 yards to the beach.

50.125732, -5.092977

Falmouth Bay/Pennance Point

This is the entrance to the third deepest natural harbour in the world – and the deepest in western Europe.

➤ **Find** Maenporth Beach (see above), then walk NE 1 mile to the point for a full view of the bay.

50.134140, -5.074086

Swanpool

Explore the brackish pool severed from the sea by a shingle bar. Try to visit on a spring tide to see the floodwaters breach the shingle and empty into the fresh water – yin and yang. Woods to the N of the pool are best at dawn in low sunlight when the shade is still cool.

➤ **Find** Swanpool Beach Car Park (Swanpool, TR11 5JL), then walk E 100 yards to the beach.

50.141058, -5.077546

Gyllyngvase Beach, Falmouth

Head here for low-tide swims and rock pooling. Smell the flowers at Queen Mary Gardens. The main beach is sandy and sheltered – good for kayak or paddleboard launch.

➤ **Find** the car park at Queen Mary Gardens (Falmouth, TR11 4NB), then walk 300 yards E to the beach.

50.144493, -5.067430

SWANPOOL BEACH CAFE, SWANPOOL

Cafe close to the sand and shingle beach serving up home-made cakes, hot and cold sandwiches and a range of quirky ice cream flavours.

Swanpool, Falmouth, TR11 5BB
www.swanpoolbeach.co.uk

FALMOUTH BAY GUEST HOUSE, FALMOUTH

Guest house with sea views over Falmouth Bay, and just a couple of mins' walk from Swanpool Beach and nature reserve.

8 Pennance Rd, Falmouth, TR11 4EA
www.falmouth-bay.co.uk

POLTAIR GUEST HOUSE, FALMOUTH

All-year B&B guest house 5 mins' walk from the seafront. Ask for a seaview breakfast on the balcony.

4 Emslie Rd, Falmouth, TR11 4BG
www.poltair.co.uk

THE FALMOUTH HOTEL, FALMOUTH

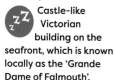

Castle-like Victorian building on the seafront, which is known locally as the 'Grande Dame of Falmouth'.

Castle Beach, Falmouth, TR11 4NZ
falmouthhotel.co.uk

Pendennis Point, Falmouth

Taste raw fallen chestnuts in autumn or collect them to roast at the beach over a low-tide campfire. Watch seals at low tide around Black Rock.

➤ **Find** Pendennis Head Car Park (Falmouth, TR11 4WZ), then walk S 20 yards to the point.

50.143946, -5.043171

Pendennis Castle, Falmouth

Touch the tunnels under the castle that was built by Henry VIII to guard the entrance to the River Fal. There are views from Pendennis Point across the river to St Anthony Lighthouse.

➤ **Find** Pendennis Point (see above), then walk N 50 yards on the SWCP with the estuary on your L shoulder.

50.146658, -5.046702

St Just In Roseland Church, St Just

This is a beautiful church on St Just Creek. It's best in winter on a misty day at high tide when you'll have it all to yourself. Explore the boatyard and gardens and find a cream tea.

➤ **Find** St Just Church Cafe (St Just in Roseland, TR2 5HZ. From the car park opposite, walk towards the church and river before turning L and walking 3 miles to St Mawes Castle (see below).

50.182221, -5.015216

St Mawes Castle, St Mawes

A 16th-century castle built in the shape of a cloverleaf.

➤ **Find** St Just Church Main Car Park (St Just in Roseland, TR2 5HZ), then walk 40 yards W to the riverside. Turn L at the water and walk 2 miles S along the river walk.

50.155806, -5.02533

St Anthony's Church, St Anthony-in-Roseland

Explore the cemetery at dusk to better take in the atmosphere and watch the bats feed. The stone inscriptions are interesting.

➤ **Find** NT St Anthony Head car park (Military Rd, St Anthony-in-Roseland, TR2 5HA). Walk N on the SWCP 1½ miles to the church.

50.149544, -5.004285

Cellars Beach, Roseland Peninsula

Pick and forage rock samphire along the beach edge and headland.

➤ **Find** St Anthony's Church (see above), then walk 400 yards N on the SWCP to the beach.

50.152844, -5.007525

THE GREENBANK HOTEL, FALMOUTH

 Hotel nestled on Falmouth Harbour, serving afternoon teas, lunches, brunches and dinners.

Harbourside, Falmouth, TR11 2SR
www.greenbank-hotel.co.uk

THE WATERSIDE, FLUSHING

 Breakfasts, lunches and dinners on a working quay. Boat to plate: this family business has connections in farming and fishing.

53 Trefusis Rd, Flushing, TR11 5TY
Facebook:
@TheWatersideFlushing

THE WATCH HOUSE, ST MAWES BAY

 Local food on the harbourside along the Roseland Peninsula. Try lobster from St Mawes Bay or purple sprouting broccoli from the local farm.

1 The Square, St Mawes, TR2 5DJ
www.watchhouse stmawes.co.uk

THE LEMON ARMS, MYLOR BRIDGE

 Pub on the edge of the River Fal.

Lemon Hill, Mylor Bridge, TR11 5NA
www.lemonarms.co.uk

Great Molunan, Roseland Peninsula

Snorkel and swim over reef, rocks and seaweed. The two sheltered beaches are best at low tide.

➤ **Find** NT St Anthony Head car park (Military Rd, St Anthony-in-Roseland, TR2 5HA). Walk N on the SWCP 500 yards.

50.145218, -5.015594

St Anthony Head View, St Anthony-in-Roseland

Listen for choughs. They perform a unique display during the spring mating season. Look for bats at sunset in between views back to Falmouth and the River Fal.

➤ **Find** NT St Anthony Head car park (Military Rd, St Anthony-in-Roseland, TR2 5HA). Walk W 200 yards to the view.

50.141637, -5.014263

St Anthony Lighthouse, St Anthony-in-Roseland

The lighthouse is set on a breathtaking rock peninsula that hooks towards Falmouth, without quite getting there. The gap means the traveller must walk the 40 miles to get around the River Fal and its estuary. Alternatively, take a 1-mile walk to the headland point and views around the lighthouse.

➤ **Find** NT St Anthony Head car park (Military Rd, St Anthony-in-Roseland, TR2 5HA). From the car park, walk towards St Anthony Head Battery and, with the battery on your L shoulder, keep walking towards the lighthouse.

50.141077, -5.016105

Zone Point, St Anthony-in-Roseland

Watch gannets come to catch inshore shoals of fish. Grey seals can also be seen along one of the best coastal sections for seabirds and fish.

➤ **Find** St Anthony Head View (see above), then walk SE 500 yards on the SWCP.

50.139561, -5.009885

Porthbeor Beach, Roseland Peninsula

Swims and rock snorkelling are yours for the taking along this large beach. Cliff collapses to the N are hazardous but if they are explored from a distance, they may reveal much of interest.

➤ **Find** NT Porth Farm Car Park (Truro, TR2 5EX), then walk SE 200 yards to Towan Beach (see page 218). Turn R on to the SWCP and walk 1 mile W to the beach.

50.149393, -4.991797

TREWINCE FARM TOURING SITE, PORTSCATHO

 Camp pitches, free showers, sea views and dog friendly. Camping pods are available for tentless walkers.

Unnamed Rd, Portscatho, TR2 5EU
www.trewincefarm.co.uk

THE ROYAL STANDARD GERRANS, PORTSCATHO

 18th-century inn for ploughman's, Sunday roast and discount ferry tickets on the River Fal. Dog friendly.

5 The Square, Portscatho, TR2 5EB
www.royalstandard-gerrans.co.uk

THE HIDDEN HUT, PORTHCURNICK BEACH

 This cafe in a hut on the SWCP near Porthcurnick Beach serves fresh food al fresco style at lunchtime, and puts on open-air feast nights during the summer. Access is only possible by foot, over rugged ground. When the SWCP meets the granite steps leading down to the beach, carry on up the other set of steps over the brow of the hill to locate the hut.

SWCP, Porthcurnick Beach, TR2 5EW
www.hiddenhut.co.uk

Porthmellin Head, Roseland Peninsula

Look for peregrine falcons and fulmars - rarely in the same airspace. There are fantastic views back to the W coast.
➤ **Find** Porthbeor Beach (see page 217), then walk 400 yards E to the head.

50.149934, -4.984421

Towan Beach, Portscatho

Sheltered bay for low-tide swims, rock pools, sand and a low-tide lagoon created by an offshore bar.
➤ **Find** NT Porth Farm Car Park (Truro, TR2 5EX), then walk SE 200 yards to the beach.

50.157367, -4.982784

Porthcurnick Beach, Portscatho

The beautiful sands of Porthcurnick Beach are worthy of a few hours' rest - day or night.
➤ **Find** the car park (New Rd, Portscatho, TR2 5HT), then walk N 400 yards on the SWCP to the beach.

50.185538, -4.971027

Pendower Beach

Creek Stephen Point, Trewithian

Look for the Dartmoor ponies that graze on the scrub and bracken.

➤ **Find** the car park (Rocky Ln, Truro, TR2 5LW), then walk W on the SWCP 1 mile to the creek.

50.196660, -4.962704

Creek Stephen, Trewithian

Bracken-lined cliffs, where the ponies can't get, are all that's left of woodland that once surrounded the bay. There are good views until the bracken gives way to birch and new woodland starts up again.

➤ **Find** Creek Stephen Point (see above), then walk 400 yards E on the SWCP.

50.198355, -4.961349

Pendower Beach, Veryan

Walk barefoot over sand and shingle on to Gerrans Bay at the mouth of a freshwater stream that runs across the beach. The sea is shallow, allowing for safer swims. Loos, parking and ice cream are available, but it's often quiet. Walk SE to Nare Head (see page 220) for views back over the bay.

➤ **Find** parking at the end of the lane (Pendower Rd, Veryan, TR2 5PE), then walk down to the shore.

50.206324, -4.944019

THE SHIP INN, PORTLOE

Pub with a beer garden. Try the crab salad or home-made burgers. Good portions.

Portloe, TR2 5RA
Facebook: @The Ship Inn, Portloe

THE LUGGER, PORTLOE

17th-century inn surrounded by cliffs and headlands on the SWCP at Portloe.

Portloe, TR2 5RD
www.luggerhotel.co.uk

PEBBLES CAFE AND CRAFTS, E PORTHOLLAND

Hamlet hideaway and a walkers' favourite, situated close to a lovely beach and on the SWCP.

3 The Tce, E Portholland, St Austell, PL26 6NA
Facebook: @pebblescafeandcrafts

Carne Beach, Veryan

Touch the shell fossils in the rock towards the middle of the bay at low tide. Trilobite fossils dating from 500 million years ago can also be found, but are rare. Walk 1 mile between Carne and Pendower beaches at low tide.

➤ **Find** Pendower Beach (see page 219), then walk 400 yards E along the sand.

50.206252, -4.935707

Nare Head, Veryan

Look for low-tide shipwrecks in the bays and reefs either side of Nare Head – the remnants of those who never made it to the safety of Falmouth Bay. Listen for the birds that circle from Gull Rock and the crags of Nare Head.

➤ **Find** Carne Beach (see above), then walk 1 mile SE on the SWCP.

50.195800, -4.921180

Jacka Point, Portloe

This spot provides fine views on the approach to the unspoilt fishing village of Portloe and its tiny harbour.

➤ **Find** the car park (Portloe, TR2 5RD), then walk S on the road and SWCP 400 yards to the point via the N edge of the village's beach.

50.217258, -4.891135

Portloe Point, Portloe

Basking sharks occasionally come to the surface in late spring.

➤ **Find** Jacka Point (see above), then walk 400 yards N and then SE on the SWCP to Portloe Point.

50.217258, -4.891135

PEOPLE OF THE PATH

The Fishermen, Porthoustock, South Cornwall

We use lures to catch mackerel and wrasse. There tends to be more fish from July.

SEASPRAY COTTAGE & CABIN, ST AUSTELL

Choice of B&B in a cabin or a cottage that fronts on to the bay. In fact, it's so close that the spray comes up to the door! The sea wall is two steps from your private front door.

St Austell, PL26 6NA
seaspraycornwall.co.uk

CAERHAYS BEACH RESTAURANT, CAERHAYS

Beach cafe on tap for fresh fish, hot and cold drinks, cakes, ice cream and pasties.

Caerhays Beach,
St Austell, PL26 6LY
Facebook:
@caerhaysbeachcafe

Caerhays Castle, St Michael Caerhays

Smell magnolias in summer and spring around the castle gardens. They are also edible.
➤ **Find** Caerhays Beach Restaurant (see left). The castle is across the road.

50.238796, -4.847184

Porthluen Cove, Caerhays

Wonderful sheltered bay under the shadow of Caerhays Castle (see above). Caerhays Beach Restaurant (see left) is to the E side of the cove.
➤ **Find** the car park (St Michael, Caerhays, St Austell, PL26 6LX), right beside the beach.

50.236963, -4.842426

Hemmick Beach, Dodman Point

Steep FPs lead down to this wonderful quiet beach.
➤ **Find** NT The Dodman car park (St Austell, PL26 6NY). Leave the car park and turn R. After a few yards, find the FP L and walk ⅓ mile down to meet the SWCP and beach.

50.2316, -4.8144

Dodman Point

The most important coastal land ridge in these parts features Iron Age ramparts and ditches to walk. There are also views from here to Lizard Point in the W, and Berry Head in the E. The vast cliff headland is sometimes associated with 'Dead Man' and the Briton 'dodman' mystics – the ancient holy men or women, wizards or wise women (aka witches) who once practised here. There are stunning pebble beaches a 1-hr walk away on either side: Hemmick Beach or Bow Beach. Both are good for snorkelling.
➤ **Find** NT The Dodman car park (St Austell, PL26 6NY). Leave the car park and turn L on the road, then straight on at the bottom into the FP. Continue S 1.8 miles to the point.

50.219851, -4.803549

Flat Rock, Dodman Point

Look for the Shetland and Dartmoor ponies that graze along the FP here.
➤ **Find** Dodman Point (see above), then walk ½ mile NE on the SWCP to the rock.

50.227225, -4.798389

COAST PATH CAFE, GORRAN HAVEN

Home-made cakes, cream teas, teacakes, filled rolls, soups, the best view and yes, a loo ... right on the SWCP.

SWCP, Gorran Haven, PL26 6JQ
Facebook:
@Coast Path Cafe

THE MERMAID BEACH CAFE, GORRAN HAVEN

Cafe beside Gorran Haven Beach where you can sip your coffee or slurp your ice cream while dipping your toes in the sea. Open Easter until October, depending on the weather.

Church St,
Gorran Haven, PL26 6JH
www.themermaid
cafe.co.uk

Little Perhaver Point, Gorran Haven

Two beaches for one at low tide... They are also quieter then, and there's access via the staircase off Cliff Rd.

➤ **Find** Gorran Haven Car Park (2 Canton, Gorran Haven, PL26 6JR), then walk E 300 yards to the beach.

50.241511, -4.787383

Vault (or Bow) Beach, St Goran

Feel the evening cold thrown over the beach by Dodman Point. Vault Beach is supposed to get its name from the shadow 'of death' cast by the point. The beach's S end is used by naturists in summer. It's pleasant to sit in the fields above the beach.

➤ **Find** Flat Rock (see page 221), then walk ½ mile N on the SWCP.

50.233355, -4.792354

Maenease Point, St Goran

Star watch or admire the daytime views over Gorran Haven.

➤ **Find** Vault Beach (see above), then walk ⅔ mile NE on the SWCP.

50.237767, -4.781014

Gerrans Point

BODRUGAN BARTON, MEVAGISSEY

 Self-catering cottages on a working farm and family home, complete with cows and sheep and an indoor heated pool, and a garden BBQ for cooking fish from the harbour. Walk though fields to a secluded cove and rock pools.

Mevagissey, PL26 6PT
www.bodrugan.co.uk

HARBOUR TAVERN, MEVAGISSEY

 Independently run bar and kitchen on the water's edge, overlooking Mevagissey Harbour.

Jetty St, Mevagissey, PL26 6UH
www.harbourtavern.com

THE LITTLE CORNISH B&B, MEVAGISSEY

 Accommodation by the SWCP. Enjoy an à la carte candlelit breakfast 1920s style. Unique.

1–2 River St, Mevagissey, PL26 6UG
www.littlecornishbandb.co.uk

PENTEWAN PLAICE, PENTEWAN

Chips by the beach. Licensed bar. Vegan options. Car parking is free after 6pm.

Pentewan Sands, PL26 6BT
pentewan-plaice.business.site

Turbot Point, Gorran Haven

Lookout point for watching dolphins and porpoises.

➤ **Find** Little Perhaver Point (see opposite), then walk 1½ miles E on the SWCP.

50.253738, -4.768446

Colona Beach, Gorran Haven

A sheltered beach protected on three sides by reef and cliffs, where you can forage for shore crabs at low tide.

➤ **Find** Turbot Point (see above), then walk 200 yards S on the SWCP.

50.255289, -4.768746

Portmellon Cove, Portmellon

Touch the sunken forest that can be seen on a spring low tide here and just to the N on Polkirt Beach (see below). The alder, birch and oak have been identified as being more than 2,000 years old. Paddle or bathe in the rock and sand pools.

➤ **Find** Colona Beach (see above), then walk 1 mile N on the SWCP.

50.262071, -4.784422

Polkirt Beach, Mevagissey

Fish for shoals of mackerel from June until November as they come inshore in large shoals to feed on sand eels. Cast from the beach or kayak.

➤ **Find** Portmellon Cove (see above), then walk 300 yards N on the SWCP.

50.264821, -4.783714

Mevagissey Harbour Lighthouse, Mevagissey

Working harbour where you can rest and watch the world go by at high tide. You can fish-watch in the clear waters, or try crabbing at low tide.

➤ **Find** Polkirt Beach (see above), then walk ⅓ mile N on the SWCP.

50.269155, -4.782104

Pentewan Beach, Pentewan

Take in views of undulating fields as you head down to the white stretch of Pentewan Beach beyond.

➤ **Find** Pentewan Sands Car Park (Pentewan, PL26 6BT), then walk 400 yards S to the beach.

50.289804, -4.777775

THE SHIP INN, PENTEWAN

A base for beach walks and valley strolls, with indoor and outdoor seating. Ingredients for the menu are sourced from Cornish farmers and fishermen – there are also Cornish ales, cider and lager. It's dog friendly, with a large beer garden overlooking the harbour.

31–33 W End,
Pentewan, PL26 6BX
www.theshipinn
pentewan.co.uk

THE RISING SUN INN, PORTMELLON

Waterside, 17th-century inn on the edge of Portmellon Cove providing a restaurant and rooms. Dog friendly.

2 Portmellon Park,
Portmellon, PL26 6PL
therisingsuninn.com

PORTMELLON COVE GUEST HOUSE, PORTMELLON

Five-star hotel overlooking the sandy cove, 15 mins walk from the fishing village of Mevagissey.

121 Portmellon Park,
Portmellon, PL26 6XD
www.portmellon-cove.com

Hallane Mill Beach, St Austell

Walk the wooded FP to Hallane Mill Beach: a good place for a picnic.

➤ **Find** Pentewan Beach (see page 223), then walk 1 mile NE on the SWCP.

50.300627, -4.762501

Black Head, St Austell

Cormorants and fulmars nest on the tree-lined cliff ledges at Ropehaven. Walk 1 mile S to the natural platform that has historically served as a fort and sea defence, where there are remnants of an Iron Age cliff castle. There are views of Coverack Bay, the Fal Estuary, Nare Head and Dodman Point.

➤ **Find** Small Car Park (St Austell, PL26 6BH), over Ropehaven Beach and the trees. Walk towards the sign on the L of the road marked 'Trenarren'. Take the L fork and continue on along the SWCP for 1 mile.

50.299276, -4.754854

Gerrans Point, St Austell

Wooded FP over white-rock cliff that provides places in which to hide and take cover.

➤ **Find** Small Car Park (St Austell, PL26 6BH), then walk ½ mile SE on the lane and the SWCP.

50.305077, -4.755895

Ropehaven Cliffs Reserve, St Austell

Look for fossils that are thought to date back more than 400 million years. Shelter in woodland on stormy days. Fulmars nest here.

➤ **Find** Small Car Park (St Austell, PL26 6BH), then walk 400 yards NE on the SWCP.

50.309643, -4.762147

Phoebe's Point/Higher Porthpean Cliffs, St Austell

After the rain and mist have passed, leave the scented trees of Ropehaven to inhale clear views over St Austell Bay.

➤ **Find** Ropehaven Cliffs Reserve (see above), then walk ½ mile N on the SWCP.

50.315458, -4.763727

Phoebe's Point

Coombe Haven

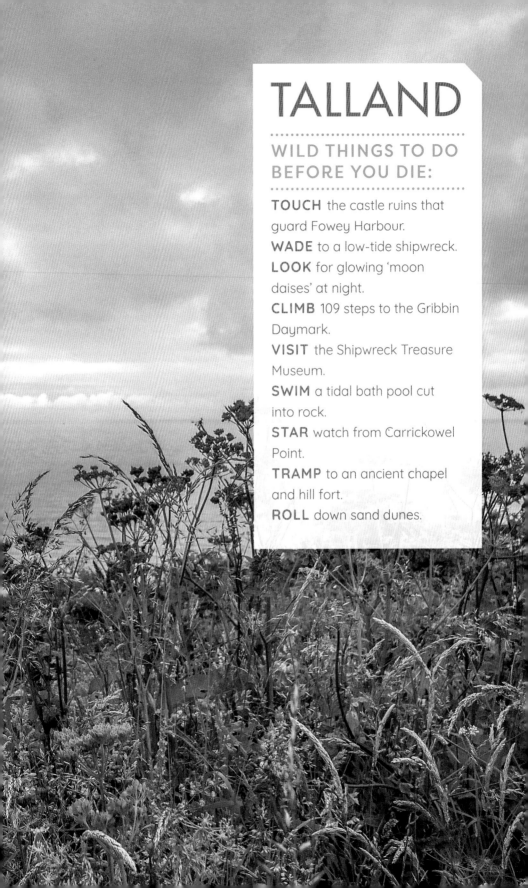

TALLAND

WILD THINGS TO DO BEFORE YOU DIE:

TOUCH the castle ruins that guard Fowey Harbour.

WADE to a low-tide shipwreck.

LOOK for glowing 'moon daises' at night.

CLIMB 109 steps to the Gribbin Daymark.

VISIT the Shipwreck Treasure Museum.

SWIM a tidal bath pool cut into rock.

STAR watch from Carrickowel Point.

TRAMP to an ancient chapel and hill fort.

ROLL down sand dunes.

THE LONGSTORE, CHARLESTOWN

Steaks and seafood, locally sourced on land and at sea.

Charlestown Harbour, Charlestown, PL25 3NJ
www.thelongstore.co.uk

THE GALLEY, CHARLESTOWN

Nibble on snacks while taking in harbour views.
Dog friendly.

45 Charlestown Rd, Charlestown, PL25 3NJ
restaurantwebexperts.com/TheGalley/

THE RUM SAILOR, CHARLESTOWN

This bar tucked away into Charlestown Harbour is a hidden gem.

The Eastern Bloc, Inner Harbour, Charlestown, PL25 3NJ
Facebook: @therumsailor

CHARLESTOWN FISH CO, CHARLESTOWN

It's a chip shop, but the thick-cut cod and crispy chips, plus its great location, make it worth a visit while you're passing.

Charlestown, PL25 3NT
Facebook: @Charlestownfishco

Lower Porthpean, Porthpean

Explore bays and mini islands by kayak or paddleboard. Line-catch bass, wrasse and mackerel on lures and feathers. Beach barbecue with nettles tips over lemon. Forage for condiments in the low-tide rock pools.

➤ **Find** the car park (Porthpean Beach Rd, St Austell, PL26 6AX), then walk 300 yards E to the beach.

50.323050, -4.766200

Carrickowel Point, Porthpean

Head here for star watching by night, and daytime hammocks in a wooded plateau. Look for gaps in the trees so you can spy over Duporth and Lower Porthpean.

➤ **Find** Lower Porthpean (see above), then walk 300 yards N on the SWCP.

50.324584, -4.762938

Charlestown Harbour, Charlestown

Visit the Shipwreck Treasure Museum (Quay Rd, Charlestown, PL25 3NJ), which houses wrecks, artefacts and stories.

➤ **Find** Charlestown Car Park (Barkhouse Ln, Charlestown, PL25 3NH), then walk 200 yards E to the harbour.

50.331387, -4.755973

Landrion Point, Carlyon Bay

The National Coastwatch Station is on Landrion Point.

➤ **Find** Charlestown Harbour's E side, then walk ½ mile E on the SWCP to the point.

50.331716, -4.745629

Carrickowel Point

HARBOUR LIGHTS, CHARLESTOWN

Not cheap ... but special. Right next to the beach, with a hot tub. The garden views are superb.

Harbour Lights,
Quay Road,
Charlestown, PL25 3NX
Facebook: @
harbourlightscharlestown

PORTH AVALLEN HOTEL AND REFLECTIONS RESTAURANT, CARLYON BAY

Family-run hotel in a cliff top location over St Austell Bay. Dine al fresco on the sea-facing terrace.

Sea Rd, Carlyon Bay,
PL25 3SG
www.porthavallen.co.uk

THE CARLYON BAY HOTEL, CARLYON BAY

Posh cliff top hotel over Carlyon Bay. There are two restaurants.

Sea Rd, Carlyon Bay,
PL25 3RD
carlyonbay.com

THE SHIP INN, PAR

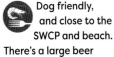

Dog friendly, and close to the SWCP and beach. There's a large beer garden.

Polmear Hill,
Par, PL24 2AR
Facebook: @shipinnpar

Par Beach and Harbour, Par

Explore and roll bare skin in the warm, sunny dunes of Par Sands. On June days, when the mist evaporates, find the shade to cool down in cold sand.

➤ **Find** the car park 300 yards S of the Ship Inn (see below left), then walk S 200 yards on to the beach and 500 yards around the SWCP beach FP to the harbour.

50.343369, -4.701206

Polkerris Harbour Quay, Polkerris

Sit and watch a working harbour from dawn 'til dusk.

➤ **Find** Par Beach (see above), then walk ½ mile SE to the harbour.

50.337085, -4.682321

Gribbin Daymark, Fowey

Touch the red-and-white striped daymark (a tower used as a daytime aid to navigation), which was built in 1832 to warn sailors not to mistake St Austell's Bay, with its shallow treacherous waters, for the deep-water harbour of Falmouth 17 miles further on. Inspiration for the horror story *The Birds* came from a farmer being attacked by gulls while in his field close to the daymark. A flag flies when it is open for viewings. Smell the overwhelming scent of wild garlic in elm woodland either side of the daymark after climbing the 109 steps.

➤ **Find** Polkerris Harbour Quay (see above), then walk 2 miles S on the SWCP. Alternatively, find Menabilly Beach car park (Par, PL24 2TN), then walk S on the road ⅔ mile to the SWCP. Turn R (SW), then walk ½ mile to the tower.

50.317100, -4.673051

Polridmouth Cove, Fowey

Find the shipwreck of the three-masted vessel *Romanie* at low tide. It beached here in 1930.

➤ **Find** Menabilly Beach car park (Par, PL24 2TN). Walk S on the road ⅔ mile to the SWCP and then turn L (E) straight on to the cove.

50.323024, -4.665692

Coombe Haven, Fowey

Visit at night to find ox-eye daisies, known as 'moon daises', which glow in the dark, or go for a midnight dip in the secluded bay.

➤ **Find** Polridmouth Cove (see above), then walk 1 mile E on the SWCP.

50.326510, -4.651905

APPLECROFT B&B, CARLYON BAY

 Rooms high above St Austell Bay, close to the beautiful harbour of Charlestown. Large driveway with plenty of parking.

90 Beach Rd, Carlyon Bay, PL25 3SB
www.applecroftbedand
breakfast.co.uk

RASHLEIGH INN, POLKERRIS

Between the SWCP and Polkerris Beach, this pub serves up seafood specials. Try Fowey mussels and crab.

Polkerris, Par, PL24 2TL
therashleighinn.co.uk

FOWEY HOLIDAY COTTAGE, FOWEY

Cottage on the river's edge, with views across the river to the village of Bodinnick.

30 Passage St,
Fowey, PL23 1DE
www.foweyriverviews.co.uk

KING OF PRUSSIA HOTEL, FOWEY

A 17th-century house, named after the smuggler and privateer John Carter, nicknamed 'the King of Prussia', who is said to have lived here. The hotel is on Fowey Quay, with estuary views from the bar and all six bedrooms.

Town Quay,
Fowey, PL23 1AT
www.kingofprussia
fowey.co.uk

St Catherine's Castle, River Fowey

Touch the castle ruins that once guarded Fowey Harbour as part of Henry VIII's S coast defences. Swim in the cove at the mouth of the River Fowey with wooded walks and ruins. The views are more impressive than the remains of the castle, but it's still worth the climb. Readymoney Cove (see below) is sheltered and fun to explore at low tide for youngsters who can't face the climb up.

➤ **Find** Readymoney Long Stay Car Park (Tower Park, Fowey, PL23 1DG), 1 mile S of Fowey, Walk away from the road towards the FP along the car park, turning L (S), then walking 400 yards to the cove. Walk anticlockwise around the cove through the woodland and follow the SWCP ten mins to the castle point.

50.3291, -4.6445

Readymoney Cove

An ancient crossing location to Polruan on the E bank was used by seafarers and traders, and reinforced by links to the Saints' Way FP.

➤ **Find** St Catherine's Castle (see above), then walk N 100 yards on the SWCP to the cove.

50.329211, -4.645260

Fowey

Best seen by moon and starlight. JM Barrie, the author of *Peter Pan*, described Fowey as being like 'a toy town ... that of a moonlight night it might pass for a scene in a theatre.' Indeed.

➤ **Find** Readymoney Long Stay Car Park (Tower Park, Fowey, PL23 1DG), then explore at will.

50.334541, -4.640497

Fowey Harbour

THE LUGGER INN, POLRUAN

Dog friendly, on Polruan Quay, close to the Fowey-Polruan foot ferry. A hatch offers hot takeaway food, plus beer, wine and hot drinks. Enjoy Fowey Estuary mussels and locally caught fish and fresh meats right by the river.

The Quay, Polruan, Fowey, PL23 1PA
www.luggerpolruan.co.uk

HORMOND HOUSE B&B, POLRUAN

Stylish B&B, open all year.

55 Fore St, Polruan, Fowey, PL23 1PH
www.hormondhouse.com

COOMBE FARM B&B, FOWEY

There are two double rooms here from which to watch the fishing boats returning to Fowey. This is a NT-owned working farm, above the valley of Coombe Hawne. Smuggling tales suggest that the last ever recorded 'run of spirits' in Fowey took place at Coombe on 9 August 1845. There is a cavity between the kitchen and dining room that's reputed to have been used as a smugglers' hole. It's also one of the few places in Fowey that offers a guaranteed parking space...

Coombe Farm, Lankelly Lane, Fowey, PL23 1HW
coombefarmbb.co.uk

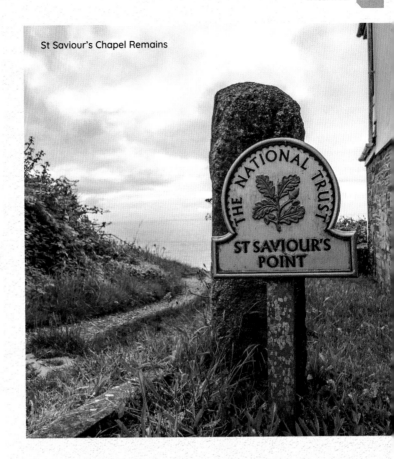

St Saviour's Chapel Remains

St Saviour's Chapel Remains, Polruan

This stone hill over Fowey Harbour offers 360-degree views, though you need to move around. It's best at sunrise.

➤ **Find** Polruan Hill Car Park (St Saviour's Hill, Polruan, PL23 1PZ), then walk S 50 yards to the top of the point.

50.326983, -4.636996

Pencarrow Head, Lanteglos

Views from Pencarrow Head are across the sandy cove of Lantic Bay, which is backed by wild plants. You can also see to the Lizard Peninsula and Bolt Head to the E.

➤ **Find** NT Car Park (Lantic Bay, Fowey, PL23 1NP), then cross the road to the FP 100 yards to the R. Follow the FP ⅔ mile to the coast and head.

50.324840, -4.598792

Lansallos Cove, Lansallos

Touch tombstones that tell fascinating stories. St Ildierna's Church is a little way above the pebble and sand beach, next to the even smaller Parson's Cove (see below).

➤ **Find** Highertown Farm Campsite (see left). From the car park opposite, facing the campsite, walk L down the road to St Ildierna's Church 220 yards away. Take the FP L of the church and follow the lane along the wooded spring for ⅔ mile.

50.3319, -4.5785

Parson's Cove, Lansallos

Snorkelling, seaweed collecting and admiring the waterfall are all options here. The stream to the W falls into Lansallos Cove, also known as West Coombe.

➤ **Find** Pencarrow Head (see page 231), then walk 1½ miles NE on the SWCP to the cove.

50.331419, -4.576584

Blackybale Point, Lansallos

Look for the natural rock arch at Blackybale Point from the cliffs overhead.

➤ **Find** Parson's Cove (see above), then walk 1½ miles E on the SWCP to the point.

50.324251, -4.547740

Chapel Pool, Polperro

This is a tidal bathing pool cut into the rock, which warms up quickly in summer sunshine. The climb down the steps after high tide is as invigorating as the swim.

➤ **Find** Blackybale Point (see above), then walk 1½ miles E on the SWCP to the pool.

50.329778, -4.516068

Polperro Harbour Heritage Museum of Smuggling and Fishing, Polperro

Be thrilled by smuggling and fishing tales in an old pilchard warehouse.

➤ **Find** 4 The Warren, Polperro, PL13 2RB
www.museumsincornwall.org.uk

50.331582, -4.516573

Polperro Harbour, Polperro

The harbour is privately owned, which is a shame … but it is no less stunning for that.

➤ **Find** Chapel Pool (see above), then walk N and E 400 yards to the harbour.

50.330835, -4.516446

THE CLAREMONT HOTEL, POLPERRO

 Adult-only, dog-friendly hotel in the centre of Polperro.

The Coombes, Polperro, PL13 2RG
www.theclaremont
hotel.co.uk

THE PLANTATION TEAROOM & RESTAURANT, POLPERRO

 Pasta, pints and plants. Try the elderflower lemonade if in season.

The Plantation, The Coombes, Polperro, PL13 2RG
Facebook: @theplantationtea roompolperro

PENRYN HOUSE HOTEL, POLPERRO

 Seasonal B&B in the village close to the working harbour and whitewashed cottages.

The Coombes, Polperro, PL13 2RQ
www.penrynhouse.co.uk

TALLAND BAY HOTEL, PORTHALLOW

 Hotel facing the sea, framed by wooded hills in a quiet nook of Talland Bay. Afternoon teas, beds, food and Talland Bay gin are all on offer.

Porthallow, PL13 2JB
www.tallandbayhotel.co.uk

Downend Point

Downend Point, Polperro

Touch the WWI granite cross memorial at Downend Point. The SWCP out of Talland Bay is alive with insects: an alley of butterflies flitting about the edges of invasive Japanese knotweed, buddleia and flowering bramble.
➤ **Find** the car park (Talland Bay, Bridals Ln, Looe, PL13 2JA). Walk to the shore and, facing the water, turn R and walk ⅔ mile SW on the SWCP to the point.

50.331455, -4.501262

Talland Bay

A snapshot of a gentler inlet that on a calm day has more in common with an outdoor lido than a torrent of waves. Care is nevertheless still needed while swimming.
➤ **Find** the car park (Talland Bay, Bridals Ln, PL13 2JA), then walk 100 yards S to the beach.

50.337233, -4.497405

Talland Church, Talland Bay

Perfectly positioned, ancient church dedicated to St Tallanus. It's worth spending some time here.
➤ **Find** Talland Bay (see above), then, facing the water, turn L up the hill and then immediately R on the SWCP. Follow the SWCP for 300 yards but after that leave it and continue on the lane up the hill another 300 yards to the church.

50.338103, -4.490749

THE OLD SAIL LOFT RESTAURANT, WEST LOOE

One of Looe's oldest buildings, known locally as 'the run' because of its smuggling heritage, which dates back more than 400 years. Nowadays, it is better known for its steaks or local fish on the quayside overlooking the harbour.

Quay St,
West Looe, PL13 1AP
oldsailloftlooe.co.uk

THE PORT GAVERNE HOTEL, WEST LOOE

17th-century restaurant and hotel set over a secluded cove. Food? Fresh off the boat, straight from the farm, foraged this morning.

Quay Rd,
West Looe, PL13 2BU
portgavernehotel.co.uk

JOLLY SAILOR INN, WEST LOOE

This claims to be one of the UK's oldest and most historic pubs, established in 1516. Beams are from the Spanish Armada fleet, which was shipwrecked off Looe Island in 1588. The main beam in the bar was taken from HMS *Indefatigable* at the Battle of Trafalgar in 1805. Ships once moored alongside the pub, until land was reclaimed to build the cottages next door.

Princes Square,
West Looe, PL13 2EP
www.jollysailorlooe.co.uk

Talland Bay

Aesop's Bed, Talland Bay

Gorse and grass tower above the headland in late summer, but there are better views in March when access is less impeded by foliage.

➤ **Find** Talland Bay (see page 233), then walk E on the SWCP ⅔ mile to the headland. Keep walking another ½ mile to Home Stone (50.333166, -4.474248) for views over Looe Island.

50.334186, -4.484720

Looe Island

Take the breathtakingly steep, slippery trail out into a world of offshore birds and sycamore woodland. It's the home of Cornwall's largest breeding colony of great black-backed gulls, and there are also grey seals and dolphins. Boat trips are available if the ⅔-mile trek is flooded at high tide.

➤ **Find** the Hannafore Kiosk (Marine Dr, Looe, PL13 2DJ), then keep going until the road ends after 330 yards. Wait anywhere along here for the tide to go out. Keep walking ⅔ mile if the tide is in to look out over Samphire Beach (50.340429, -4.462909).

50.342846, -4.454347

St Germanus' Church, Rame

This is not as impressive as St Michael's Chapel on Rame Head (see page 238), but it's still a beautiful church worthy of a stopover and reflection inside and around the graveyard. Parking spaces are available if you arrive early, which is when you can best enjoy the peaceful calm.

➤ **Find** Ramehead Ln, Rame, PL10 1LG
www.achurchnearyou.com/church/2557/

50.119240, -5.700679

1 THE OLD SIGNAL HOUSE, PENLEE

 Built at the turn of the last century to house the families of the lighthouse keepers at Eddystone Lighthouse, this property is now available for holiday lets. Set on the headland at Penlee Point, it has amazing sea views and is next to a sandy beach. Access is via a private woodland lane.

1 The Old Signal House, Penlee, PL10 1LB
www.theoldsignal house.com

THE BAY BAR & RESTAURANT, CAWSAND

 Good food in the historic smugglers' bay of Cawsand. Sea views are available from every table.

The Bound, Cawsand, PL10 1PG
thebaycawsand.co.uk

THE DEVONPORT INN, KINGSAND

 Antique interior, and a sea view exterior across Kingsand Bay. Good food.

The Cleave, Kingsand, PL10 1NF
devonportinn.com

THE RISING SUN, KINGSAND

Backstreet favourite. Large portions.

The Green, Kingsand, PL10 1NH
Facebook: @The Rising Sun Kingsand

Penlee Battery, Penlee

A gunsite ruin that exudes tranquillity, set among coastal grassland, woods and caves. Look out for bee orchid flowers, whose lower lips resemble the body of a queen bee in colour and shape. After taking in the views, walk W along the cliff to St Germanus' Church (see opposite).

➤ **Find** the end of Military Rd (Torpoint, PL10 1LB). The FP in the furthest corner leads to the battery 765 yards away.

50.321032, -4.198362

Penlee Point, Penlee

There's a 19th-century folly on this point, built for a princess who enjoyed walking here. It's a fairytale scene – great for photos.

➤ **Find** Penlee Battery (see above), then keep walking 100 yards to the point.

50.318050, -4.189408

Kingsand Beach

Explore and bathe in rock pools. Forage for seaweed in the shallows.

➤ **Find** Cawsand car park (3 New Rd, Cawsand, PL10 1PA), then walk NE 300 yards to find the beach.

50.332995, -4.200702

Aesop's Bed

THE OLD BAKERY, CAWSAND

 Freshly baked sourdough bread and pizza, cuppas and cakes beside the SWCP.

Garrett St, Cawsand, PL10 1PD www.theoldbakery-cawsand.co.uk

THE HALFWAY HOUSE INN, KINGSAND

 Dog-friendly B&B. It's named 'the halfway' as the stream at the back of the premises once marked the border between Devon and Cornwall. The pub holds a Cask Marque Award for quality real ale.

Fore St, Kingsand, PL10 1NA www.halfwayinnkingsand.co.uk

SEATON BEACH CAFE, SEATON

 Sample deluxe hot chocolate and snacks for every diet, from vegan to gluten-free, overlooking the sea. The owners provide doggy towels to pooches when they come out of the sea, and you can also buy doggy ice creams.

Looe Hill, Seaton, Torpoint, PL11 3JQ www.seatonbeach cafe.com

Seaton Beach

A wash of dark sand, fresh water and tidal wave, surrounded by wooded tips to the N along the Seaton Valley. It's worthy of a non-tidal diversion, and is a great place to paddle when it's hot.

➤ **Find** Seaton Park Car Park (6 Seaton Park, Seaton, PL11 3JF).

50.363904, -4.387042

Downderry Beach

Explore and soak in wide, shallow rock pools at low tide.

➤ **Find** Seaton Beach (see above), then walk ⅔ mile E on the SWCP.

50.360592, -4.370648

Cargloth Cliffs, St Germans

Watch fulmars over the Long Stone stack.
➤ **Find** Downderry Beach (see opposite), then walk 1 mile E on the SWCP.

50.359873, -4.338661

Britain Point, Sheviock

Enjoy wide views of the tiny harbour of Portwrinkle from Britain Point.
➤ **Find** Finnygook Beach car park (Portwrinkle, PL11 3BP), then walk ½ mile W on the SWCP to the point.

50.361000, -4.320358

Seaton

THE VIEW RESTAURANT, WHITSAND BAY

Perched high on the Rame Peninsula cliffs over Whitsand Bay, this restaurant has westerly views as far as Goonhilly on the Lizard Peninsula.

Military Road,
Torpoint PL10 1JY
www.theview-restaurant.co.uk

EDDYSTONE CAFE, WHITSAND BAY

Sip on a cuppa on one of the best surfing beaches in S Cornwall, at the bottom of Tregonhawke Cliff. There are occasional BBQs and activities. The RNLI hut is next door. Hot water is available for anyone who has stepped on a weaver fish. There are also apartments for rent, which are listed as ideal places for storm watching. Bliss.

Tregonhawke Cliff,
Millbrook, PL10 1JX
Facebook:
@EddystoneCafe

SEASCAPE, FREATHY

Cabin for sleeping on Freathy Cliff. There's a side gate on to the cliff FP to reach the beach. Sea views, with Looe to the W, Rame Head to the E. Free off-road parking.

Freathy,
Whitsand Bay, PL10 1JT
www.seascapecabin.com

Portugal Pump, Sheviock

Superb views of the 4-mile stretch of Whitsand Bay.

➤ **Find** Finnygook Beach car park (Portwrinkle, PL11 3BP), then walk 500 yards E on the SWCP to the point.

50.359475, -4.303633

Sharrow Grotto, Sharrow

The man-made cave next to Sharrow Point was apparently dug out in the early 1780s by a seaman attempting to cure his gout.

➤ **Find** Sharrow Point car park on the coast road (Torpoint, PL10 1JW), then walk 300 yards down to the beach and then turn R to find the grotto.

50.347509, -4.260333

The Grotto, Freathy

A series of coves for snorkelling and swimming. Steep cliffs can make getting down tricky. Occasionally closed due to erosion or firing range activity, in which case walk 1 mile L (SE) to Whitsand Bay.

➤ **Find** Sharrow Point car park on the coast road (Torpoint, PL10 1JW). Cross the road and, looking to the sea, walk L along the SWCP looking for FPs down.

50.3464, -4.2521

Captain Blake's Point, Rame

An ancient chapel ruin on a sacred Celtic site. A priest used to keep a fire beacon burning for passing ships.

➤ **Find** the National Coastwatch Institution at the end of Ramehead Ln (Rame, Torpoint, PL10 1LH).

50.327885, -4.221991

Rame Head, Rame

St Michael's Chapel tops the naze at the widest entrance to Plymouth Harbour. Stop awhile to admire unbeatable sunset views over Whitsand Bay. The chapel rests on the site of an old hill fort. If it's open, the chapel is often lit by candlelight. Many people who drowned at sea are buried in the churchyard, where Dartmoor ponies graze.

➤ **Find** the National Coastwatch Institution at the end of Ramehead Ln (Rame, Torpoint, PL10 1LH). Walk with the Coastwatch building to your L and continue down the FP to St Michael's Chapel and the cliff edge.

50.312464, -4.223250

PENMILLARD FARM B&B, RAME

 Family-run guest house on the Rame Peninsula bordering Mt Edgcumbe House and Country Park (see right).

Cot Valley, St Just, Torpoint, PL10 1LG www.penmillard.co.uk

RAME BARTON GUEST HOUSE AND POTTERY, RAME

 This 18th-century farmhouse offers B&B with 2 acres of gardens. It claims to be the 'premier house' in Rame. Whether or not that's true, there's no doubt about the views over the gardens to Whitsand Bay's vast sandy beach. One of the owners is renowned ceramic designer Paul Cardew.

Military Rd, Rame, PL10 1LG www.ramebarton.co.uk

THE FARRIERS CAFE, CREMYLL

 Family-run cafe on Mt Edgcumbe estate for everything from traditional breakfasts to innovative bakes.

Mt Edgcumbe House and Country Park, Cremyll, PL10 1HZ www.mountedgcumbe. gov.uk/shop-eat/the-farriers-cafe/

Porthpean

Rame Head Common, Rame

Listen out for screeching peregrine pairs as they hunt around the cliff face and head.

➤ **Find** Rame Head (see opposite), then walk 200 yards NE along the SWCP towards Bull Cove (50.315151, -4.218515) to look out for hunting birds.

50.312527, -4.220511

Mt Edgcumbe House and Country Park, Cremyll

This park offers a respite from the wild coast and a place in which to shelter. The gardens include a Picklecombe Seat, made of carved stone from nearby Stonehouse.

➤ **Find** Dry Walk Car Park (Mt Edgcumbe House, Cremyll, PL10 1HZ), then walk E 300 yards to the mount.

50.352967, -4.174576

Wilderness Point, Cremyll

Watch and listen to the sound of the historic ferry running the Tamar between Cremyll and Stonehouse.

➤ **Find** Cremyll Car Park (1 St Julians Cres, Cremyll, PL10 1HU), then walk E 400 yards along the road to the point.

50.358436, -4.171308

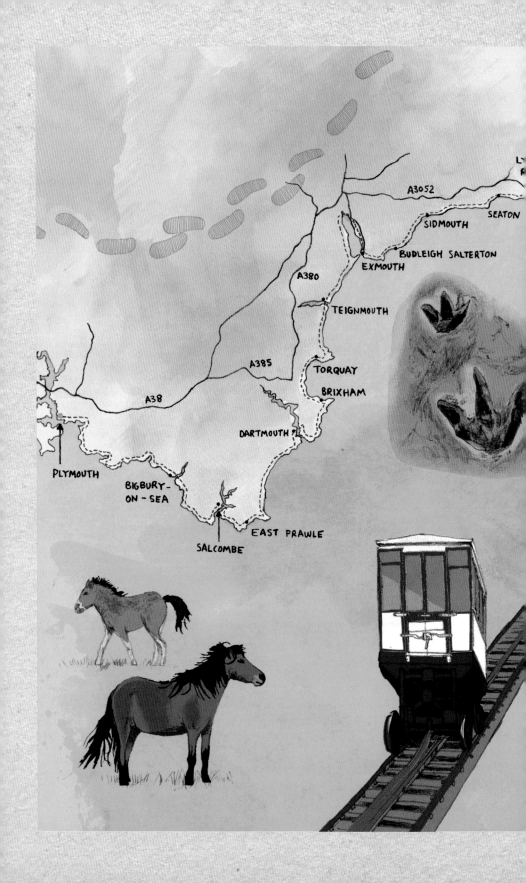

SOUTH DEVON

TASTE THE AUTUMN – they crowded around her on the flooded path into Budleigh Salterton. The mist rose over the Otter Estuary as seawater cooled the sunrise. She looked for signs of trespass or error. But it didn't matter right now; it only mattered that she hadn't expected the company: a shower of swallows following and pirouetting. Then she saw why. Her sandalled feet flushing insects into September air. An early breakfast before final call.

Bantham Sand

NOSS MAYO

WILD THINGS TO DO BEFORE YOU DIE:

TRAMP the harbour where 140,000-year-old human bones were found in a cave.
EXPLORE Devon's largest reed beds.
LISTEN to the melodic rhythm of spring water and stonechats.
WADE Mothecombe Beach to pick rock samphire.
VISIT a pub with four winter fires.
SMELL pine woodland above the River Erme.
TOUCH the tower where Bronze Age trade once entered Britain.
LOOK for lizards over grass-covered dunes.
CATCH a ferry across the River Avon.
ENJOY a pint beneath beams of a wrecked ship from the Spanish Armada.

ELVIRA'S CAFE, STONEHOUSE

 This hidden gem is ace for budget snacks and brekkies.

7 Admiral's Hard, Stonehouse, PL1 3RJ
Facbeook: @
ElvirasCafePlymouth

THE WATERFRONT, PLYMOUTH

 Formerly the base for the famous Royal Western Yacht Club, this restaurant serves fresh, local and seasonal food – everything from breakfasts to evening meals, lunches and afternoon teas.

9 Grand Pde, Plymouth, PL1 3DQ
www.waterfront-plymouth.co.uk

THE DOCK CAFE, BAR & RESTAURANT, PLYMOUTH

 Escape for a few hrs, and watch the marina traffic from this family-run cafe and restaurant. Open all day for drinks, coffees and cakes.

King Point Marina, Brunel Way, Plymouth, PL1 3EF
www.thedock plymouth.co.uk

PREZZO, PLYMOUTH

 Italian food with sea views.

Mills Bakery, Unit 16/17, Royal William Yd,Plymouth, PL1 3GE
www.prezzorestaurants. co.uk/restaurant/ plymouth/

Royal Citadel, Plymouth

Dramatic 17th-century fortress that's still in use today. It was built to defend the coastline from the Dutch.

➤ **Find** Elphinstone Car Park (Madeira Rd, Plymouth, PL1 2NU), then walk 200 yards W along the SWCP to the fortress.

50.363645, -4.136282

Sutton Harbour, Coxside

The oldest human bones ever found in England are 140,000 years old. They were discovered here in a cave. The cave is now a marina and a place from which to launch a kayak. Visit the city museum to find out more about the bones. Ask the harbour office about launching a kayak.

➤ **Find** Royal Western Yacht Club, in the car park at Queen Anne's Battery (Plymouth, PL4 0TW). Facing the marina, walk R to explore Sutton Harbour or to cross the marina on to the other side. Walk L along the SWCP for a view of the industrial wharves.

50.365143, -4.130250

Mount Batten Tower, Mount Batten

This is the site where most Bronze Age trade entered Britain, and was the 17th-century defensive point for the developing Plymouth Harbour.

➤ **Find** Mount Batten Gravel Car Park (Mount Batten, Plymouth, PL9 9SA), then walk N a few yards to the tower.

50.359182, -4.129115

Plymouth Fort

SEA BREEZES GUEST HOUSE, PLYMOUTH

There are six rooms at this B&B, serving up sea views and the option of takeaway brekkie.

28 Grand Pde, Plymouth, PL1 3DJ
Facebook: @Sea Breezes Guest House, Plymouth

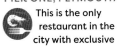

PIER ONE, PLYMOUTH

This is the only restaurant in the city with exclusive views that were once enjoyed by visitors to Plymouth's historic pier. Range of balcony views and floor-to-ceiling windows.

135 Hoe Rd, Plymouth, PL1 3DE
www.pieroneplymouth.co.uk

LINER LOOKOUT CAFE, PLYMOUTH HOE

Small cafe. Big views. Above Plymouth Hoe.

Plymouth Hoe, PL1 2PU
Facebook: @linerlookoutcafe

Jennycliff Bay

Look for spider crabs around the pebble beach. They are small, but tasty. There are views across Plymouth Sound, along with rock pools to explore, and swimming.

➤ **Find** Jennycliff Car Park (Staddon Ln, Plymouth, PL9 9SW), for the beach. It's a steep climb down.

50.350804, -4.122291

Rams Cliff, Bovisand

Forage and chew hawthorn florets in May and June on the steep shrub slope. The cliff is just ahead/past Mount Batten breakwater, with Plymouth views.

➤ **Find** Bovisand Car Park (Bovisand Ln, Wembury, PL9 0AD), then walk 800 yards N on the SWCP.

50.343231, -4.126575

Fort Bovisand, Bovisand

A 19th-century fort, converted to posh housing, beside Bovisand Harbour. Parking nearby. It's 1½ miles S of Mount Batten and 5 miles S of Plymouth.

➤ **Find** Bovisand Car Park (Bovisand Ln, Wembury, PL9 0AD), then walk 100 yards E on the SWCP.

50.336520, -4.126618

Bovisand Bay

Listen for the 'plop' of an occasional common tern fishing the shore edge. Snorkel and swim in the sandy, sheltered bay. Best explored at low tide. There are beach views across to Rame Head in Cornwall, and bus access and parking.

➤ **Find** Bovisand Car Park (Bovisand Ln, Wembury, PL9 0AD), then walk SE 300 yards on the SWCP.

50.335429, -4.120846

PEOPLE OF THE PATH

The Cafe Owners, Branscombe Bay, South Devon

There's a secret cave east of here at Hooken Cliff with rope access. We used to climb the rope and play there as kids. Our son went looking for the rope yesterday. We also used to play in the sea underneath upturned rowing boats. I wouldn't do it now!

ARTILLERY TOWER, STONEHOUSE

This restaurant sits in the 15th-century tower overlooking the sea. It once protected the deep-water passage at the N end of Plymouth Sound, between Drake's Island and the main waterfront. Choose from vegan options and super sweets.

Durnford St, Stonehouse, PL1 3QR
www.artillerytower.co.uk

NEW CONTINENTAL HOTEL, PLYMOUTH

Family-run Victorian hotel with 99 bedrooms and a restaurant.

Millbay Rd, Plymouth, PL1 3LD
www.newcontinental.co.uk

PORT O CALL, PLYMOUTH

Belly-buster breakfasts, steak sandwiches and pies are among the great dishes served here.

23 Bishops Place, Plymouth, PL1 3BW
01752 265501

OLD PIER GUEST HOUSE, PLYMOUTH

Budget three-star accommodation with six rooms, less than 1 mile from Plymouth city centre.

20 Radford Rd, Plymouth, PL1 3BY
old-pier-guest-house.
bestplymouthhotels.
co.uk/en/

Crownhill Bay

Pick spring sea beet and chew it awhile around the sandy cove.
➤ **Find** Bovisand Car Park (Bovisand Ln, Wembury, PL9 0AD). It's a steep climb down via steps and over rocks. There's parking and loos.

50.331976, -4.119732

Andurn Point

Somewhere to listen out for peregrine falcons. The tough walking gets a bit easier after this.
➤ **Find** Bovisand Bay (see page 245), then walk on the SWCP 900 yards S and W.

50.327569, -4.124849

Heybrook Bay

Dartmoor ponies graze on Wembury cliffs. It's a shallow, rocky bay where the spring water of Hey Brook empties into the sea, 9 miles S of Plymouth.
➤ **Find** Andurn Point (see above) and walk ⅔ mile S.

50.319482, -4.118187

Wembury Point, Wembury Bay

Watch nesting guillemots on the Great Mew Stone.
➤ **Find** Wembury Point car park (Wembury, PL9 0HR), then walk W on the SWCP 1 mile.

50.312995, -4.105242

Wembury Bay

Find shore crabs at low tide. Forage for dry seaweed in winter. There are rock pool rambles provided by Devon Wildlife Trust in the summer.
➤ **Find** Wembury Point (see above). The rocky bay is 200 yards E.

50.316852, -4.101021

St Werburgh's Church, Wembury

Stunning church and graveyard by the beach and rocks.
➤ **Find** The Old Mill Cafe (Church Rd, Wembury, PL9 0HP). The church is next to the large public car park overlooking Wembury Beach. NB there's no graveyard access for wheelchairs.

50.317207, -4.084982

Crownhill Bay

THE MESS ROOM, PLYMOUTH

 Restaurant in Yacht Haven Quay serving all-day breakfasts, sandwiches, light snacks and home-made cakes.

Breakwater Rd, Plymouth, PL9 7HJ
Facebook: @TheMessRoomCafe

HOTEL MOUNT BATTEN, MOUNT BATTEN

Rooms with sea views and dining on the historic Mount Batten peninsula. The carvery is pick of the menu.

Lawrence Rd, Mount Batten, Plymouth, PL9 9SJ
www.hotelmount batten.co.uk

The Tomb, Wembury

Look for basking sharks off the rocky outcrop. It's also a good spot from which to see dolphins.

➤ **Find** Wembury Point car park (Wembury, PL9 0HR), then walk 900 yards E on the SWCP to High Cliffs.

50.314782, -4.071764

Season Point, Wembury

Peregrine falcons nest and hunt along the cliffs here. Head just E of the wooded coast to shelter and watch boat traffic at the estuary entrance to the River Yealm.

➤ **Find** The Tomb (see above), then walk 400 yards E on the SWCP.

50.312255, -4.069297

NO 2 OLD COASTGUARDS COTTAGE, WEMBURY

 Georgian coastguard cottage that sleeps two and has rowing boat access (provided) from Newton Ferrers. There's mooring if you carry your own packraft, plus a secluded terrace on the Wembury side of the River Yealm, overlooking the creeks.

Warren Ln, Wembury, PL9 OEJ
Facebook: @OldCoastguards Cottage (No 2)

EDDYSTONE INN, WEMBURY

Here you'll find a roaring log burner for winter walkers, and a raised terrace with sea views for fine weather. The menu changes regularly, but favourites that appear now and then are Asian noodle broth with sea bass, and oven-roasted fillet of hake. It's just a few yards off the SWCP.

Heybrook Dr, Heybrook Bay, Wembury, PL9 OBN
www.eddystoneinn.co.uk

SEAHORSES B&B, WEMBURY

Budget accommodation on the SWCP and Two Moors Way. Ideal for walkers who want sea views without soaring prices. Close to Wembury Beach and surf.

10 Hawthorn Park Rd, Wembury, PL9 ODB
seahorsesbb.yolasite.com

PEOPLE OF THE PATH

The Local, Sidmouth, South Devon
Like most kids, I played in a derelict tunnel shaft at the east end of the bay. It's been eroded out now. Most people do love naughtiness.

Warren Point, Wembury

Look for seals and fin whales. Wild herbs and flowers grow here, including rock sea lavender, shore dock and pennyroyal.
➤ **Find** Season Point (see page 247), then walk ⅔ mile E on the SWCP. There's a seasonal ferry across the River Yealm.

50.312663, -4.054068

Yealm Pool, Wembury

Natural harbour surrounded by trees. Good water access and some summer ferry activity, 1½ miles E of Wembury.
➤ **Find** Warren Point (see above), then walk 200 yards E on the SWCP.

50.312589, -4.053268

Ferry Wood, Newton Creek

Wooded coastline overlooking the busy river and Yealm Pool, ½ mile W of the pub and parking at Noss Mayo. Take a dusk walk to spot barn owls that often hunt here.
➤ **Find** Noss Mayo Tidal Car Park (Foundry Ln, Plymouth, PL8 1EB), then walk ⅔ mile N and W along the coast road and FP into where the wood meets the SWCP.

50.311799, -4.050800

Cellar Beach, Wembury

Secluded fishing cove. Access can be tricky when the weather's wet. Collect morning driftwood and catch mackerel to eat later over a beach BBQ.
➤ **Find** Ferry Wood (see above), then walk 1 mile E and S to the beach.

50.310407, -4.064649

SHEARWATER B&B, WEMBURY

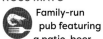

Sea view and rooms 500 yards from the SWCP and Wembury Beach in an 1830 cottage surrounded by NT land. A dog may be allowed, by prior arrangement.

146 Church Rd, Wembury, PL9 0HR
shearwaterbandb wembury.weebly.com

THE SWAN INN, NOSS MAYO

Family-run pub featuring a patio, beer garden and terrace over the creek. Home-cooked food in a waterside location. Dog friendly.

Pillory Hill, Noss Mayo, PL8 1EE
www.swaninnnoss mayo.com

EASTERN LODGE B&B, MEMBLAND

This is a remarkable building, with chimneys to match. Check online as its status and usage changes.

Membland, Newton Ferrers, PL8 1HG
heybedbreakfast. co.uk/07196017/B&B_ at_Eastern_Lodge

THE SHIP INN, NOSS MAYO

Stunning waterside pub for local beers and home-made food. Sit riverside in summer or beside the log fires in winter.

Noss Mayo, PL8 1EW
www.nossmayo.com

Brakehill Plantation, Wembury

Collect chestnut and beechnut windfalls around the SWCP in autumn at dawn. They can be cooked on a beach BBQ or in a portable kettle for lunch. Look for the fire starter – known as King Alfred's cakes, coal fungus or cramp balls – on dead or dying ash branches, to use as fuel.

➤ **Find** Cellar Beach (see opposite), then walk 400 yards into the wood to find the old oak and ash plantation.

50.308236, -4.066807

Gara Point, South Hams

Listen for the peregrine falcons and gulls that hunt here. There are views from the lookout hut E to Newton Ferrers and W from the mouth of the River Yealm to Rame Head and Wembury Gara Point.

➤ **Find** NT Warren Car Park, off Hannaford Rd (Plymouth, PL8 1EL). Walk SW on the FP with your back to the road and find the SWCP 400 yards on. Turn R facing the coast and walk 1 mile NE to the point.

50.303261, -4.074146

The Warren, South Hams

Look out for seals along this rocky 1-mile strip, which offers wonderful views and inaccessible coves.

➤ **Find** Gara Point (see above), then walk 700 yards W on the SWCP.

50.303028, -4.063589

Saddle Cove, South Hams

Basking sharks can be seen along this stretch between Saddle Rock and Netton Island (1 mile W). It's a small sandy cove, best explored at low tide.

➤ **Find** Warren Car Park, off Hannaford Rd (Plymouth, PL8 1EL), walk to the SWCP and then turn L facing the coast. Walk 400 yards to the cove.

50.296790, -4.052901

Stoke Down, Revelstoke

Keep looking for dolphins. There are also views E and W from the rocky outcrop, ⅔ mile from the NT car park (50.300886, -4.028671), ½ mile S of the Church of St Peter the Poor Fisherman (see page 250).

➤ **Find** Stoke Car Park (Plymouth, PL8 1HE; 50.301167, -4.029366) and walk down the FP with the car park on your L shoulder and the main road to your back. Walk ½ mile S to the SWCP and the down.

50.295707, -4.020736

BATTISBOROUGH HOUSE, BATTISBOROUGH CROSS

Self-catering or catered holiday home for larger families and groups.
Battisborough House,
Battisborough Cross,
PL8 1JX
www.battisborough.co.uk

SURFING COW ICE CREAM, BATTISBOROUGH

Artisan ice cream made less than 110 yards from the milking parlour where the cows graze, and overlooking Mothecombe Beach.
South Battisborough Farm, Holbeton, PL8 1JY
www.surfingcowice cream.co.uk

PIER MASTERS HOUSE, PLYMOUTH

Historic pier converted into a restaurant. Light lunches are great value, and by the waterside.
12-13 Madeira Rd,
Plymouth, PL1 2NX
www.piermasters house.com

THE KINGS ARMS, ORESTON

Traditional pub on the quayside and SWCP. Serves breakfasts all day. Perfect.
The Quay,
Oreston, PL9 7NE
Facebook:
@The Kings Arms,
Oreston

Church of St Peter the Poor Fisherman, Revelstoke

Medieval church ruin on the cliffs over Church Cove.

➤ **Find** Stoke Car Park (Plymouth, PL8 1HE; 50.301167, -4.029366). Follow the FP towards the sea away from the road, then bear L as it loops up and around the cliff top towards the church, and in front of the caravan park to the church and church cove 1 mile away.

50.3005111, -4.0174631

Wadham Rocks Beach, South Hams

This is a remote, rocky beach.

➤ **Find** Stoke Down (see page 249), then walk 1²⁄₃ miles E on the SWCP to the beach.

50.305157, -3.997286

Blackaterry Point, Newton & Noss

Pick sea beet to chew while exploring the rocky beach on a steep climb down.

➤ **Find** Wadham Rocks Beach (see above), then walk 300 yards E to the point and neighbouring beach.

50.305797, -3.994274

Carswell Cove, Holbeton

Hidden beach, which can't be seen from directly above, 2 miles W of Mothcombe. A beach hut is available to hire for two-night breaks.

➤ **Find** Blackaterry Point (see above), then walk 600 yards E on the SWCP.

50.306706, -3.982770

Saddle Rock Caves, Holbeton

Look for basking sharks in the English Channel.

➤ **Find** the caves 200 yards E of Carswell Cove (see above).

50.307150, -3.984358

St Anchorite's Rock, Holbeton

There are wonderful views from Saddle Rock Caves (see above) on the approach to St Anchorite's Rock – a spot favoured by wintering hen harriers.

➤ **Find** Carswell Cove (see above), then walk 400 yards E on the SWCP.

50.307707, -3.982770

The Grove

SCHOOLHOUSE
RESTAURANT,
MOTHECOMBE

 Seafood
restaurant, cafe
and takeaway a
few mins from the beach.
Tapas and live music in
summer.
Mothecombe, PL8 1LB
schoolhouse-devon.com

Bugle Hole, Mothecombe

Crystal-clear water in a cove set in rocks that tower out of the bay. Care is needed by swimmers and snorkellers.

> **Find** the car park (Mothecombe, Plymouth, PL8 1LB). Facing the road, turn L and walk 400 yards to the coast. Turn R on the SWCP and walk just over 1 mile to the hole.

50.305053, -3.965690

The Grove, Holbeton

Smell the scent of pine. This is a good section of the SWCP for shelter and lazy hammocks.

> **Find** the car park (Mothecombe, Plymouth, PL8 1LB), then walk down the lane to the coast and then ½ mile W to the grove on the SWCP.

50.307808, -3.955712

Mothecombe Beach, Holbeton

This is a great spot for rock pools and rock samphire.

> **Find** The Grove (see above), then walk 400 yards E to the beach. Busy in summer.

50.309657, -3.9524664

Owen's Hill, Holbeton

Woodland E of Mothecombe Beach and rock pools. Busy in summer.

> **Find** Mothecombe Beach (see above), then walk 200 yards E to the hill.

50.309939, -3.949526

Owen's Hill

Erme Mouth, Holbeton

Low-tide FP across the River Erme, surrounded by fast water and wonderful wet sands.

➤ **Find** Schoolhouse Cafe (Mothecombe, PL8 1LB). Walk down through the car park keeping the cafe on your R-hand side. The beach and water are 250 yards away.

50.311851, -3.947625

Aylestone Brook, Kingston

Swim in Aylestone Brook where it forks with the River Erme at the end of a tiny wooded lane through Tor Wood. There's a BW on the other side of the river from Orthseton Wood up towards Holbeton. There is a 1½ mile diversion from the SWCP at Wrinkle Wood (see opposite).

➤ **Find** the church next to The Dolphin Inn (Kingston, TQ7 4QE). With your back to the church gate, turn L and walk 110 yards before taking the first lane R. Walk on for 1 mile to the brook down an increasingly narrowing FP to the edge of the River Erme.

50.322851, -3.935087

This 13th-century pub is in an area known as the South Hams. There are four fires to enjoy in the winter, as well as a conservatory and a large beer garden for warmer months.
Ringmore, TQ7 4HL
www.thejourneysend
inn.co.uk

THE DOLPHIN INN,
KINGSTON

16th-century olde worlde country pub between the thatched cottages of Kingston. There's en suite B&B accommodation, a beer garden, home-cooked food and free parking.
Kingston, TQ7 4QE
www.dolphin-inn.co.uk

FISHERMAN'S
COTTAGE,
BURGH ISLAND

Rooms with sea views on the water's edge. Drive over the hard sand at low tide.
Burgh Island, Bigbury-on-Sea, TQ7 4BG
www.fishermanscottage
bigbury.co.uk

Wrinkle Wood, Kingston

Woodland cliff 600 yards N of the stunning sands of Wonwell Beach. Beware fast tides; the current can be fast and unpredictable.
➤ **Find** Ayrmer Cove Car Park (Ringmore, TQ7 4HR), then take the BW or FP by the car park ½ mile to the SWCP. Turn R facing the coast and walk 3 miles to the wood. Alternatively, find the car park (Mothecombe, PL8 1LB), then cross the river at low tide into the wood. Care is needed; it's not always safe.

50.313267, -3.939604

Muxham Point, Kingston

Come to this spot for cloud watching and views out to sea and along the River Erme.
➤ **Find** Wrinkle Wood (see above) and walk ⅔ mile S on the SWCP.

50.306573, -3.946677

The Beacon Beach, Kingston

Grey sand and rock bay with tricky access down.
➤ **Find** Muxham Point (see above), then walk 1 mile S on the SWCP.

50.297654, -3.942570

Hoist Beach, Kingston

Listen to the melodic rhythm of the running spring water and stonechats.
➤ **Find** directions for Wrinkle Wood (see above) from Ayrmer Cove Car Park, but walk 1¼ miles on the SWCP.

50.296775, -3.927160

Westcombe Beach, Kingston

One of three beaches in a row. There's swimming and rock pools to explore. Mostly quiet.
➤ **Find** Hoist Beach (see above), then walk 400 yards E on the SWCP.

50.295864, -3.917116

Ayrmer Cove, Kingston

Facility-free grass-dune cove and stone beach with parking a ten-min walk away. Look out for lizards sunbathing on some very strange-shaped rocks. The stream to the S end of the cove flows into the sea. Cirl buntings nest here.
➤ **Find** cove 700 yards E of Westcombe Beach (see above).

50.215723, -3.690348

THE PILCHARD INN, BURGH ISLAND

 Traditional pub, which can be accessed on foot at low tide. You can pay to keep the drinking glasses as souvenirs, if you like.

Burgh Island, Bigbury-on-Sea, TQ7 4BG
www.burghisland.com/tactical_box/pilchardinn/

BURGH ISLAND HOTEL, BURGH ISLAND

 This hotel claims to be one of the most renowned seafood restaurants in the South West. There's no doubt about the rugged cliff top setting and sea views. Pre-booking is required for both meals and the fishing experience on offer; fishing trips include fly and bass fishing.

Bigbury-on-Sea, TQ7 4BG
www.burghisland.com

Challaborough Beach, Bigbury

A lovely sandy cove, but busy in summer.

➤ **Find** the cove ⅔ mile E of Ayrmer Cove (see page 253).

50.287492, -3.898321

The Warren, Bigbury

Best seen at low tide and sunset when the light casts magic shows across the ripples and stone.

➤ **Find** the point 400 yards S of Challaborough Beach (see above).

50.283338, -3.897892

Burgh Island Fort, Burgh Island

Low-tide FP out to wonderful Burgh Island at the mouth of the River Avon. Sometimes there's tractor access when the tide is in. There's a former chapel set on an island peak at its centre, reached by FPs. Wonderful views over Warren Point to the N and Avon Mouth to the SE. Rock pooling and kayaking are options.

➤ **Find** parking next to Venus Cafe (Warren Rd, Bigbury-on-Sea, TQ7 4AZ). Walk to the island at low tide.

50.279518, -3.900286

Cockleridge, Bigbury

Summer ferry across the Avon to Bantham. Some people try to wade at low tide but it's deep.

➤ **Find** Burgh Island Fort (see above) and walk 1¼ miles E on the SWCP.

50.281432, -3.873489

Bantham Sand, Bantham

Surf and paddleboard the shallow water and sands at the mouth of the River Avon.

➤ **Find** Thurlestone car park (Kingsbridge, TQ7 3AN), then walk 200 yards W on to the dunes.

50.279833, -3.882506

Loam Castle, Thurlestone

Rocky headland with a narrow, hazardous FP.

➤ **Find** Bantham Sand (see above), then walk ⅖ mile SE on the SWCP.

50.268333, -3.873249

GASTROBUS BEACH FOOD, THURLESTONE

Street food at the beach. Breakfast baps from 10am are the best.
Thurlestone, TQ7 3AN
www.gastrobus.co.uk

THE VILLAGE INN, THURLESTONE

Enjoy a pint beneath the beams of wrecked Spanish Armada ships in this bar, which is part of Thurlestone Hotel. Outdoor seating and bedrooms are available.
Parkfield,
Thurlestone, TQ7 3NN
www.thurlestone.co.uk/dining/the-village-inn

LOWER GOOSEWELL COTTAGE, THURLESTONE

Family-run self-catering cottage with sea views.
Ilbert Rd, Thurlestone, TQ7 3NY
www.lowergoose wellcottage.co.uk

BEACHHOUSE, SOUTH MILTON

Simple seafood and takeaway cafe just yards from the sand.
South Milton, TQ7 3JY
beachhousedevon.com

Burgh Island

Leas Foot Sand, Thurlestone

Good place to look for spider crabs at low tide on foot, or high tide with a snorkel and mask.

➤ **Find** South Milton Sands car park at the N end of the beach (Thurlestone Sands, TQ7 3JY), then walk 300 yards N.

50.264067, -3.862691

Thurlestone Sand Lake, Thurlestone

Large beach and bridge across the lake and marsh, which is home to one of largest reed beds in Devon.

➤ **Find** Leas Foot Sand (see above), then walk 300 yards S.

50.260379, -3.857073

Thurlestone Rock Archway, Thurlestone

Touch the 'thurled stone' at low tide that gave the village its name. Care is needed on seaweed and wet rocks. Best seen by snorkel and mask on a calm day.

➤ **Find** Thurlestone Sand Lake (see above), then walk 400 yards S and E to the rocks.

50.257990, -3.860820

Beacon Point, South Huish

Rocky outcrop at the N end of a deserted beach.

➤ **Find** South Milton Sands Car Park (Thurlestone Sands, TQ7 3JY) and walk ⅔ mile S to the point.

50.250790, -3.861324

Gara Rock

BOLT HEAD

WILD THINGS TO DO BEFORE YOU DIE:

LISTEN to sika deer in rutting season.

VISIT a Gothic-style lighthouse.

FORAGE for spider crabs.

TOUCH standing stones at Prawle Point.

CLIMB down rope to a pebble beach.

TASTE shrimps netted at Steeple Cove.

SWIM Leek Cove.

CATCH a Salcombe Harbour ferry.

WATCH greater horseshoe bats.

HAMMOCK over a wooded dell.

Bolt Head

THE COTTAGE HOTEL & RESTAURANT, HOPE COVE

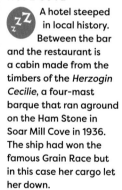

A hotel steeped in local history. Between the bar and the restaurant is a cabin made from the timbers of the *Herzogin Cecilie*, a four-mast barque that ran aground on the Ham Stone in Soar Mill Cove in 1936. The ship had won the famous Grain Race but in this case her cargo let her down.

Cottage Hotel,
Hope Cove, TQ7 3HJ
www.hopecove.com

Hope Cove

Fishing-village cove for swimming and kayaking across two beaches, situated 8 miles NW of Salcombe and 3 miles SE of Thurlestone. Find huge mugwort plants on the way into the cove in June. Pick a few leaves for tea on the beach and sweet dreams later.

➤ **Find** Thurlestone Rock Archway (see page 255) and walk ½ mile S on the SWCP.

50.243092, -3.861688

Bolt Tail Hill Fort, South Huish

Look for greater horseshoe bats around this wild and open naze. Watch the sunset over Bigbury Bay and the SW coast. Bracken lines the FPs that once trailed through forest. Some of the Iron Age fort banking is still on view, but most has been eroded and lost.

➤ **Find** The Sun Bay Hotel & Restaurant (Hope Cove, TQ7 3HH). From the public car park, walk down and then L towards the beach ramp. Climb the staircase and follow the FP through the woods and around the cliff top to the naze 765 yards away.

50.24229, -3.86655

KARRAGEEN CARAVAN & CAMPING PARK, BOLBERRY

 Small family-run caravan and camping park near Hope Cove Beach.
Karrageen House, Bolberry, TQ7 3EN
www.karrageen.co.uk

OCEANS RESTAURANT, BOLBERRY DOWN

 Perfect setting for a cuppa, ice cream or a plate of locally caught fish.
Unnamed Rd, Kingsbridge, TQ7 3DY
oceansrestaurant.co.uk

SOAR MILL COVE HOTEL, MALBOROUGH

Cafe and restaurant for afternoon teas or lunches. This family hotel also has a shop selling jams, and gin that is distilled and bottled on site.
Soar Mill, Salcombe, Kingsbridge, TQ7 3DS
soarmillcove.co.uk

Graystone, South Huish

Watch peregrine falcons hunt here.
> **Find** Bolt Tail Hill Fort (see opposite), then walk ⅔ mile SE on the SWCP to the stone.

50.235416, -3.859021

Bolberry Down, Malborough

Hear the sound of male sika deer in rutting season. Experience cliff top views from 150 yards above sea level. Listen, too, for skylarks, meadow pipits and the rare Dartford warbler.
> **Find** Graystone (see above), then walk ½ mile SE on the SWCP to the down. Alternatively, find the public car park (50.231545, -3.838786) close to Oceans Restaurant (see left), then walk NW ½ mile on the SWCP.

50.231902, -3.845113

Waterfern, Malborough

Sit beside flowering thrift, white clover and marguerites, while sipping cleaver-infused water. Cleaver grows here from February. Infuse it in a bottle of water for 90 mins for a subtle, cooling drink.
> **Find** the public car park (50.231545, -3.838786) close to Oceans Restaurant (see left), then walk 100 yards N to the cliff.

50.231230, -3.839275

Soar Mill Cove, Malborough

Explore the plunge and rock pools at low tide. A cream tea at Soar Mill Cove Hotel (see left) is a short walk away. Look for mica schist rock formations.
> **Find** Soar Mill Cove Hotel and car park (see left), then walk 700 yards on the FP E to the SWCP. The cove is below.

50.221874, -3.827370

PEOPLE OF THE PATH

The Clothes Maker, Orcombe Point, South Devon
I make clothes that encourage children away from TV and phone screens out to the beach. I'm here to take photos of my clothes and the beach. Orcombe Point is a wonderful place for people to come. Especially children.

Steeple Cove, Malborough

Come here for shrimping and fishing for early evening beach BBQs. Large bass on small lures are best in July.

➤ **Find** Soar Mill Cove (see page 259), then walk SE ⅔ mile on the SWCP to the cove.

50.216217, -3.816403

Bolt Head, Malborough

Look out for dolphins. Whales are also reported here sometimes.

➤ **Find** Soar Mill Cove (see page 259), then walk SE 2½ miles on the SWCP to the cove. Alternatively, find East Soar NT Car Park (Unnamed Rd, Kingsbridge, TQ7 3DR), and walk E on the FP just N of the car park. Walk 1½ miles to the SWCP and head.

50.209712, -3.787978

Starehole Bay, Malborough

Sheltered cove with only walking or boat access. As a natural rock harbour, the water is often calm and clear.

➤ **Follow** directions for Bolt Head (see above) but walk only 1¼ miles.

50.214174, -3.786218

Sharp Tor View, Salcombe

Watch fulmars with their vast wings glide on the thermals. This spot offers one of the best views along this section of the SWCP.

➤ **Find** Starehole Bay (see above), then walk 700 yards N and E to the tor.

50.216330, -3.783557

Fir Wood, Salcombe

Listen for the hoot of tawny owls that like to roost and hunt along this section of wooded coastline.

➤ **Find** Overbeck's Sharpitor Museum (see below), then walk N around the house 300 yards to the SWCP. Facing the sea, turn R and walk 400 yards into the woodland.

50.220326, -3.783621

NT Overbeck's Sharpitor Museum, Salcombe

Best in autumn when parts of the garden fill with the smell of flowering ginger lilies and sea air. Otto Overbeck's museum and garden are filled with nautical exhibitions of model sailing ships and photographs of boats and shipwrecks. The subtropical garden has incredible estuary views.

➤ **Find** the car park at Overbeck's (Sharpitor, Salcombe, TQ8 8LW).

50.223152, -3.784031

BO'S BEACH CAFE, SALCOMBE

Somewhere to relax, chat and eat while enjoying the atmosphere of beach and paddle sports. The cafe is located next door to Sea Kayak Salcombe in the old lifeboat house, where paddle enthusiasts meet to get on the water and take in Salcombe views.

Salcombe, TQ8 8LL
seakayaksalcombe.co.uk/
bos-beach-cafe

THE WINKING PRAWN BEACH CAFE, SALCOMBE

Buckets of prawns and platters of shellfish, plus juicy steaks. This is a shabby-chic beach restaurant buzzing with people for breakfast, lunch and dinner.

Beadon Rd,
Salcombe, TQ8 8LD
winkingprawngroup.
co.uk/winking-prawn/

SALCOMBE HARBOUR

Posh 50-room boutique hotel and spa, located on the shores of the picturesque Salcombe Estuary.

Cliff Rd, Salcombe,
TQ8 8JH
www.harbourhotels.co.uk/
salcombe

Tor Woods, Salcombe

A woodland diversion just W of NT Overbeck's Sharpitor Museum. Walk up the FP at dusk to catch a glimpse of barbastelle bats.

➤ **Find** NT Overbeck's Sharpitor Museum (see opposite), then walk 400 yards E on the FP away from the coast.

50.223681, -3.789889

South Sands, Salcombe

There are kayaks to rent, and especially soft sand. Water taxis run in summer to neighbouring beaches and Salcombe, but this place is best in winter.

➤ **Find** NT Overbeck's Sharpitor Museum (see opposite), then walk 500 yards N on the SWCP.

50.225658, -3.783471

Fort Charles and Salcombe Castle, Salcombe

Fort ruin built by Henry VIII, to defend the Kingsbridge Estuary against pirates.

➤ **Find** South Sands (see above), then walk 700 yards N on the SWCP.

50.228513, -3.780295

Salcombe Harbour

The cream of Salcombe is its harbour. Bask in the sunshine and river traffic in the late afternoon. It's a lovely place to cool your heels under the trees or to go for a swim. Walk to Rickham Common (50.223871, -3.772463) for views over The Bar to the wonderfully named Stink Cove.

➤ **Find** parking with sea views at the hairpin in the road at E Portlemouth (Salcombe, TQ8 8FD). Follow the FP down and bear L ⅔ mile through the trees to the beach.

50.229035, -3.766134

Whitestrand Quay, Salcombe

Take the ferry from Salcombe to East Portlemouth, just N of Small's Cove, from this quay. The ferry runs daily throughout the year. For more details, tel 01548 842061/842364.

➤ **Find** Creek Car Park (off Gould Rd, Salcombe, TQ8 8DU), then walk ⅔ mile S around the quay.

50.236357, -3.766304

THE MARINE QUAY, SALCOMBE

Luxury apartments for rent right on the water's edge.

Cliff Rd, Salcombe, TQ8 8JH
www.marinequay.com

VENUS CAFE, EAST PORTLEMOUTH

Hand-crimped artisan pasties, toasted panini and wraps to go, with views over Salcombe. There are garden tables with estuary views.

Ferry Steps, Millbay Rd, East Portlemouth, TQ8 8PU
www.lovingthebeach.co.uk

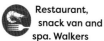

THE RESTAURANT AT GARA ROCK, EAST PORTLEMOUTH

Restaurant, snack van and spa. Walkers are welcome for lunch or dinner, or drinks on the terrace.

Gara Rock, East Portlemouth, TQ8 8FA
www.gararock.com/eat-drink/restaurant/

Small's Cove, East Portlemouth

Tiny idyllic beach of sand surrounded by trees and blue water.
➤ **Find** the small car park at the bend in the road, East Portlemouth (Salcombe, TQ8 8PE; 50.233992, -3.759364). Walk 300 yards W on the BW. At the waterfront, turn L and walk 200 yards.

50.233647, -3.765139

Mill Bay, East Portlemouth

Quiet beach opposite Salcombe with a tree-lined backdrop, and rock pools for shrimp and crabbing. Ferry service nearby in summer, and a NT car park.
➤ **Find** Small's Cove (see above), then walk 500 yards S on the SWCP.

50.230572, -3.767650

Sunny Cove, East Portlemouth, Batson Creek

This place is a favourite with boaters. Best after dusk when the water is warm and clear.
➤ **Find** Mill Bay (see above), then walk ½ mile S on the SWCP.

50.230572, -3.767650

Gara Rock Beach, East Portlemouth

Clean, sandy beach with big waves, 500 yards from the car park. Rocks to explore and climb. Find strawberry anemones (they look like strawberries …) in rock pools at low tide here, and at Abraham's Hole (Seacombe Sands) next door.
➤ **Find** Leek Cove (see opposite), then walk 1½ miles E on the SWCP.

50.217986, -3.747651

Deckler's Cliff, East Portlemouth

Visit at dawn or dusk to catch a glimpse of the ancient field systems that were among the first to be used in England – perhaps as early as 3,500 years ago. The light shows up the banks of earth and stone walls that remain behind, which were once fertilised with seaweed collected from Gara Rock Beach (see above), then carted on salt FPs known as 'hollow ways', which are still in existence today. Similar field systems are found on Dartmoor and Bodmin moors.
➤ **Find** Gara Rock (see above), then walk 600 yards E on the SWCP.

50.217088, -3.743740

GARA ROCK, EAST PORTLEMOUTH

Lunches or overnight stays in cottages and apartments. There is a caravan right on the SWCP serving pasties, sandwiches and hot drinks. The food is mostly from the kitchen garden or local farms and fishermen.

East Portlemouth, TQ8 8FA
www.gararock.com

 ## Leek Cove, East Portlemouth

There are beautiful sandy beaches below, which will tempt you down for a swim or some hopeful fishing for dinner.
➤ **Find** Sunny Cove (see opposite), then walk 700 yards S on the SWCP.

50.223063, -3.771942

 ## Venerick's Cove, East Portlemouth

Look for spider crabs by climbing down Deckler's Cliff (see opposite) via rope to access the hidden pebble beach located 3 miles W of East Prawle and 3 miles E of Portsmouth.
➤ **Find** Deckler's Cliff (see opposite), then walk 600 yards E on the SWCP.

50.214383, -3.737443

 ## Maceley Cliffs and Cove, Chivelstone

Feel low-tide sand shingle beneath tired, bare feet. Visit early in the morning as the road to the car park is extremely narrow.
➤ **Find** East Prawle Car Park (Kingsbridge, TQ7 2BX). Walk downhill to the SWCP, turn R and walk 1 mile along the SWCP.

50.207165, -3.731063

 ## Gammon Head, East Portlemouth

Touch the jagged stone of this mica schist and look for the white quartz that runs through the rock, still pulsing with energy. The rare six-banded nomad bee *Nomada sexfasciata* has been seen here on flowers. There are lovely views over Elender Cove (see page 264).
➤ **Find** Maceley Cliffs and Cove (see above). Gammon Head is the rocky point that separates them; the cove to the E and the cliffs to the N.

50.207954, -3.726449

PEOPLE OF THE PATH

The Cyclist, Orcombe Point, South Devon

My favourite place along the coast is the small harbour at Lympstone. I can cycle from Orcombe Point all the way to the estuary cafe for a cuppa on the cycle path. It's about five miles.

Prawle Point

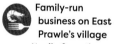

Elender Cove, Chivelstone

Listen out for the trilling 'ti – ti – ti – ti -ti' sound of the cirl bunting. These rare birds look a bit like a small yellowhammer. They sing and chirp quite loudly in and around the blackthorn and gorse bushes on this stretch of the SWCP.

➤ **Find** Gammon Head (see page 263), then walk 300 yard E to the cove.

50.208057, -3.726319

Prawle Point, East Prawle

Touch and walk rows of standing stone known as 'orthostats', which are thought to be thousands of years old. No one really knows what they were for, but they look and feel important. Devon's most southerly point is best for views of cliff-side wild flowers in early summer and spring: swarms of sea campion, bluebells and thrift. Look out for small pearl-bordered and dark green fritillary butterflies.

➤ **Find** East Prawle Car Park (Kingsbridge, TQ7 2BX), then walk 700 yards W along the SWCP.

50.202116, -3.721382

Lookout Station, East Prawle, English Channel

Volunteer-managed coast watch surrounded by WWII radar bunkers. The shipwreck of the *Demetrios* can be seen just NW of the point at low tide. Fulmars and cormorants are common.

➤ **Find** Prawle Point (see above), then walk 100 yards E along the SWCP.

50.202576, -3.721638

Langerstone Point, Chivelstone, English Channel

Noisy peregrine falcons nest and hunt here. Listen to the rattling call of male cirl buntings in summer. They're rare. Flocks of the birds roost here in winter when the peregrines aren't looking.
➤ **Find** East Prawle Car Park (Kingsbridge, TQ7 2BX). After walking down to the SWCP, turn L and walk ½ mile E to the point.

50.205592, -3.708554

Horseley Cove, Chivelstone

A sprawling ½-mile stretch of beach and rock that's ideal for shelter from the N wind.
➤ **Find** Langerstone Point (see above), then walk ½ mile E on the SWCP.

50.210774, -3.702730

Stinking Cove, Chivelstone

Look out for porpoises.
➤ **Find** Horseley Cove (see above), then walk 1 mile E on the SWCP.

50.219367, -3.685326

Evator Cove, Chivelstone

Smell the scent of elderflower around the rocks in June and July.
➤ **Find** Horseley Cove (see above), then walk 1 mile E on the SWCP.

50.219367, -3.685326

Lannacombe Beach, Stokenham

This is one of the most isolated sandy beaches on the SWCP, with limited car access and facilities. Perfect.
➤ **Find** Start Point Car Park (Stokenham, Kingsbridge, TQ7 2ET). Walk E towards the point and turn R as it joins the SWCP, then walk E for 2 miles.

50.222380, -3.678578

Mattiscombe Sands, Stokenham

A sandy treasure. Take the long walk from Start Point (see page 266) for some of the best Devonshire views.
➤ **Find** Start Point Car Park (Stokenham, Kingsbridge, TQ7 2ET). Walk S (with the gate to the lighthouse on your L) towards the bay, which is 1 mile W.

50.220301, -3.659617

THE CRICKET INN, BEESANDS

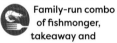 Village inn serving up award-winning food and ales. There are seven bedrooms for stopovers. Beesands village derived its name from the term 'Bay Sands' and was first inhabited in the late 18th century, once pirates had stopped raiding the coast.

Beesands, TQ7 2EN
www.thecricketinn.com

BRITANNIA @THE BEACH, BEESANDS

 Family-run combo of fishmonger, takeaway and licensed cafe/restaurant.

Beesands, TQ7 2EH
www.britanniaatthe
beach.co.uk

VALSEPH B&B, BEESANDS

Rooms overlooking the beach and a short walk from the pub and chippy.

Beesands, TQ7 2EJ
www.beesandsbandb.
co.uk

Ravens Cove, Stokenham

Get blown off your feet, literally. SW gales have been known to knock people over. This is part of the shipwreck coast that epitomises the treacherous nature of the lonely wild.

➤ **Find** Mattiscombe Sands (see page 265), then walk ⅔ mile E on the SWCP.

50.219217, -3.653501

Start Point, Start Bay

Watch white horses. The crested waves rise at Start Point just before low tide. As the last of the water ebbs out of the bay, it is squeezed between the shore and the rock coral shelf known as Skerries Bank. This water rush is known as a tidal race: white horses in full gallop. At low tide, try fishing down in the bay over the 7ft rock reef that runs 4 miles NE from the point.

➤ **Find** Start Point Car Park (Stokenham, Kingsbridge, TQ7 2ET), then walk ⅔ mile downhill.

50.222644, -3.642561

Start Point Lighthouse, Start Bay

This 92ft Gothic-style lighthouse, built in 1836, is located SE of Freshwater Bay and car park. It's open in summer, and offers great views N over Slapton Sands, even as far as the Isle of Portland on a clear day.

➤ **Find** Start Point (above). The lighthouse is 50 yards back from Start Bay.

50.222539, -3.641147

Ravens Cove

Hallsands

 ## Shoelodge Reef, Start Point

Look for the on- and offshore rock formations.

➤ **Find** Start Point Car Park (Stokenham, Kingsbridge, TQ7 2ET), then walk ½ mile NW on the SWCP.

50.225720, -3.650440

 ## Hallsands, Start Bay

Listen to the colony of breeding kittiwakes that nest on the cliffs and ruined buildings. The fishing village was wiped out by storms in 1917. Strete Undercliffe nearby went at the end of the 18th century. What remains is 1½ miles of beach coves and pools.

➤ **Find** Hallsands Village Car Park (Stokenham, TQ7 2EY). Walk 300 yards E along the road to the beach and then walk S a few yards.

50.240050, -3.658702

 ## Widdicombe Ley, Beesands

Small freshwater lake, or 'ley', behind Beesands. Shelter in a bird hide when the weather turns foul.

➤ **Find** the beach car park (Beesands, TQ7 2EJ). Walk 200 yards N to the ley.

50.257088, -3.656618

 ## Beesands Quarry, Beesands

Wonderful wooded dell for sheltering, hammocking and exploring.

➤ **Find** the beach car park (Beesands, TQ7 2EJ), then walk ½ mile N.

50.261891, -3.655077

Dartmouth

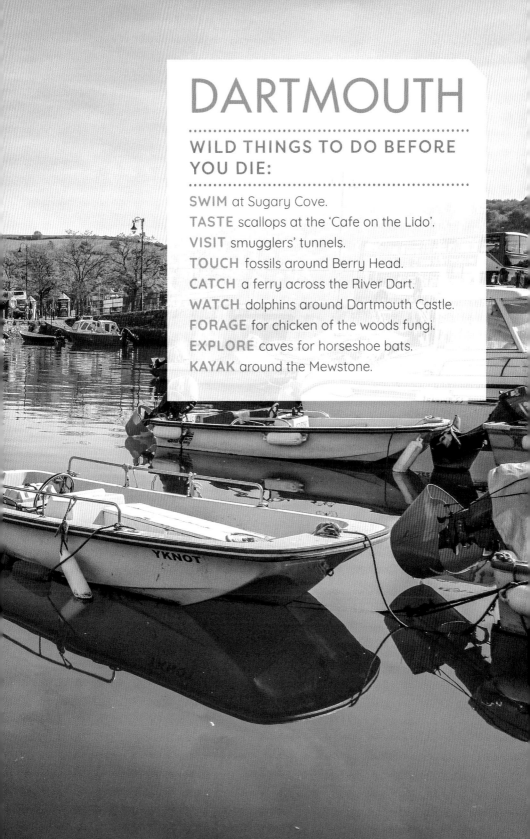

DARTMOUTH

WILD THINGS TO DO BEFORE YOU DIE:

SWIM at Sugary Cove.

TASTE scallops at the 'Cafe on the Lido'.

VISIT smugglers' tunnels.

TOUCH fossils around Berry Head.

CATCH a ferry across the River Dart.

WATCH dolphins around Dartmouth Castle.

FORAGE for chicken of the woods fungi.

EXPLORE caves for horseshoe bats.

KAYAK around the Mewstone.

QUEENS ARMS, SLAPTON SANDS

Home-cooked food and great pints.

Slapton Sands, TQ7 2PN
www.queensarms
slapton.co.uk

THE LIME COFFEE CO., SLAPTON SANDS

This cafe on the beach at Strete Gate takes its name from the limestone quarries and kilns that once lined the coastline. It serves up award-winning pasties and fine coffee.

Strete Gate, TQ6 0RR
www.limecoffeeco.com

THE KINGS ARMS, STRETE

Community pub with a beer garden and Devon-style BYOB (Bring Your Own Blanket) right beside the SWCP.

Dartmouth Rd, A379, Strete, TQ6 0RW
kingsarmsatstrete.co.uk

MANOR FARM CAMPING, STRETE

A naturist-friendly campsite with a special feel. Somewhere to throw off your cares ... and clothes.

Strete, TQ6 0RU
www.naturistdirectory.
com/UK/3/Manor-Farm

Slapton Ley, Torcross

Filled by the sound of the River Gara, this fascinating freshwater lake straddles coast and country, with Widdecombe Ley less than 1 mile S. It's a wonderful walk or drive with water either side. Listen out for the plop of water voles. Kayak trips are sometimes available. The neighbouring shore beach is stony.

➤ **Find** Slapton Sands Memorial Car Park (Kingsbridge, TQ7 2QW). Either cross on to the beach or walk along the road into Sands Rd to explore the lake. Slapton Sands Camping & Caravanning Club Site (see page 267) is a ten-min walk from here.

50.277063, -3.649410

Shiphill Rock Waterfall, Strete

Crashing waterfall on the S side of Forest Cove (see below).
➤ **Find** Slapton Sands Memorial Car Park (Kingsbridge, TQ7 2QW), then walk 2 miles N.

50.308769, -3.622137

Forest Cove, Strete

Super views from the fields above Forest Cove towards Slapton and Start Point.
➤ **Find** Shiphill Rock Waterfall (see above), then walk 500 yards N.

50.311840, -3.619141

Landcombe Cove, Strete

This cove with a stream is a diversion 220 yards from the SWCP. Pick sea beet to chew on the climb back up.
➤ **Find** Venus Cafe (see opposite). Walk through the large public car park, away from the cafe, on to the beach after the tide has gone out. Keep walking ⅔ mile to the cove. If the tide comes in, walk back on the incredibly beautiful SWCP walk, crossing the road at 50.315261, -3.619009. Be wary walking back on the A379. Although it's less than ⅓ mile, there is no pavement, and the road can be busy throughout the year.

50.314201, -3.615900

Jenny Cole's Cove, Blackpool Sands

Secluded S section of Blackpool Sands. Care is needed as it's possible to get cut off by the tide.
➤ **Find** Blackpool Freshwater Lake (see opposite), then walk 300 yards W.

50.316358, -3.613217

**VENUS CAFE,
BLACKPOOL SANDS**

Full breakfast and baps served up to 11.30am.
Set the alarm. Head here for a cuppa and kayak hire on a wonderful beach. Takeaway is available, too.

Blackpool Sands,
TQ6 0QR
www.lovingthebeach.co.uk

Blackpool Freshwater Lake, Strete

Spring-fed natural water palace. Best at midday. Kids love it.
➤ **Find** the car park (Blackpool Sands, TQ6 0QR), then walk 300 yards to the river and lake.

50.318030, -3.613153

Blackpool Sands, Blackpool

Kayak over shingle beach and clear water.
➤ **Find** the car park (Blackpool Sands, TQ6 0QR), then walk E on to the beach.

50.319447, -3.609987

Redlap Cove

Old smugglers' haunt with no public land access and tunnels allegedly into the cliff face.
➤ **Find** a kayak and paddle in from Little Dartmouth coves 1 mile E. Experience is needed as the route can be hazardous.

50.325999, -3.584429

Warren Point, Dartmouth

This point gets its name from rabbits that were once bred here in vast warrens, for fur and meat. There are great views to Start Point Lighthouse on Start Bay. Watch guillemots and cormorants fishing here.
➤ **Find** Little Dartmouth NT Car Park (Redlap Ln, Dartmouth, TQ6 0JR), then walk ½ mile S to the point.

50.324947, -3.576550

PEOPLE OF THE PATH

The Retired Weather Woman/The Camper, Orcombe Point, South Devon
We're having a retirement party on the beach. Our favourite place on the path is the view from Eype campsite. We go there in our campervan.

DARTMOUTH ARMS, DARTMOUTH

Pub on Bayard's Cove in Dartmouth. Fresh, home-made food seven days a week.

26 Lower St, Dartmouth, TQ6 9AN
thedartmoutharms.co.uk

THE CRAB AND BUCKET, DARTMOUTH

Harbourside pub for a sandwich and a pint.

5 S Embankment, Dartmouth, TQ6 9BH
Facebook: @The Crab And Bucket

Western Combe Cove, Dartmouth

Beautiful S-facing beach, steps and cove, where you can forage for seaweed to dry or eat raw. There are also several larger coves, including neighbouring Willow Cove. Best tramped at low tide.

➤ **Find** Little Dartmouth NT Car Park (Redlap Ln, Dartmouth, TQ6 0JR), but walk through the lower car park on to the Serly FP. After ⅓ mile, the FP bears L. Continue on the final ⅓ mile to Combe Point and Shinglehill and Willow coves.

50.3264, -3.5728

Compass Cove, Dartmouth

Touch or collect chicken of the woods fungi that grow around the base of large oaks on the cove's W face. The dark sand and shingle beach is surrounded by shade. Access is often restricted because of landslips, so even more care than normal is needed around this bit of coast.

➤ **Find** Western Combe Cove (see above), then walk 1 mile N on the SWCP to the cove.

50.333783, -3.568557

Deadmans Cove, Dartmouth

It's a steep climb through woods above Deadmans and Sugary coves. Good place for sun and storm shelter. Sniff out sweet cicely, which grows here.

➤ **Find** Compass Cove (see above), then walk 600 yards N on the SWCP to the cove.

50.337819, -3.565339

KINGSWEAR COFFEE CO, KINGSWEAR

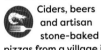

Coffee shop beside the ferry, steam train station, sailing club and post office. Somewhere to buy local produce, too: coffee from Exeter's Exe Coffee Roastery, bread from 5 Doors Up in Brixham, local jams and marmalade from Clare's Preserves based in Bovey Tracey, and ice cream tubs from Surfing Cow.

2A The Square, Kingswear, TQ6 0AA
www.kingswearcoffee. co.uk

STEAM PACKET INN, KINGSWEAR

Ciders, beers and artisan stone-baked pizzas from a village inn overlooking the River Dart and Dartmouth.

Fore St, Kingswear, TQ6 0AD
steampacketinnkings wear.co.uk

Dartmouth Castle, Dartmouth

Look for dolphins in the bay. This coastal fort guards the Dart Estuary and is the strategic port of Dartmouth. There's a tearoom and coastal church, too.

➤ **Find** the corner at Redcap Ln (Dartmouth, TQ6 0JR), then walk between the two car parks on the E-facing and E-pointing BW. Follow the lane 1.2 miles on Castle Rd to the edge of the river and the castle. Explore Deadmans Cove, Sugary Cove and Castle Cove. There is a small car park here (Castle Rd, Dartmouth, TQ6 0JN), but it's often busy and the walk (or cycle) from Redcap Ln is lovely. Consider walking on another 1 mile along the coastal roads and the B3205 to Dartmouth's centre.

50.34203, -3.56829

Bayard's Cove, Dartmouth

Walk and feel the cobbles beneath your feet. This was one of the last stops for the Pilgrim Fathers before they set sail for America in 1620.

➤ **Find** Dartmouth Castle (see above), then walk 1 mile N.

50.347965, -3.577620

Bommerock Remains, Kingswear

Ferry trip across the River Dart from Dartmouth to Kingswear.
➤ **Find** Steam Packet Inn (see left), then walk 1 mile S on the SWCP.

50.343963, -3.561076

Kingswear Castle, Kingswear

Walk up and out of the castle through Monterey and Corsican pines between views across the River Dart.
➤ **Find** Bommerock Remains (see above), then walk 300 yards S on the SWCP.

50.341853, -3.559766

Mill Bay Cove, Kingswear

Walk across hard sand at low tide for a dip in turquoise waters, framed by green banks of rock and forest. Collect seaweed around the cove to dry or eat raw.
➤ **Find** the car park at Darthaven Marina & Services (Volvo Penta Centre) (Brixham Rd, Kingswear, TQ6 0SG) and walk 1½ miles S on the SWCP to the cove. Alternatively, find Kingswear Castle (see above), then follow the SWCP 500 yards S and then E.

50.342744, -3.556826

Newfoundland Cove, Kingswear

Look for the hobby falcons that hunt around the rear of the cove and sometimes just offshore.

➤ **Find** Mill Bay Cove (see page 273), then walk ⅔ mile SE on the SWCP to the cove.

50.338527, -3.547302

Inner Froward Point, Kingswear

Grey seals rest at low tide around The Mewstone, 400 yards offshore. It's owned by the NT but closed to the public for conservation reasons. Good site for kayaking, and from which to see shags and cormorants.

➤ **Find** Newfoundland Cove (see above), then walk 400 yards SE on the SWCP to the point.

50.335964, -3.543696

The Tower Day Beacon, Kingswear

Listen to linnets, skylarks and the rare cirl bunting on the walk to the daymark erected in 1864 as a navigational aid.

➤ **Find** Inner Froward Point (see above), then walk N ½ mile on the FP that leaves the SWCP towards the beacon.

50.342289, -3.542730

Old Mill Bay, Kingswear

Look for the Dartmoor and Exmoor ponies that sometimes graze along this section of the SWCP.

➤ **Find** Inner Froward Point (see above), then walk ⅔ mile E on the SWCP to the bay.

50.338280, -3.534038

Kelly Cove, Kingswear

Listen for crickets in the open grassland bordering the FP. It's a wild flower and dark green fritillary butterfly hotspot on warm June days. Eat a primrose petal or two.

➤ **Find** Old Mill Bay (see above), then walk ⅔ mile E on the SWCP to the cove.

50.339499, -3.532986

Pudcombe Cove, Kingswear

Take the plunge and go for a night-time swim and listen to tawny owls hooting from the trees overhead. Lovely views.

➤ **Find** the car park off Brownstone Rd (Kingswear, TQ6 0EQ; 50.350737, -3.534033), then walk ⅔ mile to the SWCP. Turn R facing the sea and walk ⅔ mile W to the cove.

50.344139, -3.531097

Castle Cove

NT Coleton Fishacre House & Gardens, Kingswear

NT garden, cafe, shop and toilets. Look for common blue butterflies in summer grassland and rare sea views from the terraces. Colonies of ants have nested in the garden for several centuries – it may be worth checking them out.

➤ **Find** Brownstone Rd, Kingswear, TQ6 0EQ
www.nationaltrust.org.uk/coleton-fishacre

50.352484, -3.514863

Downend Point, Kingswear

Look out for wild ponies. This place is also great for butterflies and foraging for cleaver for making a water bottle infusion.

➤ **Find** the car park off Brownstone Rd (Kingswear, TQ6 0EQ; 50.350737, -3.534033), then walk ⅔ mile E to the SWCP and the point.

50.352484, -3.514863

Scabbacombe Sands, Kingswear

It's a steep cliff walk down to this naturist beach, where you'll find a whole cove for rock pooling, crabbing and snorkelling.

➤ **Find** Downend Point (see above), then walk ½ mile N on the SWCP to the beach.

50.357720, -3.521141

Long Sands, Kingswear

Sit down next to bird's-foot trefoil and early purple orchids so you can listen to white-tailed bumblebees around the June flowers.

➤ **Find** Scabbacombe Sands (see above), then walk ½ mile N on the SWCP. See also Man Sands on page 276.

50.361852, -3.519005

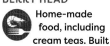

Man Sands, Kingswear

Look for Cetti's warbler and reed warbler in the reed bed and pools just inland of the existing coastline. It's a unique area of brackish plain and farmland that has been allowed to flood into the sea, the wall defences having not been replaced.

➤ **Find** the car park (Scabbacombe Ln, Kingswear, TQ6 0EF), then walk ⅔ mile down the lane to the SWCP above Long Sands. Turn L facing the sea and walk 1 mile N to the sands.

50.370964, -3.514927

Southdown Cliffs, Kingswear

Wild flowers abound all about the limestone meadows from May to August.

➤ **Find** Man Sands (see above), then walk 500 yards N on the SWCP.

50.376495, -3.514111

Sharkham Point, Brixham

Feel the pain on one of the steepest climbs on the SWCP, but also experience some of the best views.

➤ **Find** Sharkham Point car park (Brixham, TQ5 9FH), then walk 400 yards E to the point.

50.381962, -3.496752

Berry Head Nature Reserve, Brixham

Look for greater horseshoe bats, which hunt in caves and crevices around this limestone head. It also hosts the largest guillemot colony on the S coast of England. Look for harbour porpoises and seals.

➤ **Find** Sharkham Point (see above), then walk 200 yards N on the SWCP.

50.383447, -3.498075

St Mary Bay, Brixham

Access to the secluded shingle beach can be difficult, but it's worth the effort to look for fossils.

➤ **Find** Berry Head (see opposite), then walk 500 yards NW on the SWCP.

50.387239, -3.503348

Durl Head, Brixham

Listen out for nesting kittiwakes and guillemots (known locally as the 'Brixham penguin').

➤ **Find** the car park (Gillard Rd, Brixham, TQ5 9AP), then walk 500 yards S on the SWCP to the head.

50.391895, -3.492727

SHOALS CAFE, BRIXHAM

The 'Cafe on the Lido' over the wonderful Shoalstone Sea Water Pool (Brixham, TQ5 9FT). There are sea views from the outdoor terrace, and fish from the family-owned trawler. Try local scallops direct from Brixham Fish Market. There are also meat and vegetarian dishes.

10 SWCP, Brixham, TQ5 9FT
www.shoalsbrixham.co.uk

FISHCOMBE COVE CAFE, BRIXHAM

Dog friendly, al fresco beach hut cafe for cakes, home-baked cream tea and freshly ground coffee.

Fishcombe Cove, Brixham, TQ5 8RU
Facebook: @Fishcombe Cove Cafe

Berry Head

Find coral reef fossils around the rocky head, which was formed 400 million years ago. The reef is evidence of Berry Head's former tropical climate, when it sat almost on the Equator before drifting.

➤ **Find** Durl Head (see opposite), walk ⅔ mile N on the SWCP and then take the FP to the head.

50.399531, -3.482942

Shoalstone Point

Look out for stunning fulmars gliding about the sandstone wave platforms.

➤ **Find** Berry Head (see above), then walk ⅔ mile W on the FP, and then the SWCP, to the point.

50.401270, -3.495961

Fishcombe Cove, Brixham

Cove surrounded on all sides by tall cliffs and wooded hillsides. The beach is sheltered and ideal if you want to escape the crowds of Brixham. Steps lead down through woodland, and open out to reveal a small low tide beach.

➤ **Find** the car park (Fishcombe Rd, Brixham, TQ5 8RU) and walk 150 yards NW through Battery Gardens to the cove.

50.402287, -3.522072

Durl Head

Preston Sands

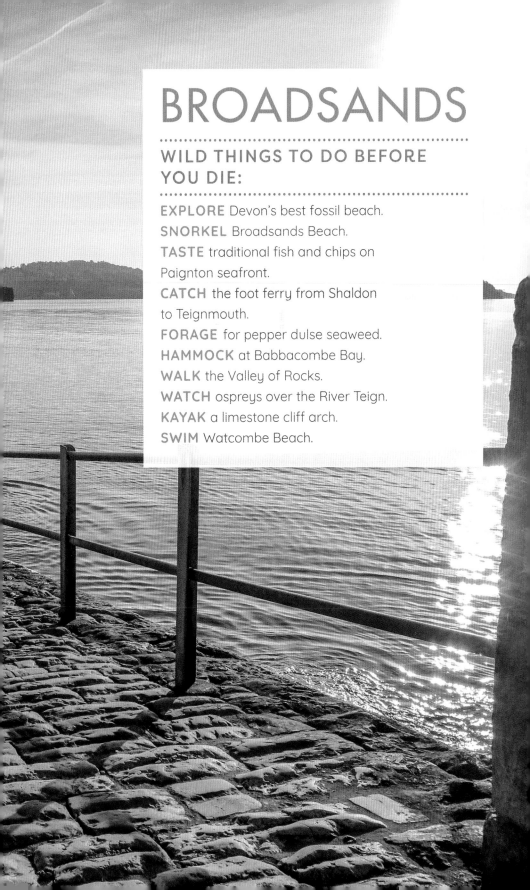

BROADSANDS

WILD THINGS TO DO BEFORE YOU DIE:

EXPLORE Devon's best fossil beach.

SNORKEL Broadsands Beach.

TASTE traditional fish and chips on Paignton seafront.

CATCH the foot ferry from Shaldon to Teignmouth.

FORAGE for pepper dulse seaweed.

HAMMOCK at Babbacombe Bay.

WALK the Valley of Rocks.

WATCH ospreys over the River Teign.

KAYAK a limestone cliff arch.

SWIM Watcombe Beach.

VENUS CAFE, BROADSANDS BAY

Recently opened as a Venus cafe, serving up breakfasts, lunches, coffees and cakes right on the beach.

SWCP, Paignton, TQ4 6HL
www.lovingthebeach.co.uk

SOUTH SANDS BEACHSIDE CAFE, SOUTH SANDS

Beachside cafe for ice creams and hot chocolate.

S Sands, Paignton, TQ4 6NB
07960 259152

THE SANDS, PAIGNTON

Four-star hotel with sea views, close to the harbour.

32 Sands Rd, Paignton, TQ4 6EJ
Facebook: @thesandshotelpaignton

THE HARBOUR INN, PAIGNTON

Pub with views over Paignton Harbour.

59 Roundham Rd, Paignton, TQ4 6DS
harbourinnpaignton.com

Broadsands Beach, Paignton

Sandy beach for snorkelling. It's also easy to launch a packraft or kayak here.

➤ **Find** Broadsands Car Park (Broadsands Rd, Paignton, TQ4 6HX), then walk 100 yards N to the beach.

50.407366, -3.554147

Broadsands Viaduct, Broadsands Bay

Touch Brunel's legacy, especially when a steam train passes overhead. Limestone for the viaduct came from neighbouring Churston. The railway was opened on 1 August 1859, six weeks before Brunel's death.

➤ **Find** Broadsands Car Park (Broadsands Rd, Paignton, TQ4 6HX), then walk ⅔ mile up Broadsands Rd to where the viaduct crosses the street.

50.402260, -3.559479

Torquay Harbour, Torquay

A natural harbour, tamed by engineers to become a coastal resort. Still naturally beautiful.

➤ **Find** Daddyhole Plain Car Park (5 Daddyhole Rd, Torquay, TQ1 2EF), then walk 1 mile W to the harbour.

50.460548, -3.527203

Broadsands Viaduct

MOLLYS, PAIGNTON

Snacks and drinks beside Paignton Harbour.

Roundham Rd, Paignton Harbour, TQ4 6DT
Facebook: @Mollystheharbour

MEADFOOT BEACH CAFE, TORQUAY

Cafe for coffee and brekkies and peaceful views across Meadfoot Bay.

Meadfoot Sea Rd, Torquay, TQ1 2LQ
Facebook: @meadfootbeachcafe

MERRITT HOUSE B&B, PAIGNTON

B&B right on the SWCP. Super food and service.

7 Queen's Rd, Paignton, TQ4 6AT
www.merritthouse.co.uk

THE SPINNING WHEEL INN, PAIGNTON

Nibbles, main meals and meat-free menus.

19 Espl Rd, Paignton, TQ4 6BE
www.spinningwheel inn.co.uk

PAIGNTON PIER CHIPPY CO., PAIGNTON

Traditional fish and chip shop and restaurant on Paignton seafront.

SWCP, Paignton, TQ4 6BW
www.paigntonpier chippy.com

Beacon Cove, Torquay

Swim cove reserved for ladies only until 1903. Agatha Christie swam here as a child.

➤ **Find** the cove 200 yards E of Beacon Quay Car Park (Beacon Hill, Torquay, TQ1 2BG).

50.457369, -3.523568

London Bridge, Torquay

Paddle through this natural arch in the limestone cliff S of Torquay Harbour. The neighbouring cave is popular, too - with kayakers and bats.

➤ **Find** Beacon Cove (see above), then walk ½ mile SE on the SWCP to the arch.

50.454374, -3.519141

Daddyhole, Torquay

Dawn views over Tor Bay. Catch the sunrise and then walk down for a swim at Meadfoot Beach (see below).

➤ **Find** London Bridge (see above), then walk 600 yards NE on the SWCP.

50.455331, -3.510903

Meadfoot Beach, Torquay

Head here for low-tide swims and rock pooling. Launch a kayak from the ramp over the beach at high tide. The beach is best at low tide.

➤ **Find** Daddyhole (see above), then walk ½ mile to the beach.

50.459295, -3.503121

PEOPLE OF THE PATH

The Hikers, Warren Point, South Devon

Our favourite places after 400 miles of walking have been the villages either side of Lizard Point. And the same around Lannacombe Bay. They tend to be places people are less likely to drive to.

Hope's Nose

BEST WESTERN LIVERMEAD CLIFF HOTEL, TORQUAY

Hotel with direct and private access to the beach, a short walk from the marina seafront.

Torbay Rd,
Torquay, TQ2 6RQ
www.livermeadcliff.co.uk

THE LIVERMEAD HOUSE HOTEL, TORQUAY

One of Torquay's most historic hotels.

Torbay Rd,
Torquay, TQ2 6QJ
www.livermead.com

THE GRAND HOTEL, TORQUAY

Torquay's landmark hotel comes with Victorian architecture, elegant interiors, a fantastic seafront and award-winning food.

Sea Front, Torbay Rd,
Torquay, TQ2 6NT
grandtorquay.co.uk

Hope's Nose, Torquay

A naze from which to watch seals. Popular with anglers. It's also one of the best locations in Devon for fossils, which can be found on the foreshore at low tide.

➤ **Find** the coastal road along Ilsham Marine Dr (Wellswood, Torquay, TQ1 2PH). At its junction with Thatcher Av, bear L off the road on to the FP and walk ⅓ mile to the end of the rocky peninsula. There's limited parking sometimes in Ilsham Marine Dr so consider instead finding Babbacombe Cricket Club (Walls Hill Rd, Torquay, TQ1 3LZ), where there's a public car park (and a lovely beach). With your back to the car park, walk R along Walls Hill Rd and just keep on to Walls Hill and the SWCP. Turn R from here and follow the old SWCP 1¼ miles back to Ilsham Marine Dr, and on to Hope's Nose.

50.46347, -3.48159

Brandy Cove and Hope Cove, Torquay

Listen to nesting kittiwakes, with views over Thatcher's Rock. Coral fossils can be found here, too.

➤ **Find** Hope's Nose (see above), then walk ½ mile E and N to the head on the SWCP.

50.464794, -3.489749

Black Head, Babbacombe Bay

Forage for mallow flowers in June while walking through the woodland around Black Head.

➤ **Find** Brandy Cove (see above), then walk 500 yards N to the head on the SWCP.

50.468415, -3.491552

LAS IGUANAS - TORQUAY, TORQUAY

Latin American menu and cocktails with views across the Riviera.

4 Abbey Sands, Abbey Crescent, Torbay Rd, Torquay, TQ2 5FB
www.iguanas.co.uk/ restaurants/torquay

TQ2 CAFE AND BAR, TORQUAY

Pit stop for coffee with food beside the marina.

2 Princess Pier, Torquay, TQ1 2BB
Facebook: @TQ2club

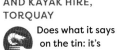

ANSTEY'S COVE BEACH CAFE AND KAYAK HIRE, TORQUAY

Does what it says on the tin: it's a beach cafe and kayak hire joint! Breakfasts, panini and freshly ground coffee.

Anstey's Cove Rd, Torquay, TQ1 2JB
ansteyscove.info

THE BABBACOMBE HOTEL, BABBACOMBE

Large hotel with 80 beds overlooking the famous Babbacombe Downs, with views across Lyme Bay.

Babbacombe Downs Rd, Babbacombe, TQ1 3LH
www.thebabbacombe hotel.co.uk

Long Quarry Point, Torquay

This point affords you the best view of Torquay. Fin whales sometimes swim offshore. Also look out for dolphins.
➤ **Find** Black Head (see opposite), then walk 1 mile N on the SWCP to the point.

50.475807, -3.497583

Withy Point, Torquay

Porpoises arrive here in July to feed with their calves.
➤ **Find** Long Quarry Point (see above), then walk ½ mile NW on the SWCP to the point.

50.479297, -3.506339

Oddicombe Beach, Oddicombe

Cliff railway runs overhead in summer. Walk down to swim, then catch the train back. Look for oval-shaped coral fossils trapped in the sandstone 'breccia' blocks used to make the building walls at the bottom of the cliff railway. The surrounding red-rock breccia cliffs are a kind of sandstone formed 250 million years ago in desert conditions.
➤ **Find** Withy Point (see above), then walk 600 yards NW on the SWCP to the beach.

50.481861, -3.515096

Petit Tour Beach, Torquay

Forage and collect pepper dulse seaweed. Nosy seals come in to look about in summer.
➤ **Find** Oddicombe Beach (see above), then walk 600 yards N on the SWCP to find the FP going E towards the coast. Walk another 700 yards to the cliff above the beach.

50.488117, -3.514385

PEOPLE OF THE PATH

The Four Sisters and Friend, Warren Point, South Devon

The best beach around here is Sugary Cove. It's the first one into Little Dartmouth. The best cream teas are by the castle.

Babbacombe

DEVON PALMS, MAIDENCOMBE

Holiday cottages and apartments set in 1 acre in Maidencombe, a short walk from the SWCP and coves.

Teignmouth Rd, Torquay, TQ1 4TH
devonpalms.co.uk

CAFE RIO, SUP AND KAYAK HIRE, MAIDENCOMBE BEACH

Ice cream, pasties, cakes, kayaks and paddleboards ... perched on the cliff side!

Maidencombe Beach, Steep Hill, Torquay, TQ1 4TS

Watcombe Beach, Torquay

Swim and snorkel. Feel the mud clay that was once considered the best in England for pottery that was known as Devon Motto Ware.

➤ **Find** Watcombe Beach Rd Car Park (Watcombe Beach Rd, Torquay, TQ1 4SH), then walk 500 yards on the FP to the beach.

50.496028, -3.514675

Giant Rock, Valley of Rocks, Babbacombe Bay

Walk the Valley of Rocks, once part of the estate owned by Isambard Kingdom Brunel. Giant Rock is obscured by trees, but was visible in the Victorian era and was a tourist attraction. Touch and taste coconut-flavoured gorse flowers in July. Star watch above Watcombe Beach.

➤ **Find** Watcombe Beach (see above), then walk 500 yards N on the SWCP.

50.497692, -3.517839

Maidencombe Beach, Torquay

Swim and snorkel in clear water.

➤ **Find** Watcombe Beach (see above), then walk 1⅓ miles N to the beach. Alternatively, find Maidencombe Beach Car Park (off Rock House Ln, TQ1 4TS), then walk 300 yards to the beach.

50.506112, -3.513082

THE FERRY BOAT INN, SHALDON

Dog-friendly pub next to Shaldon Beach.

4 Strand, Shaldon, TQ14 0DL
www.theferryboatinn.co.uk

THE STRAND CAFE, SHALDON

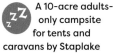

Savour cake, barista coffee or loose-leaf tea in a garden with delightful sea views.

1 Strand, Shaldon, TQ14 0DL
www.thestrandcafe
bistro.co.uk

HUNTERS LODGE CARAVAN AND CAMPING SITE, STARCROSS

A 10-acre adults-only campsite for tents and caravans by Staplake Brook, which empties into the River Exe 1,000 yards away. The Exe Estuary Cycle Trail runs through Starcross. A passenger ferry runs to Exmouth in summer.

Starcross, Exeter, EX6 8FL
www.hunterslodge-
camping.co.uk

Mackerel Cove, Maidencombe

Catch mackerel on rod and line with a feather, and barbecue them later on the beach. There's a wooded walk overhead, should you require shelter.

➤ **Find** Maidencombe Beach (see opposite), then walk ½ mile N to the beach.

50.511246, -3.510997

Labrador Bay, Shaldon

This isolated stretch of coast is famous for its Devon sandstone cliffs. Dolphins, basking sharks and nesting peregrine falcons can all be seen. Dartmoor ponies chew their way through scrub and woody growth; they're allowed to graze here to protect the grassland from being lost to scrub.

➤ **Find** The Ness Car Park (Shaldon, TQ14 0DP). Facing the water, turn R on to the SWCP and walk ⅔ mile to Smugglers Cove and Labrador Bay.

50.52956, -3.50199

The Ness, Shaldon

Look for ospreys in March and April on their migration N. Views to Shaldon.

➤ **Find** The Ness Car Park (Shaldon, TQ14 0DP), then walk 400 yards SE.

50.537536, -3.497029

Shaldon

THE THORNHILL, TEIGNMOUTH

 Elegant Georgian B&B situated by a sandy beach, with a heated public lido.

Mere Lane, Teignmouth, TQ14 8TA
www.thethornhill.co.uk

EAST CLIFF CAFE, TEIGNMOUTH

 Toasties and coffee on the SWCP.

The Sea Front, East Cliff Walk, Teignmouth, TQ14 8SH
east-cliff-cafe.edan.io

THE MOORINGS B&B, TEIGNMOUTH

 Great sea views and hospitality.

33 Teignmouth Rd, Teignmouth, TQ14 8UR
01626 770400

SALTY DOG KIOSKS, HOLCOMBE

 Ice cream, coffee and fresh sea air.

Smugglers' Ln, Holcombe, Dawlish, EX7 0JL
saltydogkiosks.business.site

THE SMUGGLERS INN, DAWLISH

 Pub famous for its 'Farmers Feast Carvery': a delicious roast consisting of three local meats and a minimum of five seasonal vegetables.

27 Teignmouth Rd, Dawlish, EX7 0LA
thesmugglersinn.net

Shaldon, River Teign

Take the foot ferry from Shaldon to Teignmouth. If there's no ferry, you can cross the bridge into Teignmouth.

➤ **Find** The Ness (see page 285), then walk 600 yards NW on the SWCP.

50.540449, -3.503554

Langstone Rock, Dawlish

Watch cormorants sunbathe on the red rock stacks.

➤ **Find** the car park next to Dawlish Station (EX7 0NF), then walk ½ mile S along the railway track FP.

50.592663, -3.442693

Dawlish Inner Warren

This stunning sand spit at the mouth of the River Exe is one of only two places in Britain where you can find the tiny Warren crocus in spring. Thousands of birds feed here and at the surrounding mudflats as part of their migratory stopovers. Look out for Sandwich and Arctic terns.

➤ **Find** Warren Golf Club (Dawlish Warren, Beach Rd, Dawlish, EX7 0NF), next to the large public car park and Dawlish Warren Station. Exit the car park at the bottom, heading E with your back to the railway line, towards the public toilets. Keep walking to the beach and then choose whether to walk along the sand or the FPs to Dawlish Warren Point 1⅓ miles away. Return along the point's NW shore for a view across the entire natural harbour.

50.605461, -3.435713

St Clement's Church, Powderham

Touch the brick and stone church next to the River Exe. It's worth the 2-mile hike N of the FP via Starcross station. Fields to the E of the church have been eroded by the tide. Good cycle path to Exeter.

➤ **Find** St Clement's Church (1 Church Rd, Powderham, EX6 8JJ). Facing the River Exe, turn L along the FP and walk riverside 1.4 miles for a delightful stop at the Turf Hotel right beside the water.

50.650396, -3.4546013

THE BEECHES B&B, DAWLISH

 B&B set on a no-through road with sea views to the rear and only a 10–15-min walk down the hill to the beach. There are sea views from some of the rooms.

15A Old Teignmouth Rd, Dawlish, EX7 0NJ
www.thebeechesbandb.co.uk

ROCCIA ROSSA CAFFE, DAWLISH

 Cafe and coffee shop located on the SWCP near Dawlish Warren.

SWCP, Dawlish, EX7 0NF
Facebook: @Roccia Rossa Caffe – Red Rock

LANGSTONE CLIFF HOTEL, DAWLISH

 Family-run hotel set in 19 acres of woodlands overlooking the Exe Estuary, and a short walk from sandy beaches and the Warren.

Mount Pleasant Rd, Dawlish Warren, Dawlish, EX7 0NA
www.langstone-hotel.co.uk

MOUNT PLEASANT INN, DAWLISH

 Traditional pub and lodgings beside the SWCP.

Mount Pleasant Rd, Dawlish Warren, Dawlish, EX7 0NA
www.mountpleasantinn.com

SANDAYS B&B, DAWLISH WARREN

 B&B on the Exe Estuary trail and the SWCP, a short walk to the beaches.

Warren Rd, Dawlish Warren, Dawlish, EX7 0PQ
sandays-devon.co.uk

Dawlish

Sandy Bay

SIDMOUTH

WILD THINGS TO DO BEFORE YOU DIE:

LISTEN to starling murmurations at dusk.
CATCH and cook mackerel.
SMELL green-winged orchids.
FORAGE for hazelnuts.
TASTE beach-brewed limpets and Alexanders.
TOUCH the Geoneedle.
TRAMP the red cliffs of Orcombe Point.
FIND the 'Frog Stone'.
SNORKEL Pinhay Bay.

THE ANCHOR INN, COCKWOOD

Pub overlooking the harbour and close to Cockwood's village green, which is home to Cockwood's famous geese.

Cockwood, EX6 8RA
www.anchorinn
cockwood.com

THE GALLEON INN, STARCROSS

Pub with rooms close to the station and riverside.

The Strand,
Starcross, EX6 8PR
www.galleoninn.co.uk

THE ATMOSPHERIC RESTAURANT, STARCROSS

Good choice of beers and a roaring fire. Located opposite the station.

The Strand,
Starcross, EX6 8PA
www.atmosphericpub
restaurant.co.uk

THE BEACH PUB, EXMOUTH

Pub next to Exmouth Marina, a few yards from the seafront.

Victoria Rd,
Exmouth, EX8 1DR
www.heavitreebrewery.
co.uk/pubs/the-beach-
hotel/

Exe Estuary

Starling murmurations at dusk and dawn over the Exe Estuary are best seen from the Topsham side of the River Exe or from the FP under the M5. Also look out for sand martins and avocets.

➤ **Find** the very end of Station Rd at the Lions Rest Eco Park (Exminster, EX6 8DZ). Facing the Exeter Canal, turn L on to the FP and walk 1 mile towards the M5 road bridge. Continue on under the bridge for a longer walk. Less than ⅓ mile from Station Rd, a ferry sometimes runs across the River Exe to Topsham, with several cafes along the shorefront.

50.684658, -3.474056

Starcross Jetty, Starcross

Ferry across the Exe Estuary to Exmouth.
➤ **Find** Starcross Car Park (Starcross, EX6 8PJ), then walk 400 yards S on the SWCP.

50.626814, -3.445593

Cockle Sands, Exmouth

Go at low tide and look out for the rare Cetti's warblers, as well as black-tailed godwits and wigeons.

➤ **Find** the car park (The Royal Ave, Exmouth, EX8 1BZ), 500 yards N of the SWCP ferry crossing, then walk another 400 yards along the East Devon Way to view the sands at low tide.

50.627746, -3.421336

Exmouth Beach

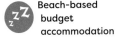

Pole Sand, Exmouth

Forage for limpets around the River Exe's rock pools at low tide.
➤ **Find** Queens Drive Echelon Car Park (Queen's Dr, Exmouth, EX8 2AY), then walk 500 yards E on the SWCP.

50.607495, -3.410011

Maer Rocks, Exmouth, River Exe

The red, red rock of the Maer. Touch it.
➤ **Find** the car park (339 Queen's Dr, Exmouth, EX8 2DB), then walk E 50 yards to the rocks.

50.609612, -3.394627

The Geoneedle, Exmouth

Landmark celebrating 180 million years (or so) of the Triassic, Jurassic and Cretaceous rock formations that make up this unique coastline. The Geoneedle is crafted from the many rocks that form the World Heritage coastline, with a 'Jurassic coast hopscotch' to enable walkers to jump through time from Triassic (red sandstone) to Cretaceous (limestone). Look for the tiny purple and white flowers of the rare bithynian vetch.
➤ **Find** Maer Rocks (see above), then walk E ⅔ mile to the Geoneedle.

50.607159, -3.387115

Orcombe Point, Exmouth

Walk the cliff around Orcombe Point. The rocks slant at a descending angle to Dorset, which means you can literally walk back through time over thousands of years as layer upon layer descends. The oldest rock layer is at Orcombe Point; the youngest at Old Harry Rocks 95 miles away.
➤ **Find** Maer Rocks (see above), then walk E 1 mile on the SWCP to the point.

50.606274, -3.384990

Sandy Bay, Exmouth

Look for purple flowers of rare green-winged orchids from late April until June.
➤ **Find** Orcombe Point (see above), then walk E ½ mile on the SWCP to Sandy Bay.

50.607500, -3.374782

Straight Point, Exmouth

Peregrine falcons hunt here. Kittiwakes nest on the red cliff ledges.
➤ **Find** Sandy Bay (see above), then walk 1 mile E on the SWCP to the point.

50.606933, -3.362133

SOUTH BEACH CAFE, EXMOUTH

Cliff top cafe over Sandy Bay Beach for food and views. It's a resort cafe, but it's open to the public.

SWCP, Devon Cliffs Holiday Parks, Sandy Bay, Exmouth, EX8 5BT
Facebook:
@South Beach Cafe

WEST END KIOSK, BUDLEIGH SALTERTON

Cuppas, ices and good views on the beach, at the bottom of Steamer Steps.

Cliff Rd, Budleigh Salterton, EX9 6JZ
Facebook:
@WestEndKioskBudleigh

LONGBOAT CAFE, BUDLEIGH SALTERTON

Beach cafe serving fresh Budleigh Salterton crab, cakes, snacks and locally sourced, award-winning Yarde Farm Devon Ice cream.

Marine Pde, Budleigh Salterton, EX9 9AL
www.longboatcafe.com

Otter Estuary

Budleigh Salterton

Touch the past. Find red sandstone rock and look for the white tube-shaped vertical lines. The fossil roots date from the Triassic period, 250 million years ago, when desert plants burrowed into the sand for water.

➤ **Find** Lime Kiln car park (Granary Ln, Budleigh Salterton, EX9 6JF), then walk 1 mile W to the cliffs.

50.625002, -3.336220

Otter Estuary, Budleigh Salterton

Listen for redshank, common sandpipers and curlews.

➤ **Find** Lime Kiln car park (Granary Ln, Budleigh Salterton, EX9 6JF), then walk 400 yards E to the estuary.

50.629983, -3.306857

Otter Ledge, Budleigh Salterton

Take a dip or a paddle. You might need a wetsuit even in summer: it's cold. The sun-baked red earth being eroded on the tide is 250 million years old. Find the red pebble mix still trapped in the red sandstone cliffs.

➤ **Find** the cliffs on the E side of Otter Estuary (see above).

50.627729, -3.306498

Ladram Rock, Otterton

Watch seabirds around the red sandstone stacks just offshore.

➤ **Find** Mutter's Moor Car Park (Peak Hill Rd, Sidmouth, EX10 0NW), then walk 500 yards down the lane to the SWCP. Turn R and walk W along the SWCP 2 miles W to the rock.

50.658913, -3.277966

THE LONG RANGE, BUDLEIGH SALTERTON

 Short stays and gardens with views over the Otter Valley.

5 Vales Rd, Budleigh Salterton, EX9 6HS
www.thelongrange hotel.co.uk

PEBBLES RESTAURANT, OTTERTON

 Restaurant with views over Ladram Bay and the sea.

Otterton, Budleigh Salterton, EX9 7BX
www.ladrambay.co.uk

High Peak, Otterton

Iron Age settlement surrounded by woodland.
> **Find** Ladram Rock (see opposite), then walk 1 mile NE on the SWCP.

50.666435, -3.270119

Sidmouth

Step in dinosaur footprints around wooded cliff face and beach. Fossils can sometimes be found around fallen boulders. The best views over the bay are from the old settlement site on High Peak (see above).
> **Find** Mutter's Moor Car Park (Peak Hill Rd, Sidmouth, EX10 0NW), then either cross the road and follow the FP opposite down to the cliff tops or walk down Peak Hill Rd ⅓ mile to the cliff top FP E (to the R). Access to the site is at low tide from the SWCP.

50.674901, -3.2573269

Salcombe Hill Cliff, Sidmouth

Watch fulmars glide between the views of N France, the Channel Islands and Portland Bill.
> **Find** Sidmouth seafront and walk E on the SWCP across the River Sid 3.4 miles to the cliff. Alternatively, walk the beach at low tide; make sure there's enough time to walk back and not get cut off by tide.

50.680536, -3.226034

PEOPLE OF THE PATH

The Beef Farmer, Little Dartmouth, South Devon

We graze the land around the path with placid breeds of bullock. They can be inquisitive. You should never slap a calf with your hand because they can kick and their legs are longer than your arm. And don't hit out with a walking stick. Just be assertive and push them back gently with a stick if they get too curious. They are intelligent, gentle animals who like routine.

THE CLOCK TOWER CAKERY & RESTAURANT, SIDMOUTH

Iconic tower on the beach serving breakfasts, lunches, cream teas and ... err ... cakes!

The Clock Tower, Connaught Gardens, Peak Hill Rd, Sidmouth, EX10 8RZ
www.clocktower
sidmouth.com

BEDFORD HOTEL, SIDMOUTH

Family-run hotel on Sidmouth seafront with views over Lyme Bay.

The Espl, Sidmouth, EX10 8NR
www.bedfordhotel
sidmouth.co.uk

ROYAL YORK & FAULKNER HOTEL, SIDMOUTH

Regency hotel with balconies offering views of Sidmouth Beach, Lyme Bay and the red-rock Jurassic cliffs.

The Espl, Sidmouth, EX10 8AZ
www.royalyorkhotel.co.uk

THE FOUNTAIN HEAD, BRANSCOMBE

Traditional pub set 700 yards back from the SWCP but worth the short trek. The food is great, especially the scallops.

Fountain Head House, Branscombe, EX12 3BG
www.fountainheadinn.com

Chapman's Rocks, Sidmouth

Find the 'Frog Stone', placed by a Royal Navy frigate helicopter on 10 April 1964. It looks, as the name suggests, like a frog...

➤ **Find** Salcombe Hill Cliff (see page 293), then walk E on the SWCP 700 yards to the rocks.

50.680607, -3.217366

Weston Mouth Beach, Sidmouth

Forage for Alexanders between February and September around the meadow of wild flowers beside the pebble beach.

➤ **Find** Chapman's Rocks (see above), then walk E on the SWCP 1½ miles to the underground spring.

50.684824, -3.184622

Weston Ebb, Sidmouth

A wooded cliff walk for when you need to take shelter.

➤ **Find** Weston Mouth Beach (see above), then walk ⅔ mile E on the SWCP.

50.684253, -3.168822

Berry Cliff Camp Hill Fort, Branscombe

See if you can see the remains of Berry Cliff Camp, an Iron Age hill fort. Three sides of the defensive bank and ditch are partially visible.

➤ **Find** Weston Mouth Beach (see above), then walk E on the SWCP 1½ miles to the fort. If you can get down to the beach, do so.

50.687530, -3.150510

Branscombe Down, Branscombe

Listen to grasshoppers around the grass top of Branscombe's red cliffs. Wood white butterflies feed here in the sunlit wooded areas.

➤ **Find** Berry Cliff Camp Hill Fort (see above), then walk E on the SWCP 600 yards.

50.688605, -3.144974

Branscombe

Stand aboard and touch the last relic here of the shipwrecked MSC *Napoli's* 14-tonne anchor. The cargo ship was grounded and controversially plundered in 2007.

➤ **Find** Branscombe Down (see above), then walk E on the SWCP 1 mile.

50.687650, -3.123841

GREAT SEASIDE B&B, BRANSCOMBE BEACH

 B&B in a 16th-century thatched farmhouse 200 yards from the beach with views over Lyme Bay. Double and family rooms are available.

Great Seaside Farm, Branscombe Vale Brewery, Branscombe, EX12 3DP
www.greatseaside.co.uk

SEA SHANTY BEACH CAFE, BRANSCOMBE BEACH

 Traditional food and drink, with an emphasis on seafood, beside the beach. Fresh crab is landed on the beach beside the cafe. Local ales come from the microbrewery nearby. Organic, free-range eggs are from Bulstone Springs farm. Salad and herbs are grown in the village. Try the home-made soup or sprats with bread and salad.

The Beach, Branscombe, EX12 3DP
Facebook: @ seashantybranscombe

ANCHOR INN, BEER

 Hotel and pub overlooking the bay of the village of Beer. Sea views from every room. Taste freshly caught fish as part of daily specials.

Fore St, Beer, EX12 3ET
www.greenekinginns.co.uk/hotels/anchor-inn/

Branscombe Mouth

Branscombe Mouth, Branscombe

Explore 1 mile of shingle beach, swim beside cliffs and paddle in pools of sea anemones.
➤ **Find** MSC *Napoli*'s anchor (see opposite), then walk E on the beach 200 yards.

50.687657, -3.122521

Hooken Beach, Beer

Deserted stone beach for mackerel fishing, and resting.
➤ **Find** Branscombe Mouth (see above), then walk ¾ mile E along the stone beach to Hooken Beach.

50.686042, -3.112122

The Pinnacles Cave, Beer

Visit at dusk to watch bats feeding on insects in summer. Climb to the chalk pillars at dawn to watch sunrise.
➤ **Find** Hooken Beach (see above), then walk ¼ mile E along the stone beach to the cave.

50.686471, -3.104445

Hooken Cliffs, Beer

Navigate between the chalk pinnacles spread along the cliff FP. Look down to the breathtaking views – this dramatic slope of woodland and white rock was formed by a landslide in 1790. Peregrine falcons hunt and nest here.
➤ **Find** Hooken Beach (see above), then look for a way up.

50.687566, -3.106477

Hooken Beach

THE DOLPHIN HOTEL, BEER

Rooms and locally caught seafood overlooking the beach.

Fore St, Beer, EX12 3EQ
www.dolphinhotel
beer.co.uk

CHAPPLE'S TEA HUT, BEER

All-day breakfast by the beach a few yards from the SWCP. Sandwiches, cakes, ice creams, main meals and hot and cold drinks are also available.

Beer, Seaton, EX12 3NE
Facebook:
@Chapples tea hut

Pound's Pool Beach, Beer

Once renowned as a wild smuggling centre, this beach is now dramatic for its cliffs, shingle beach and rock pools.

➤ **Find** Beer Head (see below), then walk S 600 yards on the SWCP to the beach.

50.688592, -3.094454

Arratt's Hill, Beer

Listen out for peregrine falcons. See where the red Triassic earth shifts to white chalk around Beer, at the mouth of the River Axe.

➤ **Find** Pound's Pool Beach (see above), then walk N 200 yards on the SWCP.

50.690754, -3.096965

Beer Head

Look for porpoises offshore. Walk and swim around Chalky Naze, off South Down Common. Hunt for ammonites on the beach around Hooken Cliff in sand and chalk. The walk down to the beach is steep.

➤ **Find** Beer Head Caravan Park (Common Hill, Beer, EX12 3AH), and the E Devon Council car park opposite. There are great views from here, but walk down towards the beach on to Little Ln and then R along the lane towards the SWCP and steep climbs to the beaches and rocks. FPs down are sometimes lost to erosion so you may need to keep walking S and W to Beer Head Point and then Hooken Beach.

50.69337, -3.09315

CLIFFSIDE CABIN, SEATON

Toasties, cuppas and chocolate brownies with cliff side views.

Seaton Hole Kiosk, Old Beer Rd, Seaton, EX12 2PX

THE HIDEAWAY, SEATON

An old ice-cream parlour, right on the promenade, for food, coffee and treats made using local, or-ganic ingredients

The Espl, Seaton, EX12 3TY www.thehideaway seaton.com

THE MARINERS HOTEL & RESTAURANT, SEATON

Seafront hotel and bistro with views over Lyme Bay, towards the chalk cliffs of Beer Head.

East Walk, Seaton, EX12 2NP www.marinershotel seaton.co.uk

River Ledge, Axmouth

Look for the hen harriers that hunt here during winter when they migrate from colder N England. Listen to freshwater springs trickling into the sea.

➤ **Find** The Orchard Rd Car Park (Beer Rd, Seaton, EX12 2PD). Walk S to the SWCP and then E ⅔ mile to Haven Cliff and then head S down to the low-tide beach and estuary.

50.701512, -3.054587

Haven Cliff, Axmouth

Naturists' beach. Isolated.

➤ **Find** River Ledge (see above), then walk 500 yards E along either the beach or the SWCP.

50.703076, -3.046131

Sparrowbush Ledge, Axmouth

This is one of the most deserted beaches along the S coast.

➤ **Find** Haven Cliff (see above), then walk 1 mile along the beach after high tide.

50.699934, -3.038402

The Landslip/Bindon Cliffs, Axmouth

Forage for hazelnuts in autumn. Look for roe deer that feed here.

➤ **Find** Sparrowbush Ledge (see above), then walk ½ mile E along the cliff.

50.701824, -3.027684

PEOPLE OF THE PATH

The Lookout, Prawle Point, South Devon

This is a wonderful piece of coastline. I enjoy looking at the different layers of prehistoric beach all the way up the hillside to the campsite at the top. I imagine what it was like when the sea waters lapped up there over the millenniums past, before the sea levels dropped so dramatically.

PEOPLE OF THE PATH

The Car Park Attendant, Mothecombe, South Devon

This is great place for bird watchers. Migrating ospreys feed on the run of fish when the trout and salmon are on. We had a sea eagle from the Isle of Wight last year. Peregrines nest along here, so you might see one.

Charton Undercliff, Lyme Regis

Coastal woodland on a shingle and sand cove. There are rock pools at low tide where you can forage for beach crabs and shrimps. Enjoy late-evening, low-tide BBQs over stone.

➤ **Find** Bindon Cliffs (see page 297), then walk 1½ miles E on the SWCP.

50.705664, -2.995504

Pinhay Bay, Uplyme

Forage for seaweed to eat raw or dry. The deep water and rocks along this sweeping cove and reef are perfect to snorkel. Best accessed from Lyme Regis at low tide. There are tree-lined cliffs at Ware or Pinhay. Find fish, ammonites and shell fossils on the beach, and in the rock and chalk.

➤ **Find** Monmouth Beach Car Park (Lyme Regis, DT7 3JN), then walk 1½ miles W on the SWCP.

50.71294, -2.96478

PEOPLE OF THE PATH

The Angler, Seaton, South Devon

Most fish are caught with a beach rod to the front of The Point Cafe. Mackerel start coming in June to feed on smaller fish. In July and August the water will literally seem to 'bubble' because there will be so many whitebait the mackerel can feed on.

Seaton Beach

DORSET

- - - - - - - - - - - - -

SCENT OF WINTER – the walkers
inhaled through their nostrils on the
climb up Chapel Hill. As the coast
slowly unfolded, they turned and
looked back without speaking. Gulls
circled on flying, white clouds over
Chesil Beach. The walkers carried
on towards St Catherine's Chapel. Both
singing snatches of tunes in between
breathlessness. A flask of coffee
in each bag.

Lyme Regis

LYME REGIS

WILD THINGS TO DO BEFORE YOU DIE:

STAND under an ammonite lamp post, in the fossil capital of England.

CATCH a glimpse of a giant sunfish.

LISTEN to swifts over Burton Bradstock.

SMELL the air on the highest cliff on the south coast.

WADE over honeycomb-shaped reef.

FORAGE for wild thyme.

VISIT the stone ruins of a 13th-century chapel.

WATCH bats hunt over collapsed cliffs.

COLLECT fossils on Monmouth Beach.

THE COBB ARMS, LYME REGIS

Pub overlooking the world-famous Cobb, with three en suite rooms and access to the Jurassic Coast. The restaurant and bar has a veranda overlooking the harbour and Lyme Bay.

Marine Pde,
Lyme Regis, DT7 3JF
www.thecobbarms.co.uk

ALEXANDRA HOTEL & RESTAURANT, LYME REGIS

With one of the best views in Dorset, this 25-bedroom hotel is set within an acre of private gardens with a grandstand view overlooking Lyme Bay.

Pound St,
Lyme Regis, DT7 3HZ
www.hotelalexandra.co.uk

Devonshire Head, Monmouth Beach

Feel the shell outline of fossil ammonites that fed and swam here millions of years ago. You'll need a hammer, safety glasses and a low tide.

➤ **Find** the RNLI Lyme Regis Lifeboat Station next to fishing trip boats at Cobb Harbour (Lyme Regis, DT7 3JJ). From the large beachside car park, facing the sea, walk R ¾ mile while exploring the beach. Keep walking an extra ¾ mile to reach Pinhay Bay.

50.71955, -2.94310

St Michael the Archangel, Lyme Regis

Cliff top church. The cemetery contains the grave of famed fossil finder Mary Anning.

➤ **Find** Church St, Lyme Regis, DT7 3DB

50.726270, -2.932153

Church Cliffs, Lyme Regis

Catch shrimps in your cupped hands from rock pools at low tide. Listen as the River Lym flows over the beach into the bay 200 yards W of the rocks.

➤ **Find** Lyme Regis Tourist Information Centre (Church St, Lyme Regis, DT7 3BS). Walk S to the beach and then E 150 yards to the cliffs on other side of the sea wall.

50.725121, -2.929882

The Spittles

TOM'S LYME REGIS, LYME REGIS

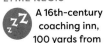 Family-run seafood restaurant on a seaside terrace.

Marine Pde,
Lyme Regis, DT7 3JQ
www.tomslymeregis.com

ROYAL LION HOTEL, LYME REGIS

A 16th-century coaching inn, 100 yards from the SWCP, with oak beams, wood panelling and an open fire.

60 Broad St,
Lyme Regis, DT7 3QF
royallionhotel.com

THE OLD MONMOUTH B&B, LYME REGIS

 16th-century Tudor-style B&B located 120 yards from the seafront.

12 Church St,
Lyme Regis, DT7 3BS
www.oldmonmouth.com

Lyme Regis, Lyme Bay

Feel the stones on the beach under your bare feet at the fossil capital of England. Even the lamp posts are shaped like ammonites. There are fossil shops, tours and museums.

> **Find** Charmouth Rd long-stay car park (Charmouth Rd, Lyme Regis, DT7 3DR), and walk down the wide steps 220 yards towards the concreted coast walk. Turn L and walk another 165 yards to the concrete staircase down on to the beach. Walk on another 220 yards for the better finds. For wheelchair access to the SWCP and great views, find Cobb Gate Car Park (Marine Pde, Lyme Regis, DT7 3QD).

50.72957, -2.92715

The Spittles, Lyme Regis

Look up to avoid straying too close to rock and mudslides. This isolated beach for fossil hunting is just ½ mile W of Lyme Regis. Take care not to get cut off by the tide.

> **Find** Lyme Regis Tourist Information Centre (Church St, Lyme Regis, DT7 3BS). Walk S to the beach and then E ½ mile to the cliffs on the other side of the sea wall. Beware the incoming tide.

50.731314, -2.921763

Timber Hill, Lyme Regis

Smell the changing scent of wooded sea cliff during sun or rain, 150 yards above water, as the SWCP leaves the shoreline. Somewhere to shelter.

> **Find** Lyme Regis Football Club (Charmouth Rd, DT7 3DW), then follow the SWCP N 500 yards where it forks once into the woodland. Leave the SWCP at the first fork L to follow the FP into the heart of the pine and broadleaf woodland.

50.735485, -2.923801

PEOPLE OF THE PATH

The Paddle Boarder, South Beach, Studland, Dorset

There are two types of seahorse that can be found here if you snorkel. The seaweed is also good to eat, either raw or cooked. It's all edible.

Charmouth

THE ROYAL OAK, CHARMOUTH

 B&B and pub serving food, 330 yards from the famous fossil beach.

The St, Charmouth, DT6 6PE
royaloakcharmouth.co.uk

 ## Canary Ledges, Lyme Regis

Look up for rockfalls at this fossil beach, similar to The Spittles, with access from Charmouth. Beware of dangers as noted above. High tides reveal fossils in the mud that can be found among the shingle and larger stones. Explore Bar Ledges rocks a few yards to the E at low tide.

➤ **Find** The Spittles (see page 305), then walk 500 yards E along the beach.

50.732124, -2.916363

 ## Black Ven, Charmouth

Watch bats at dusk fly about these collapsed cliffs, E of Lyme Regis. Relax in the sunshine by sitting still. You might even see a common lizard.

➤ **Find** the beach car park (Lower Sea Ln, Charmouth, DT6 6LS). Walk S on to the beach and turn R facing the water, then walk W along the shore ½ mile after high tide as limited or no access at full tide. Beware the incoming tide.

50.733809, -2.910275

 ## Mouth Rocks, Charmouth

Listen cliff side as the River Char trickles or gushes, depending on rain or season, into the sea at Charmouth. There's gravel beach paddling, swimming and fossils.

➤ **Find** the beach car park (Lower Sea Ln, Charmouth, DT6 6LS), then walk to the shore. Turn L facing the water and walk 100 yards E to where the river enters the sea. Cross the river bridge. After the bridge, ignore the cliff walk and move on to the beach for up to 1 mile to find the quietest parts and the best finds.

50.733266, -2.899685

Cain's Folly, Stanton St Gabriel

Touch sabellaria reef, also known as honeycomb worm, along the foreshore.

> Find Mouth Rocks (see opposite), then walk E along the beach ½ mile. Paddle the surf after high tide and beware incoming water after low tide.

50.731853, -2.882977

Broom Cliff, Stanton St Gabriel

Look out for common lizards and fossils.

> Find Stonebarrow NT Car Park (Stonebarrow Ln, Charmouth, DT6 6SD). Find the SWCP 50 yards W of the car park and follow it SE to Westhay Farm. Follow the FP 1½ miles E to the cliff.

50.729234, -2.857355

St Gabriel's Mouth and Ledge, Stanton St Gabriel

Grill barbecued mackerel caught on a simple beach rod of feathers. Fish opposite the freshwater river stream.

> Find Broom Cliff (see above), then follow the SWCP 100 yards E before taking the FP right and down to the beach.

50.726446, -2.857142

The Cove/Cann Harbour, Stanton St Gabriel

Feel the rush of water over your skin or under a wetsuit, while snorkelling in the secluded bays either side of Wear Cliffs. Catch a glimpse of sea bass in the early morning. Fish with silver or sand eel lures.

> Find St Gabriel's Mouth and Ledge (see above), then walk E on the SWCP ½ mile to Shorne Cliff and the narrow FPs down to the beach.

50.723103, -2.844536

PEOPLE OF THE PATH

The National Trust ranger, Shell Beach, Studland, Dorset

Look out for tiger beetles around the beach. They get their name because they hunt down an ant like a tiger.

EYPE HOUSE CARAVAN & CAMPING PARK, EYPE

Campsite on the SWCP for walkers and vans, with incredible views over Eype Mouth. Choice of static caravans, camping and log pods.

Mount Ln, Eype, DT6 6AL
www.eypehouse.co.uk

WINDY CORNER CAFE, WEST BAY

Family-run cafe for coffee and cakes.

Quayside, West Bay, DT6 4GZ
Facebook: @Windy Corner Cafe

WATCH HOUSE CAFE, WEST BAY

Cafe with a wood-fired pizza oven, freshly cooked pasta and a Hive Cafe micro-bakery cake counter beside West Bay Beach.

East Beach,
West Bay, DT6 4EN
www.watchhouse cafe.co.uk

THE BRIDPORT ARMS, WEST BAY

Rooms, drinks and food, right on the beach by West Bay Harbour. As seen in the ITV drama series *Broadchurch*.

West Bay, DT6 4EN
thebridportarms.co.uk

Golden Cap, Stanton St Gabriel

Inhale the sea air on the highest cliff on the S coast. There are stunning views above the ruin of St Gabriel's Chapel (see below) over Lyme Bay to Dartmoor. Scoop up ammonites from the beach on the way into Seatown. Listen for the sound of the stonechat, which gets it name from its chirp, which sounds like two pebbles being banged together.

➤ **Find** the Eype House Caravan & Camping Park (see left) and keep on to the bottom of the lane to the beach car park. Facing the sea, turn R and walk 1 mile to Golden Cap. Alternatively, walk down on to the beach. Beware incoming tides.

50.726376, -2.841311

St Gabriel's Chapel, Stanton St Gabriel

Discover the remnants of a ghost town. Touch the stone ruin of this 13th-century chapel set a few yards back from the SWCP. It was built on a former Saxon settlement to serve the hamlet, which is no more.

➤ **Find** Golden Cap (see above), then circle up and over on the FP N of the ruin. The FPs are 200 yards E and W of the Cap.

50.727854, -2.844326

Doghouse Hill, Chideock

Feel the air around one of the earliest settlements found in England – believed to date back more than 10,000 years to the Mesolithic Age. Pottery decorated with fingernail impressions has been found here.

➤ **Find** Seatown Car Park (Bridport, DT6 6JU), then walk ⅔ mile E on the SWCP.

50.720575, -2.806682

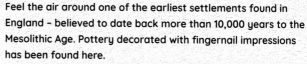

East Ebb Cove, Chideock

Magical deserted cove and shingle beaches.

➤ **Find** Seatown Car Park (Seatown, DT6 6JU), then walk E on the SWCP ½ mile to the cove via Ridge Cliff.

50.718645, -2.805515

Thorncombe Beacon, Symondsbury

Inhale sea air and views of the Jurassic Coast and Portland Bill, almost 2 miles E of Golden Cap. The beacon was one of many placed as part of a foreign invasion warning system.

➤ **Find** East Ebb Cove (see above), then walk ½ mile E on the SWCP to the beacon.

50.719503, -2.797531

THE WEST BAY HOTEL, WEST BAY

 Serving since 1739. Fine ales in the beamed bar and restaurant or the gardens a few yards from the SWCP. Ask for a room with a sea view.
3 Station Rd,
West Bay, DT6 4EW
wdlh.co.uk/plan-your-holiday/location/the-west-bay/

Eype Mouth Ford, Eype

Listen as fresh water enters the sea. Pick and chew dog rose petals from further along the beach. Road access is shocking so arrive before 5am in the summer season.

➤ **Find** Eype Beach car park (Eype, DT6 6AL), then walk 150 yards S and E to the ford.

50.712824, -2.773041

West Cliff, Eype

Taste freshly caught bass cooked on a portable stove. Look for fossils and rock pool wildlife while listening to buzzards mewing overhead. An unusual number of different blackbirds (three) sing at dusk around where the cliffs have fallen.

➤ **Find** Eype Mouth Ford (see above), then walk ½ mile E to the cliffs.

50.712824, -2.773041

East Cliff, Burton Bradstock

Listen to swifts high overhead. Keep looking for massive sunfish between here and Chesil Beach (see page 317).

➤ **Find** Quayside Car Park (Pier Tce, West Bay, DT6 4ER), then walk ⅔ mile E on the SWCP.

50.706942, -2.752439

Burton Bradstock

THE SEASIDE BOARDING HOUSE, BURTON BRADSTOCK

 Hotel, restaurant and bar overlooking the sweep of Lyme Bay.
Cliff Rd, Burton Bradstock, DT6 4RB

HIVE BEACH CAFE, BURTON BRADSTOCK

 Local seafood, home-made cakes and cuppas right on the beach at Burton Bradstock.
Beach Rd, Burton Bradstock, DT6 4RF
www.hivebeachcafe.co.uk

Burton Freshwater, Burton Bradstock

Feel the cool water underfoot as it enters the sea. Peregrine falcons hunt smaller seabirds here at dawn and dusk, close to where they nest along the cliffs.

➤ **Find** East Cliff (see page 309), then walk ⅔ mile E on the SWCP.

50.702743, -2.740504

Burton Cliff, Burton Bradstock

Sit down by purple thrift and yellow flowers of pea-like bird's-foot trefoil to look for the elusive Lulworth skipper butterfly. It's small and looks like a shaving of mahogany wood.

➤ **Find** Burton Freshwater (see above), then walk ½ mile E to the cliff.

50.699459, -2.733856

Burton Beach, Burton Bradstock

Sunglasses are needed to shield your eyes from the golden glow of Burton Cliff. Bridport sand lights up in sunshine thanks to nature's unique mixture of hard- and soft-layered rock – alchemy in action.

➤ **Find** Burton Cliff (see above), then walk 400 yards E to the beach.

50.697068, -2.726301

Burton Bradstock, Lyme Bay

Feel fossilised shark fins, shells and ammonites. Cliff falls leave the foreshore scattered with finds.

➤ **Find** the Hive Beach Cafe (see left). From the beachside car park, walk L a few yards towards the chalk cliffs. Keep going for ¾ mile along the beach to reach the beautiful Cogden Beach (see page 314).

50.69608, -2.72253

PEOPLE OF THE PATH

The Campaigner, Shell Beach, Studland, Dorset

Be aware of how tides are rising and eroding the coast.

Hive Beach, Burton Bradstock

Snorkel rocks and marine life from shingle with sandstone cliffs as a backdrop, at the long N entrance to Chesil Beach (see page 317). Busy in summer. Barbecue bass on this part of Chesil Beach. Tens of thousands of mackerel and bass breed here in summer.
➤ **Find** Burton Bradstock Hive Beach NT Car Park (Beach Rd, Burton Bradstock, DT6 4RF), then walk down on to the beach. Walk E 500 yards for quieter sections of beach.

50.695601, -2.721034

Bind Barrow, Burton Bradstock

Feel the past at this Bronze Age burial mound. Smell the scent of wild thyme. Look for pyramid and bee orchids and blue butterflies on yellow wort.
➤ **Find** Hive Beach (see above), then walk over the cliff top 200 yards.

50.696702, -2.717621

West Cliff

WEST BEXINGTON

WILD THINGS TO DO BEFORE YOU DIE:

TRAMP one of the longest stone spits in England.

TASTE a takeaway breakfast on St Catherine's Chapel mount.

LISTEN to mute swans at Abbotsbury.

FORAGE for sea kale.

PADDLE the fleet to Chesil Beach.

CATCH a glimpse of an adder.

LOOK for rare sea peas.

WATCH for porpoises.

SHADE under a tamarisk bush.

Cogden Beach, Burton Bradstock

Chew on sweet gorse and hawthorn flowers on your way down to the water, before foraging sea kale on the deserted pebble beach.

➤ **Find** Burton Bradstock Hive Beach NT Car Park (Beach Rd, Burton Bradstock, DT6 4RF), then walk 1 mile E to the beach on the SWCP.

50.691048, -2.708399

Burton Mere, Burton Bradstock

Listen to grasshoppers and warblers around the reed bed while identifying as many May flowers as possible.

➤ **Find** Cogden Beach (see above), then walk ½ mile E on the SWCP to Mere.

50.687838, -2.695168

West Bexington Nature Reserve, Puncknowle

Look for adders in spring around the beach edges. Fry dandelion flowers in oil over a portable stove.

➤ **Find** The Club House (see left) looking out on to the beach. From the beach car park, facing the sea, turn R and walk 330 yards to the reserve. Several FPs lead up from the beach around the pools.

50.678918, -2.672233

Chesil Beach E of Abbotsbury, Abbotsbury

A mass of plants grows here. Find sea holly and rare sea pea on the shingle. Blue holly flowers bloom from July to September, and there are mats of white-flowering sea campion. Look for yellow horned poppies flowering in June to brighten up the dullest day. They only flower by the beach, the yellow version of the red that blooms mostly inland. The ancients used the plant as a herb and the root was used to cure bruising.

➤ **Find** Abbotsbury Beach (see below), then walk along the shingle a few hundred yards.

50.660314, -2.628459

Abbotsbury Beach, Abbotsbury

Feel the shade under tamarisk over pebble beach on a hot summer's day. Catch mackerel at low tide ready to be cooked over a camp stove, in mustard and nettle tips.

➤ **Find** the beach car park (Abbotsbury, DT3 4LA), then walk on to the beach.

50.656985, -2.618893

St Catherine's Chapel, Abbotsbury

Stroke and feel the smooth vein on the back of dandelion leaf, while taking in the chapel views. It's a special place to enjoy a packed breakfast while sitting cross-legged in the grass and daisies.

➤ **Find** the car park off Swan Ln (Abbotsbury, DT3 4JH). Walk E on the SWCP 500 yards and then follow the trail N 300 yards up to the chapel.

50.661642, -2.606247

Abbotsbury Swannery, Abbotsbury

Listen to hundreds of mute swans at Abbotsbury Swannery. Walk around the trails for some of the best views along the N shore of the West Fleet.

➤ **Find** New Barn Rd, Abbotsbury, DT3 4JG

50.655367, -2.602224

Wyke Wood, Langton Herring

Walk the tree line at dusk in midsummer to see pipistrelle bats feed on flies. There's plenty of late-afternoon shade in which to sit, rest and watch dragonflies hunt the same insects before the bats take over as the sun vanishes.

➤ **Find** Abbotsbury Swannery (see above), then walk 2½ miles E on the SWCP to West Fleet shore.

50.634380, -2.560052

Clay Hard Point, Langton Herring

Paddle the shallows around the hard. Boats launch from the shore of West Fleet, and it's also ideal for launching a packraft, 500 yards N of Langton Slipway (see page 316).

➤ **Find** Wyke Wood (see above), then walk 1 mile S on the SWCP to West Fleet shore.

50.634380, -2.560052

Abbotsbury Swannery

EAST FLEET FARM TOURING PARK & CAMPING SHOP, CHICKERELL

Campsite for tents and caravans on a 20-acre organic farm, beside the shores of the vast lagoon overlooking Chesil Beach (see opposite). There's a decent pub and restaurant.

Fleet Ln,
Chickerell, DT3 4DW
www.eastfleet.co.uk

MOONFLEET MANOR, WEYMOUTH

A manor estate linked to a novel about smuggling and the ghost of Col 'Blackbeard' Mohune, who is said to still haunt the local churchyard. It's all fiction of course – ahem! – apart from the name of the original owners, the Mohune family. To explore this wonderful piece of coast and estate, choose either an afternoon tea of a luxury night or two in a colonial-feel room. Dog friendly.

Fleet Rd,
Weymouth, DT3 4ED
www.moonfleet
manorhotel.co.uk

Langton Hive Point and Slipway, Langton Herring

Paddle around the old crossing point over the West Fleet to Chesil Beach (see opposite), traditionally used by fishermen.

➤ **Find** Clay Hard Point (see page 315), then walk 500 yards S on the SWCP to the slipway.

50.630668, -2.558000

Herbury, Langton Herring

Look for merlins hunting over the small peninsula jutting out into the Fleet around Gore Cove's NE rim.

➤ **Find** Langton Slipway (see above), then walk 1 mile E and S on the SWCP to the slipway.

50.626218, -2.548084

Gore Cove, Langton Herring

Sit down in shingle around the Fleet lagoon's smallest inlet cove, behind Chesil Beach (see opposite).

➤ **Find** Herbury (see above), then walk 300 yards S on the SWCP to the cove.

50.626218, -2.548084

East Fleet Church, Fleet

Pick and eat new bramble tip stems from around the church edge. Scrape the soft thorns off with a knife. Keep the leaves for tea. The storm in 1824 destroyed most of the building, leaving just the chancel.

➤ **Find** Gore Cove (see above), then walk 1²/₃ miles E on the SWCP to the church ruin.

50.618970, -2.517004

Butterstreet Cove, Chickerell

One of the largest coves on the Fleet. Often visited by whooper swans.

➤ **Find** East Fleet Church (see above), then walk S on the SWCP ½ mile.

50.612192, -2.503995

The Fleet, Wyke Regis

Kayak or paddle the most important brackish lake in England. The Fleet beach was formed 6,000 years ago by rising tides that severed 18½ miles of stone pebble from the mainland, creating a magical lagoon.

➤ **Find** Butterstreet Cove (see above), then walk S 200 yards on the SWCP.

50.610514, -2.514239

Pirates Cove, Wyke Regis

Chesil Beach (see below) is severed from the mainland by a tidal lagoon, known as the Fleet, part of which includes Pirates Cove. There's low-tide access to a fossil-rich beach and safer (but rarely safe) swimming overlooking Chesil Beach.

> **Find** Martleaves Farm Campsite (see left). A FP runs down the R side of the campsite. Follow the FP for ¼ mile, with the camp on your L, to where it meets the SWCP and beaches L and R.

50.591821, -2.485627

Chesil Beach, Wyke Regis

Named 'Dead Man's Bay' by Thomas Hardy, Chesil Beach is one of England's most remarkable natural wonders. The shingle beach is 18 miles long, 600ft wide, and 50ft high. See little terns in April – the second-rarest breeding sea bird in the UK, with fewer than 2,000 breeding pairs. The best way to see the birds is from the Fleet Explorer and there are special tern-watching trips running as well.

> **Find** the Fine Foundation Chesil Beach Centre (Portland Beach Rd, Portland, DT4 9XE) and the pay-and-display car park. The boardwalk next to the Centre provides easy access to the beach. From here, it's possible to walk 8 miles along the beach to Abbotsbury Swannery (see page 315), on the site of an old monastery. Take care of rising tides and exposure.

50.57843, -2.46975

Wallsend Cove

CHESIL CHIPPIE, PORTLAND

 Traditional chippy that does what it says on the label.

1a Olde Stables, Victoria Square Roundabout, Portland, DT5 1BJ
www.chesilchippie.co.uk

THE LITTLE SHIP PUB, PORTLAND

 Pub grub and Chesil hospitality.
Try out the burgers.

Victoria Square, Portland, DT5 1AL
Facebook: @TheLittleShippub

THE COVE HOUSE INN, CHISWELL

 Right beside Chesil Beach with views over Portland. Locally caught fish and seafood include Portland crab and seared scallops. Freshly ground coffee.

91 Chiswell, Portland, DT5 1AW
thecovehouseinn.co.uk

QUIDDLES CAFE BEACH BAR, CHISWELL

 A small celebration of seafood and hot drinks, on the promenade overlooking the start of Chesil Beach.

The Espl, Chiswell, Portland, DT5 1LN
Facebook: @Quiddlesbeachcafe16

West Cliff, Portland

Look for porpoises from the top of West Cliff back along Chesil Beach and the Fleet Lagoon. Taste mallow flowers when they bloom from June to October – the leaves can be boiled.

➤ **Find** St George's Church (West St, Portland, DT5 2JP), then walk on the FP alongside the N side of the church and follow the FP E and N until it meets the SWCP. The cliff is ⅔ mile from the church.

50.552507, -2.448642

Mutton Cove, Portland

Look out for migrating ospreys in spring and autumn. There may be guillemots and cormorants, too.

➤ **Find** West Cliff (see above), then walk S on the SWCP 1½ miles.

50.539406, -2.454332

Pulpit Rock

PEOPLE OF THE PATH

The Rock Climbers, Portland Point, Dorset

We climb to stay fit and to help heal any injuries we have. We don't do more than a few feet. But we put crash mats down so we can practise more difficult climbs at low level. This is one of the best places for finding unique rock climbs.

WEYMOUTH

SWIM with spiny seahorses.

CATCH a glimpse of starling murmurations over Weymouth Bay.

SMELL wild garlic around Furzy Cliff.

LISTEN to the Portland blow hole.

VISIT a pirates' graveyard.

TOUCH fossils around Pulpit Rock.

TRAMP the walls of the Verne Citadel prison.

WATCH peregrines exchange food mid air as part of displays.

FISH for wrasse around Portland Bill.

PORTLAND BUNKHOUSE, PORTLAND

 Bunk-style accommodation with spectacular views from the top of Portland Bill. It also provides free tea and a fully equipped kitchen.

Bunkhouse, Portland Bill Rd, Portland, DT5 2JT
www.portlandbunk
house.com

THE PULPIT INN, SOUTHWELL

 Take in the views from Portland while sharing a drink or eats or staying in one of the rooms.

Portland Bill,
Southwell, DT5 2JT
the-pulpit-inn.
dorsethotels.net/en/

THE LOBSTER POT, PORTLAND

 Great food right next to the famous Portland Bill Lighthouse. Family-run business, famous for fresh locally-caught crab and Dorset cream teas. The owners claim to have an almost fanatical obsession with creating the perfect chips!

Portland Bill Rd, Portland,
DT5 2JT
www.lobsterpotrestaurant
portland.co.uk

Portland Obelisk

 ## Blow Hole, Portland

Famous. Listen … it blows hard at high tide.
➤ **Find** the car park (Portland Bill Rd, Portland, DT5 2JT), then walk 500 yards E to the hole on the cliff side.

50.518188, -2.459863

 ## Pulpit Rock and White Hole, Portland

Touch fossils in rock around the flat platforms and white wash constantly worn by waves. Best seen when it's rough.
➤ **Find** the car park (Portland Bill Rd, Portland, DT5 2JT), then walk S 400 yards to the rock.

50.514115, -2.459252

 ## Portland Bill, Portland

Fish for bass, mackerel, conger eel and wrasse in June and July.
➤ **Find** Pulpit Rock (see above), then walk 300 yards E.

50.513015, -2.456696

 ## Cave Hole, Portland

Hikers carrying mattresses are in fact … climbers. They only need to climb 3.3 yards at most over their crash mats in order to gain fitness and practise their climbing skills. They can be seen here, and all around the island hanging from rock arches.
➤ **Find** Portland Bill Obelisk (50.513279, -2.456126), then walk 1 mile NE on the SWCP to the cave hole.

50.520188, -2.443606

FISHERMAN'S SELF-CATERING COTTAGE, PORTLAND

 Classic holiday let close to Portland Bill and Church Ope Cove.

75 Southwell Rd, Portland, DT5 2JT
portlandcottages.co.uk

PORTLAND BILL CAMPING, PORTLAND

 Climb the 153 steps for great views.

Portland Bill Rd, Portland, DT5 2JT
portland-bill-camping.
business.site

EIGHT KINGS, PORTLAND

Place for a pint, cuppa or roast 300 yards from the SWCP.

40 Southwell Rd, Portland, DT5 2DP
www.eightkingsportland.
co.uk/index

Sand Holes, Portland

Look out for lizards bathing in the midday sunshine on the altar-like rock from April between Sand Holes and Cave Hole. They're usually quick but become sluggish when the sun goes in.

> **Find** Cave Hole (see opposite), then walk N on the SWCP 500 yards to the hole.

50.523927, -2.440796

Freshwater Bay, Portland

Find a way down from the FP to the bay, choosing different routes at different times. Forage for kelp to chew or dry.

> **Find** Sand Holes (see above), then walk ⅔ mile N on the SWCP to the bay.

50.529391, -2.437504

Southwell Landslip, Portland

Watch peregrine falcons exchange food in mid air. Parent birds pass prey to each other as part of their courtship ritual.

> **Find** the car park off Southwell Rd (Portland, DT5 2EG), and, facing the road, turn right on the SWCP and walk NE 400 yards to where the FP meets the cliff.

50.534626, -2.431105

Portland Museum, Portland

This museum is located just above Church Ope Cove (see page 324) and provides information on smuggling and shipwrecks.

> **Find** 217 Wakeham, Easton, Portland, DT5 1HS

50.540368, -2.430114

PEOPLE OF THE PATH

**The Singer,
St Catherine's Chapel,
Chapel Hill**

Sing when you walk. People will not think you are mad. They will want to be you. Singing will help your breathing as you walk.

Church Ope Cove

THE JAILHOUSE CAFE, PORTLAND

Staffed by prisoners, this cafe has views over Weymouth Bay and Portland Harbour.

HMP The Verne, Portland, DT5 1EQ
jailhousecafe.co.uk

CRABBERS' WHARF, CASTLETOWN

Self-catering cabins with sea views over Portland Harbour and Weymouth. The Wharf has its own Tourist Information Centre on the ground floor. A ferry service runs from April to October (weather permitting) to Weymouth.

Castletown, Portland, DT5 1BD
www.crabberswharf.co.uk

THE BOAT THAT ROCKS, PORTLAND

Marina-side restaurant and outdoor bar, which hosts regular live music events in summer.

Portland Marina, 7 Hamm Beach Rd, Portland, DT5 1DX
tbtr.co.uk

Church Ope Cove, Portland

Iconic pirates' graveyard in the shadow of a castle ruin (no access, but good for photos). A steep pebble FP leads though trees to the stone cove encircled by beach huts. It's full of fossils and calm. Access is difficult because of the rocks.

➤ **Find** Portland Museum (see page 323). The museum has a car park 88 yards along Pennsylvania Rd, on the R, under trees. Walk back to the museum and turn R into Church Ope Rd. Follow the lane all the way to Rufus Castle (see below) and the SWCP 220 yards away. Turn R along the FP, then walk another 110 yards to get down on to the cove. Walk back into the trees to explore the ruin of Portland's first parish church, St Andrew's Church.

50.53731, -2.42884

Rufus Castle, Portland

These are just the remains of the 15th-century Rufus Castle. Look for the broadleaf plantain that's common around the ruin. Pick some leaves, either to eat or to make into a poultice that treats insect bites and even broken skin wounds.

➤ **Find** Church Ope car park (Pennsylvania Rd, Portland, DT5 1HT), cross the road and then turn L and then R on to the SWCP. Walk 300 yards E to the remains.

50.539553, -2.426961

Penn's Weare, Portland

Explore this deserted boulder beach by leaving the SWCP after Rufus Castle (see above), then following the coastal FP. It's spookily quiet. There's low-tide fishing.

➤ **Find** Rufus Castle (see above), then look for the FP that runs around the N edge of Church Ope Cove (see above). There are good views over the cove before the FP leads down to a rocky and tricky FP that can be used to find the deserted stone beach.

50.540808, -2.421273

SANDSFOOT CAFE, WEYMOUTH

Peaceful cafe inside the grounds of Sandsfoot Castle (see page 326) gardens, with harbour views.

39 Old Castle Rd, Weymouth, DT4 8QE www.sandsfootcastle. org.uk

STONE PIER CAFE, WEYMOUTH

Toasties and crab sandwiches with unrivalled views next to Weymouth's old stone pier.

Weymouth Harbour, Nothe Pde, Weymouth, DT4 8TX Facebook: @Stonepier cafeWeymouth

THE SHIP INN, WEYMOUTH

Eat while watching the boats come into the harbour. Steak pie and hand-battered fish and chips are among the favourites.

Custom House Quay, Weymouth, DT4 8BE www.shipweymouth.co.uk

ROCKFISH WEYMOUTH, WEYMOUTH

Seafood restaurant for fresh, local fish either landed each day from the boat *Rockfisher* or bought from Brixham Fish Market.

48–49 The Espl, Weymouth, DT4 8DQ therockfish.co.uk

Grove Cliff, Portland

Look for guillemots, fulmars and kittiwakes, which nest here in spring.

> **Find** Penn's Weare (see opposite), then keep following the FP 400 yards until it eventually turns up the cliff to rejoin the SWCP. Some scrambling may be needed.

50.544257, -2.419630

The East Weares, Portland

Listen for feral goats that feed on the scrub beneath and around the steep cliffs. Look for rare silver-studded blue butterflies in spring. Portland is one of the best sites around the SWCP for butterflies, with more than half of all species (54) found here.

> **Find** where the Grove Cliff FP joins the SWCP and walk N ½ mile to the HM Young Offenders Institution (104 Grove Rd, Portland, DT5 1DL). After the HM site, take the FP 500 yards down to Folly Pier.

50.553838, -2.417871

The Grove Quarry, Portland

Explore, climb and touch the abandoned boulders of Grove Quarry. This 'rock' theatre was worked by convicts from 1848. They excavated 1,500 tones of Portland Stone a day to build the island's breakwater and harbour. Portland remains one of the largest man-made harbours in the world.

> **Find** New Ground Car Park (off Yates Rd, Portland, DT5 1LQ), then walk 300 yards SE on any of the many FPs.

50.554053, -2.433471

The Verne, Portland

Admire the impressive architecture of the Verne Citadel. Now used as a prison, the citadel was designed by Captain W Crossman of the Royal Engineers and enclosed an area of 56 acres on the highest point of Portland. Work began in the mid-1800s and the Great Verne Ditch took 30 years to complete. Kestrels nest here.

> **Find** New Ground Car Park (off Yates Rd, Portland, DT5 1LQ), then facing Yates Rd, turn R and walk 400 yards E to the prison.

50.559544, -2.434203

Portland Castle, Castletown

One of Henry VIII's important coastal forts, this castle was built to protect against French and Spanish invasion. It overlooks Portland Harbour.

> **Find** Liberty Rd, Castletown, DT5 1AZ.

50.56825 -2.44670

ROYAL HOTEL WEYMOUTH, WEYMOUTH

Dog-friendly hotel with 71 bedrooms, a bar and a games room, near the beach.

90–91 The Espl, Weymouth, DT4 7AX bespokehotels.com/royal-weymouth-hotel

WEYMOUTH BAY HOTEL, WEYMOUTH

Good views, next to the beach, with parking.

107 The Espl, Weymouth, DT4 7EE weymouth-bay-hotel.business.site

PREMIER HOTEL, WEYMOUTH

B&B with single and double rooms, close to the beach, esplanade and marina.

121 Brunswick Tce, Weymouth, DT4 7EP www.thepremierhotel.co.uk

JURASSIC ROCKS CAFE, WEYMOUTH

Gets busy in summer but a nice snack stopover if the chairs and queues are down.

SWCP, Weymouth, DT4 7SN www.jurassicrockscafe.co.uk

Merchants' Railway, Portland

This disused track now used as a FP provides incredible views to Portland Harbour and the cliffs of Purbeck. Portland Harbour is very sheltered and therefore an ideal home for the National Sailing Centre. It was also a natural choice as the venue for the sailing in the Olympics of 2012.

➤ **Find** The Verne (see page 325), then walk clockwise on the SWCP 700 yards to the top of the hill via steps.

50.562959, -2.440988

Sandsfoot Castle, Weymouth

16th-century castle ruins with gardens and a tea cabin (see page 325). The remains contain fragments of medieval stone from Bindon Abbey at Wool.

➤ **Find** 39 Old Castle Rd, Weymouth, DT4 8QE.

50.354812, -2.274140

Weymouth Espl, Weymouth

Swim the bay. Look for dolphins offshore, and starling murmurations at dusk in winter just before they roost for the night.

➤ **Find** Royal Hotel Weymouth (see above left), then walk down to the beach and 200 yards N towards the pier.

50.624347, -2.443688

Lodmoor Nature Reserve, Weymouth

Listen for bearded tits and Cetti's warblers in the reed beds. One of the largest common tern colonies is here.

➤ **Find** Lodmoor Car Park (off B3155, Weymouth, DT4 7SX), walk E on to the seafront SWCP and follow the FP NE 600 yards to the reserve the other side of the road.

50.628221, -2.441075

TOP CAT CAFE, WEYMOUTH

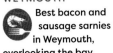

Best bacon and sausage sarnies in Weymouth, overlooking the bay.

Preston Rd Beach Kiosk, Weymouth, DT4 7SX
top-cat-cafe.edan.io

OASIS, WEYMOUTH

Stylish cafe bar with sea views for light snacks or hearty meals, inside or out.

Overcombe Corner, Bowleaze Coveway, Weymouth, DT3 6PN
www.cafeoasis.co.uk

Furzy Cliff, Weymouth

Smell wild garlic in May around the pitted ponds, shrubs and nettles. Hide among a chorus of blackbirds and chirping sparrows.

➤ **Find** Lodmoor Nature Reserve (see opposite), cross the road on to the pebble beach and walk ⅔ mile NE to the cliff.

50.635033, -2.427244

Bowleaze Cove, Weymouth

Look for spiny seahorses in sea grass. Explore erosion and landslides after a storm or high tides.

➤ **Find** the car park off Bowleaze Coveway (Weymouth, DT3 6PP), then walk S 100 yards on to the beach.

50.636150, -2.420761

THE LOOKOUT CAFE, WEYMOUTH

Try a seafood plate while gazing over the sea from Furzy Cliff (see above right). Full English and cuppas are also on the menu.

Bowleaze Coveway, Weymouth, DT3 6PL
Facebook: @Thelookoutweymouth

Bowleaze Cove

Osmington Mills

Redcliff Point, Osmington

Inhale the scent of flowering meadows in the remnants of abandoned rock quarries.

➤ **Find** Bowleaze Cove (see page 327), then walk 1 mile E on the SWCP to the point.

50.633038, -2.407520

Blackhead Spring, Osmington

Wooded valley dripping in water, ferns and old twisted timbers, more reminiscent of a living Jurassic park than any Hollywood production. It's a good place in which to escape winter storms and summer heatstroke.

➤ **Find** Redcliff Point (see above), then walk 1½ miles E on the SWCP to the spring.

50.639071, -2.382789

TOP FIELD, EWELEAZE FARM CAMPSITE, OSMINGTON

 Tent camping in August only, when the farm opens up this cliff top field. There are also two cottages available to hire all year. Sea views and access to a private beach. Campfires are allowed, with firewood available to buy.

Osmington, Weymouth, DT3 6ED

THE SMUGGLER'S INN, OSMINGTON

Famous as a smuggling HQ for the French smuggler Pierre Latour, this 13th-century inn was one of the favourite places for handling smuggled goods in the 17th century. Favourites today are steak pie, fish and chips and Sunday roasts.

Osmington Mills, DT3 6HF
www.smugglersinn osmingtonmills.co.uk

Osmington Mills, Osmington

Fabulous tree-lined cliffs and rock ledges, many of which have been used historically as natural docks for landing goods. There are ammonites along the foreshore and set into the rocks, and you can swim or do a spot of rock pooling. Look for fossilised burrows of creatures that lived in the sea here 155 million years ago, and the 90-million-year-old remains of sea creatures that have turned to dust (chalk). There's also a cafe, pub, parking and toilets. Nearby camping at Rosewall Camping.

➤ **Find** the Smuggler's Inn (see left), then the public car park and toilets opposite. With your back to the sea, turn R immediately after the Smuggler's Inn on to the SWCP and walk along the SWCP. Alternatively, walk down from the car park on the L side, facing the sea, to the beach via the narrow, steep FPs that pass by the Mills Cafe. The R-side FP from the car park offers lovely beach walks but be wary of incoming high tides.

50.63391, -2.37571

PEOPLE OF THE PATH

The Biker, Burton Bradstock, Dorset

I cycle to raise money for charity.. It seemed important to me to have a reason to explore the path.

Kimmeridge Bay

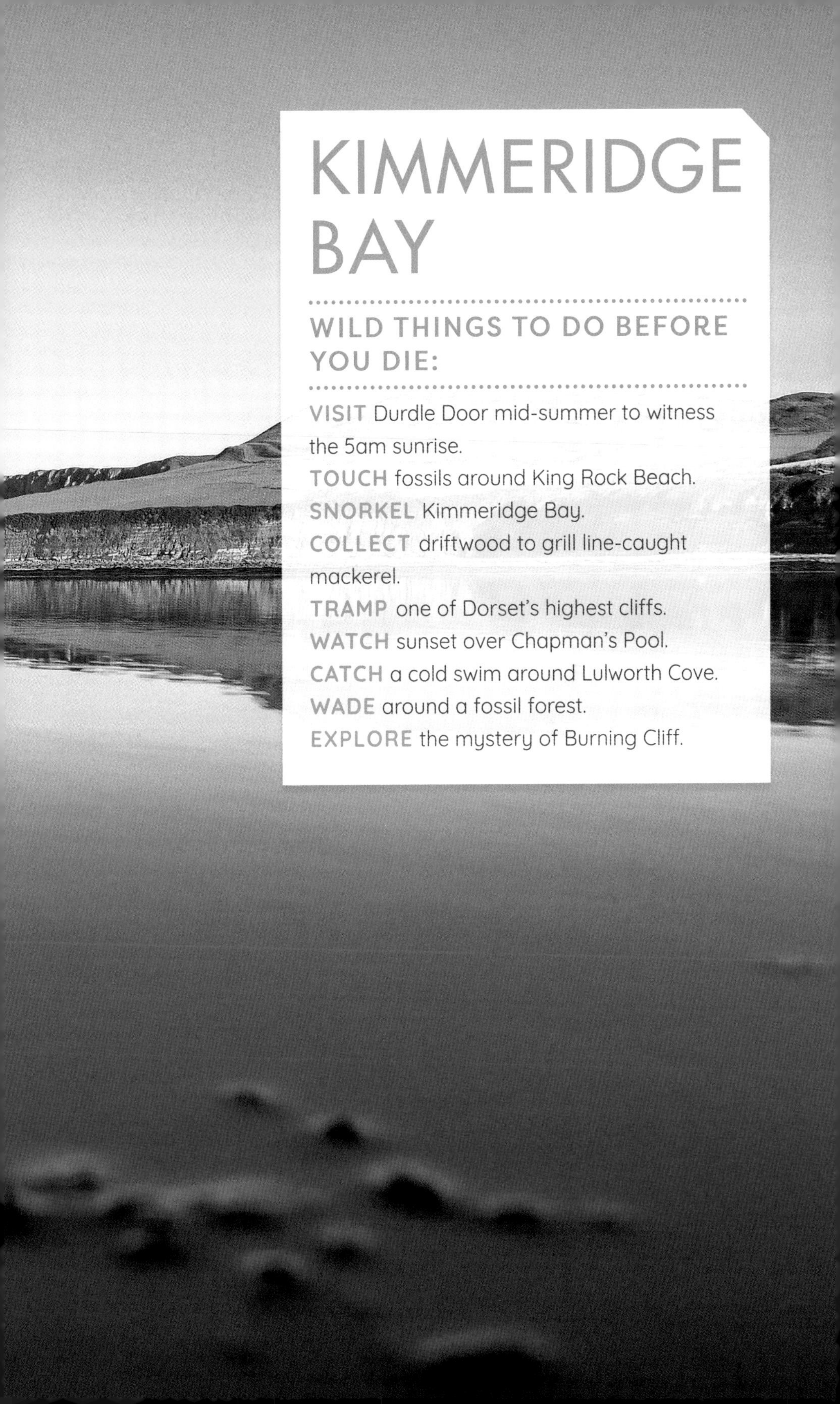

KIMMERIDGE BAY

WILD THINGS TO DO BEFORE YOU DIE:

VISIT Durdle Door mid-summer to witness the 5am sunrise.
TOUCH fossils around King Rock Beach.
SNORKEL Kimmeridge Bay.
COLLECT driftwood to grill line-caught mackerel.
TRAMP one of Dorset's highest cliffs.
WATCH sunset over Chapman's Pool.
CATCH a cold swim around Lulworth Cove.
WADE around a fossil forest.
EXPLORE the mystery of Burning Cliff.

Ringstead Ledge, Ringstead

Pebble beach for rock pooling and fossil hunting. Just east of here is the deserted medieval village of West Ringstead, where remains of the cottages and streets can still be made out.

➤ **Find** The Kiosk car park (Fishers Pl, Ringstead, DT2 8NG), then walk 200 yards S to the beach.

50.631055, -2.352028

Burning Cliff, Ringstead

Geological wonder of oil shale and iron pyrites that has been known to ... ignite and flame. Forage for shore crabs. Cook soup over a BBQ on stone, with lemon and nettles.

➤ **Find** Ringstead Ledge (see above), then walk ⅔ mile E on the pebble beach.

50.632150, -2.338644

St Catherine-by-the-Sea, Holworth

Calm place for a rest. Walk behind the chapel for the best views over the bay.

➤ **Find** the beach at Burning Cliff (see above). Walk back on to the SWCP and then head E on the path 300 yards to the church.

50.63421 -2.33706

King Rock Beach, Holworth

Previously one of the best fossil sites until a landslide allowed brambles to grow up and encase the ammonite exposures in impassable thorns. Occasional fossils can be found after landslides and high tides. The best specimens are seen at nearby museums.

➤ **Find** Burning Cliff (see above), then walk ¾ mile E on the pebble beach to the rocky point.

50.627521, -2.327640

Ringstead

Bat's Head

White Nothe, Holworth

This is one of the highest cliffs along the Dorset Coast and offers superb views of Weymouth and the Isle of Portland. Feel chalk cliffs beneath your feet with views over Weymouth Bay and Portland.

➤ **Find** King Rock Beach (see opposite). Keep walking on the beach at low tide 400 yards and find the FP up the cliff to the SWCP and cliff views. If the FP has eroded, walk back to Ringstead.

50.625300, -2.324012

Bat's Head and Bat's Hole Natural Arch, Chaldon Herring

Explore the unusual rock formations around Bat's Head. There are views of Durdle Door beyond.

➤ **Find** White Nothe (see above), then walk 1½ miles E on the SWCP to the arch.

50.622331, -2.291374

Durdle Door, Wareham St Martin

Wonder what it was like to be at Stonehenge 3,000 years ago? Head to Durdle Door: the famous limestone archway is best seen during August when the beach is packed with zealots. It's like a religio/pop concert, and that's no bad thing – it adds to the mystique. Arrive before 5am and leave no later than 3pm.

➤ **Find** Bat's Head (above), then walk ½ mile E on the SWCP to Durdle Door beach.

50.621279, -2.276815

Man o' War

Man o' War, Wareham St Martin

This is a rack of stone. Also look out for the Lulworth Skipper – the brown butterfly discovered nearby in 1832.

> **Find** Durdle Door Car Park (Wareham, BH20 5PU), then walk ⅓ mile W for a cliff view over stones.

50.620590, -2.270098

Hambury Tout Barrows, Oswald's Bay

Sacred site above beach and sand at Oswald's Bay. Explore barrows and views.

> **Find** Jurassic Coast Activities (38 Main Rd, West Lulworth, Wareham, BH20 5RQ) on the W bank of Lulworth Cove. From the public car park opposite, and with your back to the activities centre, walk W along the SWCP 660 yards, veering off R to look out for the barrow and L for better sea views.

50.622020, -2.261750

Stair Hole, West Lulworth

Best at low tide in summer when rock pools are warm and alive, and fossils are easier to find. Look for the unusual folds of rock known as the Lulworth Crumple.

> **Find** Hambury Tout Barrows (see above), then walk ½ mile E on the SWCP to the cove.

50.617946, -2.253237

Lulworth Cove

Lazy, cold swims around the healthy scent of fish and warm September sea air. Arrive and leave early … even out of season.

> **Find** Lulworth Cove car park (West Lulworth, BH20 5RS), then walk 300 yards E to the cove.

50.618750, -2.249280

LULWORTH LODGE, WEST LULWORTH

Lulworth's watermill has been converted into 12 bedrooms. Stop for a crab sandwich or cream tea on the terrace.

38 Main Rd, West Lulworth, BH20 5RQ
www.lulworthlodge.co.uk

THE BOAT SHED CAFE, WEST LULWORTH

Al fresco dining on a terrace over the beach, made from what was once a fishermen's lock-up.

Main Rd Lower, West Lulworth, BH20 5RQ
lulworth.com/visit/food-drink/boat-shed-cafe/

Lulworth Range, Lulworth

To avoid missing out on the coastal trek E out of Lulworth Cove, plan your walk for when the ranges are open – most weekends and holidays. Look for raised red flags in daytime and red-lit lamps at night to know when the military are using the coastal cliffs. For information on times, tel 01929 404712 or 01929 404806.

➤ **Find** Lulworth Cove (see opposite) and follow the SWCP E 600 yards on to the range.

50.618205, -2.243580

Pepler's Point, Wareham St Martin

Dolphins can sometimes be seen from here. There are super views back over Lulworth Cove.

➤ **Find** Lulworth Range (see above), then walk 200 yards S to the point.

50.616589, -2.245232

Bindon Hill Beach, Wareham St Martin

The 'fossil forest': the beach at the foot of Bindon Hill has one of the best Jurassic forests in the world. Look for bulbous lumps of rock near the sea, which are thought to be 135 million years old.

➤ **Find** Pepler's Point (see above), then walk 300 yards E.

50.616411, -2.240913

Mupe Rocks, Wareham St Martin

Peregrine falcons hunt here. Listen for nesting seabirds.

➤ **Find** Bindon Hill Beach (see above), then walk ⅔ mile on the SWCP to Mupe.

50.616434, -2.225029

PEOPLE OF THE PATH

The Campsite Owner, Burton Bradstock, Dorset

If you have booked a pitch and you're not going to arrive, let us know. We don't and won't charge you. We just want to know you are OK and safe.

PEOPLE OF THE PATH

The Foreman, Weymouth, Dorset

We've just upgraded the facilities and changing rooms here in Weymouth. They are fantastic. Available for all and well worth a visit for anyone coming to the beach.

Mupe Bay, Wareham St Martin

Wild flowers and butterflies abound over sweeping, quiet bays. Beware ordnance from the tank range.

➤ **Find** Mupe Rocks (see page 335), then walk 500 yards on the SWCP to Mupe.

50.616970, -2.221724

Flowers Barrow and Hill Fort, East Lulworth

Remains of an Iron Age fort, which has never been excavated.

➤ **Find** Mupe Bay (see above), then walk 1½ miles E on the SWCP to the hill fort.

50.625155, -2.192574

Worbarrow Beach and Tout, Tyneham

This area was famously evacuated of villagers so it could be used in D-Day landing tests. Sometimes, this place still feels like a ghost zone. Very strange, but beautiful. Good mackerel and bass fishing.

➤ **Find** Flowers Barrow (see above), then walk 500 yards to the beach ... and then on another 500 yards to the amazing headland. Best at sunset.

50.615000, -2.186607

Gad Cliff, Tyneham

Smell the air of trees along this sacred platform. This place has been a burial ground and lookout for thousands of years above Brandy Bay. Smugglers also used this route for centuries to reach cart tracks E and W. More recently, it was taken over by the MoD. Visit on the weekend when the area, including the abandoned village of Tyneham, and the beach, are open to the public.

➤ **Find** St Mary's Church (Tyneham, BH20 5QN). Keeping the church on your R, take the R turn down the track towards a large car park. Leave here on foot, walking S ½ mile, taking the L fork in the FP after the first 220 yards.

50.618720, -2.165772

Kimmeridge Bay

Snorkel the sunlit water for beds of pink coral weed and fields of snakelocks anemones. Plunge into freezing water to explore the 400-yard snorkel trail around the bay. Wear a wetsuit. Even in summer, it's cold. Fish for pollack and wrasse. Check tide times to gain the most reward. Nov-Mar: closed for the winter. Apr-Oct: open every day, including bank holidays, 10.30am-5pm. Some of the cliff FPs are steep in places, with slippery rock pools.
➤ **Find** the Fine Foundation Wild Seas Centre (Kimmeridge, BH20 5PF).

50.609742, -2.129967

Clavell Tower, Kimmeridge

Built in the early 1830s as a folly and observatory.
➤ **Find** Kimmeridge Bay car park (Kimmeridge, BH20 5PF), then walk 300 yards N on the SWCP to the tower.

50.607423, -2.129865

Clavell's Hard, Kimmeridge

Ancient hard and boat launch.
➤ **Find** Clavell Tower (see above), then walk 1 mile E on the SWCP to the hard.

50.599187, -2.113465

Egmont Bight Waterfall, Corfe Castle

Listen for the waterfall that tumbles into the sea, surrounded by the scent of wild flowers.
➤ **Find** Clavell's Hard (see above), then walk 1½ miles E on the SWCP.

50.594848, -2.080744

Worbarrow Tout

Clavell Tower

Houns-tout Cliff, Corfe Castle

Feel the steep climb to the top of Houns-tout Cliff, which stands at 490ft above sea level, before heading out to St Aldhelm's Head.
➤ Find Egmont Bight Waterfall (see page 337), then walk ⅔ mile E on the SWCP to the cliff.

50.594739, -2.069711

Chapman's Pool, St Aldhelm's Head

Natural harbour for swimming tucked into the W-facing armpit of St Aldhelm's Head. It's a wonderful beach walk down the cliffs, but it's a slog back up. Find loads of fossilised ammonites and shells.
➤ Find Renscombe Car Park (3 Renscombe Rd, Worth Matravers, BH19 3LL). With your back to the road, exit the car park along the FP to the L and follow it ⅔ mile down to the beach. FPs are narrow and steep.

50.593179, -2.063930

Commando Memorial, Wool

There's an incredible sunset view over Chapman's Pool and the Kimmeridge Bay coast from a stone enclosure and seating beside the memorial.

> **Find** the memorial directly above the E side of Chapman's Pool (see opposite).

50.590969, -2.059339

St Aldhelm's Chapel, Wool

Wonderfully bleak setting for this gem of a square chapel on the headland 350ft above the sea – one of the oldest churches in England.

> **Find** Chapman's Pool (see opposite), then walk 2½ miles. Alternatively, find Renscombe Car Park (3 Renscombe Rd, Worth Matravers, BH19 3LL), then walk 1½ miles on the lane S to the chapel.

50.579756, -2.056943

Worth Matravers Strip Lynchets, Worth Matravers

Medieval field terraces that can still be seen in the landscape as plough scars. They are called 'strip lynchets'. Four groups of medieval strip lynchets are situated on the slopes, either side of Winspit Bottom.

> **Find** St Aldhelm's Chapel (see above), then walk 1½ miles E on the SWCP to fields either side of the Winspit River valley.

50.585528, -2.034681

PEOPLE OF THE PATH

The Sheep Farmer, Kimmeridge, Dorset

That hill is my favourite place on the path. There is a path all the way up. The views are great and I proposed to my wife up there eight years ago.

STUDLAND

WILD THINGS TO DO BEFORE YOU DIE:

SWIM and snorkel with sea horses at South Beach.

CATCH a glimpse of the skies from the Durlston Astronomy Centre.

TOUCH the Limousin cow sculpture.

LISTEN for the whistling sound of sika deer in autumn.

FORAGE for mugwort tea.

VISIT a limestone quarry to see bats.

WATCH nesting puffins.

PADDLE a pool blasted out of rock for school children.

LOOK for bottlenose dolphins.

Seacombe Quarry, Langton Matravers

Sea quarry where limestone rock used to be dug and lowered on to boats for delivery to London and other cities.

➤ **Find** Worth Matravers car park (BH19 3LE), then walk 300 yards S onto Pikes Ln, take the first L into the FP and follow the FP 1 mile along Pillow Mounds Spring to the quarry.

50.589160, -2.021567

Seacombe Cliff

Look for rare chalkhill blue and Adonis blue butterflies in June and July.

➤ **Find** Seacombe Quarry (see above), then walk 200 yards S on the SWCP to the cliff.

50.589160, -2.021567

Dancing Ledge Caves, Langton Matravers

Explore natural caves and quarried tunnels that smugglers made use of for centuries. The fields above these caves are considered the best in Britain for the insect-like early spider orchid. Visit in April or early May and you might see a male bee attempting to mate with one. Look for nesting puffins around the cliffs either side. There are also razorbills and guillemots.

➤ **Find** Seacombe Cliff (see above), then walk 600 yards E on the SWCP to the first cave, 700 yards to the second and almost 1 mile to the third.

50.592066, -2.005866

PEOPLE OF THE PATH

The Tank Ranger, Kimmeridge, Dorset

The lost village of Tyneham and Worbarrow is my favourite place on the path. It was evacuated in December 1943 during WWII and has been deserted ever since. It's a wonderful peaceful place.

Spyway

Dancing Ledge, Langton Matravers

Take a dip or paddle in the pool that was blasted out of the rocks 200 years ago so that school children, including Ian Fleming, could swim safely. Landslips make the steep FP down difficult at times. Feel the ruts in the rock; remnants of wheel tracks from man-drawn carts that carried Purbeck limestone out to waiting boats. Listen for nesting peregrine falcons. Puffins feed and nest here, too. Watch rock climbers of all abilities tackle some of S England's most popular climbs. Good fishing or lunch spot.

➤ **Find** Dancing Ledge Caves (see opposite), then walk 200 yards E on the SWCP to the ledge.

50.591344, -2.004654

Spyway, Langton Matravers

Touch the Limousin cow sculpture by Sarah Moore in the stone wall. The sculpture was placed here to demonstrate the importance of conservation grazing and farming in managing landscapes.

➤ **Find** the sculpture on the N side of the boundary wall next to the SWCP above Dancing Ledge (see above).

50.591344, -2.004654

Blackers Hole Springs, Langton Matravers

Listen for the whistling sound of sika deer in autumn.

➤ **Find** the SWCP above Dancing Ledge (see above), then walk ²/₃ mile E to the springs.

50.591882, -1.991227

Durlston Bay

Anvil Point View, Swanage

Pick mugwort for tea and take in the sea views. Crush wild mustard leaf for its pungent scent.

➤ **Find** Blackers Hole Springs (see page 343), then walk 1½ miles E on the SWCP.

50.590853, -1.961035

Anvil Point Lighthouse, Swanage

Completed in 1881, the lighthouse is open for guided tours and can be rented as holiday accommodation.

➤ **Find** the lighthouse 100 yards NE of Anvil Point View (see above).

50.591974, -1.959908

Tilly Whim Caves, Swanage

Find bats at dusk in the remnants of three limestone quarries carved into the cliff face.

➤ **Find** Anvil Point Lighthouse (see above), then walk 300 yards E on the SWCP.

50.594812, -1.950505

Durlston Bay

Marvel at the Great Globe – a 10ft-wide, 40-tonne Portland stone globe created by George Burt, which was installed here in 1887. A journey through stone, time and water, it illustrates the Victorian view of the world.

➤ **Find** the car park at Durlston Country Park (St Catherines Rd, Swanage, BH19 2JL). From here, walk another 330 yards along St Catherines Rd, past Seventh Wave (see opposite above), where you could perhaps drop in for a coffee and cake.

50.595130, -1.951370

Swanage

SEVENTH WAVE, DURLSTON

This cafe, bar and restaurant serves up seasonal, fresh food, inside Durlston Country Park, a few yards from the SWCP.

Durlston Country Park, Lighthouse Rd, Swanage, BH19 2JL

THE 1859 PIER CAFE & BISTRO, SWANAGE

Breakfasts, sandwiches, cakes, burgers and daily specials a few yards from the harbour. Dog friendly.

Swanage Pier, Swanage, BH19 2AW www.swanagepiertrust. com/cafe

TAUNTON HOUSE B&B, SWANAGE

Dog-friendly B&B a few yards from the seafront and a short walk to the beach.

4 Taunton Rd, Swanage, BH19 2BY

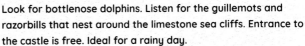

Durlston Head Castle, Durlston

Look for bottlenose dolphins. Listen for the guillemots and razorbills that nest around the limestone sea cliffs. Entrance to the castle is free. Ideal for a rainy day.

> Find The Durlston Astronomy Centre (see below), then walk 300 yards E to the castle.

50.595127, -1.953391

The Durlston Astronomy Centre, Durlston

Pay a small entrance fee to see the telescope housed in its own observatory dome. Phone ahead of time to check availability and the weather.

> Find 15 Lighthouse Rd, Swanage, BH19 2JL

50.595611 -1.957328

Peveril Point, Swanage

Look for roe deer inland of the Peveril cliffs, and kittiwakes, cormorants and fulmars offshore.

> Find Broad Rd Car Park (Broad Rd, Swanage, BH19 2AP), then walk E 700 yards on the FP.

50.607531, -1.944104

PEOPLE OF THE PATH

The Decorator, Weymouth, Dorset

The changing rooms here are great for people who want to swim. I painted these changing rooms when they were last done 20 years ago. It's good to be back.

BROOK TEA ROOMS, SWANAGE

No frills fry-ups and sea views. Dog friendly.

15 The Pde,
Swanage, BH19 1DA
brook-tea-rooms.edan.io

THE CABIN, SWANAGE

Multi-tiered beach cafe nestled in the cliffs below The Grand Hotel, with great views from the top deck.

Burlington Rd,
Swanage, BH19 1LW
Facebook: @The Cabin Swanage

THE PINES HOTEL, SWANAGE

This hotel offers sea-facing rooms, a cliff top garden and private steps to the beach.

Pines Hotel, Burlington Rd,
Swanage, BH19 1LT
pineshotel.co.uk

Swanage Bay Cliffs

Listen for burrowing bees while exploring cliff falls and landslips on the beach beyond the groynes at low tide. Beware: the Swanage cliffs are especially prone to collapse since they are made of soft rocks, sandstones and clays (known as Wealden beds). It's even possible to get cut off by a combination of landslide and rising tide. Care is therefore needed when visiting from above or below, so explore landslips from a distance.
➤ **Find** Main Beach Car Park (Information Centre, A351, Swanage, BH19 1PW), then walk E 500 yards to the beach. Walk 1 mile N to New Swanage Bay Beach and cliffs.

50.624091, -1.951962

Whitecliff Wood, Swanage

Feel the shade along the cliff top wood. Pick fresh oak tree shoots to use as tooth picks or for day-long chews.
➤ **Find** the SWCP behind Swanage Bay Cliffs (see above), then walk 200 yards E.

50.625978, -1.950052

Ballard Down Tumuli, Swanage

Look for chalkhill blue and Adonis blue butterflies on the flowers of Ballard Down.
➤ **Find** the beach FP up the cliffs at the N end of New Swanage Beach (50.623446, -1.952783). Find the SWCP and turn R, then walk N 1 mile to the tumuli. On the summit, walk 1 mile W along the Studland Hill BW to the stone seat and obelisk, where there are views over Brownsea Island and Studland Bay.

50.631578, -1.944951

Whitecliff Wood

Old Nick's Ground

Ballard Point View, Studland
Listen to the nesting razorbills, guillemots and puffins.
➤ **Find** Ballard Down Tumuli (see opposite), then walk E ⅔ mile
on the SWCP to the point.

50.631026, -1.940735

Old Nick's Ground, Studland
**Inhale and feel cold mist as it oozes over the cliff top from
below like a bucket of cold water emptying into a bath of warm
air. Vision can go from 20/20 to arm's length within less than
ten mins.**
➤ **Find** Ballard Point View (see above), then walk N ½ mile
on the SWCP to the grassy cliff top.

50.636576, -1.929786

The Pinnacle, Studland
Chalk stack where cormorants fish and sunbathe.
➤ **Find** Old Nick's Ground (see above), then walk N 200 yards
on the SWCP.

50.637266, -1.927301

St Lucas Leap Natural Arch, Studland
**Grassy platform south side of the rock, for the best views along
this section of FP.**
➤ **Find** the car park, (Manor Rd, Studland, BH19 3AU), then
walk 1¼ miles E on the SWCP.

50.641121, -1.924543

Old Harry Rocks

Old Harry Rocks, Studland

Listen for peregrine falcons that hunt close to one of the most famous pirate haunts around the south coast. Rogue bands would hide in boats behind the chalk stacks to raid trade ships of spices, jewels and even exotic animals.
➤ **Find** St Lucas Leap Natural Arch (see page 347), then walk 200 yards to the N side of the rock.

50.642496, -1.923121

The Foreland, Studland

Walk barefooted through meadows of buttercups in spring, sea side of the FP, down towards Warren Wood (see below).
➤ **Find** Old Harry Rocks (see above), then walk ½ mile W on the SWCP.

50.641026, -1.937510

King Barrow, Studland

It's possible to see remnants of land used by Celtic farmers from here. Look out for rectangular earthworks in wooded areas after/before Old Harry Rocks, in the vicinity of King Barrow.
➤ **Find** Old Harry Rocks (see above), then walk ½ mile W on the SWCP.

50.639346, -1.936589

Warren Wood, Studland

Find and taste windfall hazelnuts in autumn. The wood is a mixture of Scots pine and hazel. It's carpeted in bluebells from April.
➤ **Find** Old Harry Rocks (see above), then walk ⅔ mile W on the SWCP.

50.640467, -1.940575

Middle Beach

THE PIG, STUDLAND

 Country house by the beach. Beautiful accommodation, some of which is described as 'cheap and cheerful'; it's anything but! If the prices are a little out of range, the restaurant is worthy of a treat visit. Ingredients are grown in the kitchen garden, or sourced locally as part of The Pig's commitment to 'the 25-mile menu'. Piggy and fishy bites start at less than a fiver, with main meals reasonably priced. A kitchen garden, sea-foraged food, a FP down to the beach and roaring log fires make it pretty magical.

Manor House, Manor Rd, Studland, BH19 3AU
www.thepighotel.com

LONGMEAD COTTAGE B&B, STUDLAND

 Good food and rooms a short walk from the beach and the Fort Henry bunker (see right) overlooking Studland Bay.

Beach Rd,
Studland, BH19 3AP
01929 450472

NT MIDDLE BEACH CAFE, STUDLAND

 Sea views, bacon baps and hearty brekkies a few yards from the beach.

Marine Tce, Beach Rd,
Studland, BH19 3AX
Facebook: @Middle
Beach Cafe

South Beach, Studland

This is a beautiful swim spot lined with beach huts and woodland. Swim or snorkel the warm shallows of seaweed and clear water on any hot day in summer, looking out for cuttle- and pipefish. Feel warm sand against your feet and lie back to admire sea views over Old Harry Rocks (see page 348).

> **Find** the car park (Manor Rd, Studland, BH19 3AU), then walk 300 yards E to the beach.

50.641195, -1.941669

Fort Henry, Studland

Listen to the buzz of insects around poppies in the wildflower meadow in July, next to Fort Henry. Look for the observation window below.

> **Find** Middle Beach car park (Beach Rd, Studland, BH19 3AX), then walk E 500 yards to the R of the beach on the SWCP to the fort.

50.645453, -1.948193

Middle Beach

Snorkel through carpets of edible seaweed to see … sea horses. Two species live here.

> **Find** Marine Tce car park (Beach Rd, Studland, BH19 3AX), then walk 400 yards E.

50.646858, -1.948577

Knoll Beach, Studland

Hire a paddleboard or kayak. Chew and paddle W through 3 miles of raw seaweed, sand and warm water to the Shell Bay ferry.

> **Find** Knoll Beach car park (Ferry Rd, Studland, BH19 3AQ), then walk 400 yards E.

50.650010, -1.951059

Little Sea, Studland

Listen for plopping sounds of otters and water voles around some of the most overgrown and inaccessible parts of the freshwater lake. Look for Dartford warblers in the heath surrounding the water.

> **Find** Studland Dunes (see opposite), then walk 2 miles N across the sand.

50.658793, -1.956896

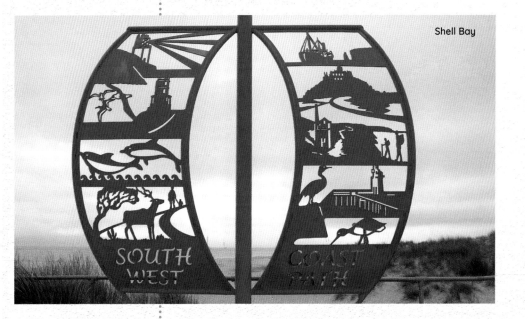

Shell Bay

SHELL BAY RESTAURANT & BISTRO, STUDLAND

 Enjoy oysters from the shell or whole lobster, mackerel and Dover sole from the fire next to Shell Bay Beach at the very end of Ferry Rd.

Ferry Rd,
Studland, BH19 3BA
shellbay.net

NT KNOLL BEACH CAFE, STUDLAND

 Relax at one of the best beaches in Dorset. Warm drinks or local ciders, beers and fruit juices.

Ferry Rd,
Studland, BH19 3AQ
www.nationaltrust.org.uk

Studland Dunes, Studland

Look for sika deer in the marshes and woodland that surround these dunes, which are held together by marram grass. Find sand earthtongue fungi in autumn where the heather meets grass. This is the only place the fungi grow in England, and they look like narrow black tongues. Some say if stewed they're OK to eat, but that they're not good raw. Either way, they are rare so best left alone.

➤ **Find** Shell Bay NT car park (Ferry Rd, Studland, BH19 3BA), then walk ½ mile N into the dunes.

50.668583, -1.946046

Shell Bay, Studland

Listen for the nightjars after dusk. Watch out for sandwich and common terns catching fish along the shoreline.

➤ **Find** Shell Bay NT car park (Ferry Rd, Studland, BH19 3BA). Looking towards the ferry terminal to Bournemouth, turn R down towards the beach and walk for 1½ miles along the glorious bay. Alternatively, cross the road at the car park and explore the S, and quietest, side of Poole Harbour.

50.675049, -1.945681

South Haven Point, Studland

Touch the blue metal sculpture beside the ferry that thousands of people before you have felt to mark the start/finish of the SWCP.

➤ **Find** the ferry ramp at South Haven Point and walk 200 yards E to the start/finish of the SWCP.

50.679489, -1.949860

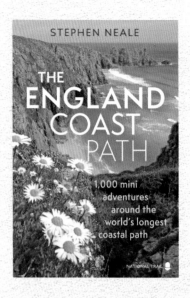

THE ENGLAND COAST PATH

1,000 Mini Adventures Along the World's Longest Coastal Path

England has opened more of its coastline to the public than any other nation in the world, and this book shows you how to make the most of it. Exploring the length of the England Coast Path, this gorgeous and inspiring guidebook highlights 1,000 mini adventures to enjoy along its entire route.

ISBN 978-1-8448-6579-6

WILD CAMPING

Exploring and Sleeping in the Wilds of the UK and Ireland

A revolutionary guide to the world of wild camping and foraging, showing how anyone can camp, sleep and wake in the UK's most secluded and beautiful places, with a Foreword by Ed Stafford.

ISBN 978-1-8448-6572-7

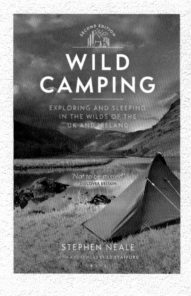

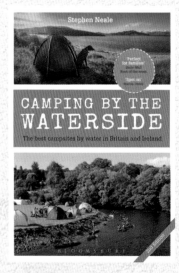

CAMPING BY THE WATERSIDE

The Best Campsites by Water in Britain and Ireland

This is the ultimate guide to camping near water – by the sea, lake, river or estuary – and covers planning your trip, gear to take, introductions to each activity (canoeing, sailing, angling etc) and the very best waterside locations in the UK and Ireland. With a Foreword by *One Man and a Campervan's* Martin Dorey.

ISBN 978-1-4729-4330-9